THE SAKYA JETSUNMAS

H.E. Jetsun Kushok transmitting (Tib. *lung*) a religious text in the mid-1990s.

The Sakya Jetsunmas

The Hidden World of Tibetan Female Lamas

Elisabeth A. Benard

SNOW LION
IN ASSOCIATION WITH THE SAPAN FUND

Snow Lion
An imprint of Shambhala Publications, Inc.
2129 13th Street
Boulder, Colorado 80302
www.shambhala.com

Cover art: H.E. Jetsun Kushok at nineteen years old,
Dolma Palace, Sakya, Tibet, 1957

Cover design: April Dolkar, Gopa & Ted2 Inc.,
and Daniel Urban-Brown

Interior design: Gopa & Ted2 Inc.

9 8 7 6 5 4 3 2 1

Printed in the United States of America

⊖This edition is printed on acid-free paper that meets the
American National Standards Institute z39.48 Standard.
♻Shambhala Publications makes every effort to print on recycled paper.
For more information please visit www.shambhala.com.
Snow Lion is distributed worldwide by Penguin Random House, Inc.,
and its subsidiaries.

LIBRARY OF CONGRESS CATALOGING-IN-PUBLICATION DATA

Names: Benard, Elisabeth, author.
Title: The Sakya jetsunmas : the hidden world of
Tibetan female lamas / Elisabeth Benard.
Description: Boulder : Shambhala, 2022. |
Includes bibliographical references.
Identifiers: LCCN 2021037100 | ISBN 9781645470915 (trade paperback)
Subjects: LCSH: Women Buddhist priest—Tibet Region—Biography. |
Vajrayoginī (Buddhist deity)—Cult—Tibet Region. | Yoginīs—Tibet
Region—Biography.
Classification: LCC BQ4890.V343 T5248 2022 | DDC 294.3092/2
[B]—dc23/eng/20211014
LC record available at https://lccn.loc.gov/2021037100

West and Central Tibet

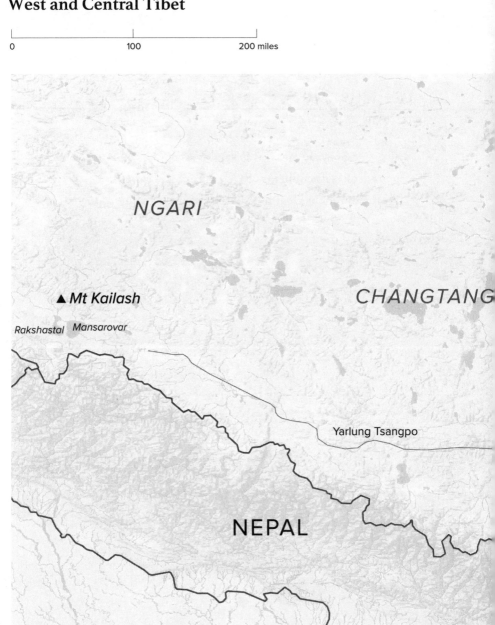

NGARI

CHANGTANG

▲ Mt Kailash

Rakshastal   Mansarovar

Yarlung Tsangpo

NEPAL

0   100   200 miles

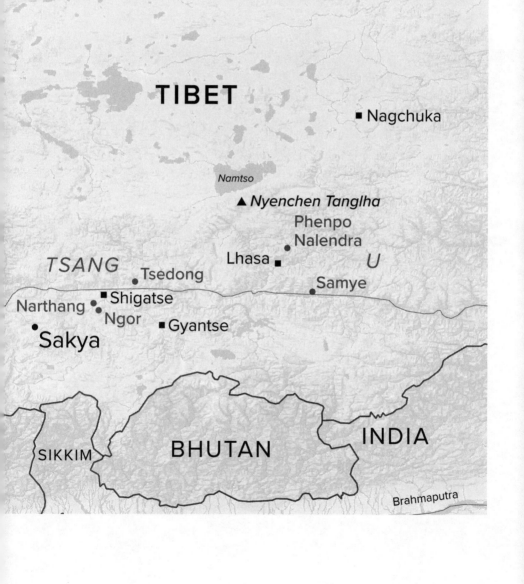

TIBET

■ Nagchuka

Namtso

▲ *Nyenchen Tanglha*

Phenpo
Nalendra

Lhasa ■   *U*

● Samye

TSANG   ● Tsedong

■ Shigatse

Narthang ●●   *Ngor*

● Sakya   ■ Gyantse

SIKKIM   BHUTAN   INDIA

Brahmaputra

Contents

Foreword

THIS BOOK PROVIDES an extensive exploration of the great female adepts of the Sakya Khon family. No scholars to date have written about them, and this is the first book written in English to present their extraordinary lives. Women's lives are rarely described in historical literature, and even then, women receive only brief mentions as mothers or consorts and often remain nameless. The sources for this book are extensive, including interviews, biographies, diaries, and oral traditions.

The most remarkable of the Khon family women throughout its entire history—Jetsunma Chime Tenpai Nyima, Jetsunma Tamdrin Wangmo, and Kyabgon Pema Trinlei—are thoroughly documented in this book. It describes the pivotal roles they played in teaching the highest and most famous lamas of their time, as well as generations to come, and their personal spiritual achievements.

Detailed descriptions are provided of the cultural, physical, historical, and spiritual fabric that comprises the Khon family lineage. This book also illustrates how these women practitioners were encouraged and supported by their families to cultivate their religious practices.

Elisabeth Benard interviewed my brother—His Holiness Sakya Kyabgon Gongma Trichen Rinpoche—and me on many occasions over several years. Her research and execution of this undertaking will inform and inspire practitioners throughout the English-speaking world.

Chimey Luding

Chimey Luding
May 7, 2020

Preface and Acknowledgments

IN 1974 I visited Nepal for the first time and met a group of people whom I instantly liked. At the time, I knew nothing about their history or their plight as refugees. I was attracted by their attitude. It is difficult to describe, but they seemed genuinely interested in knowing their fellow human beings. They were Tibetans who had fled from communism in their homeland and chose to live in exile, despite the difficulties. After a few months, I returned home and forgot about them.

But in September 1976 in New York City, interested in learning Sanskrit, I went to The Tibet Center, where a Sanskrit class was being offered. There I met three Tibetans: Khyongla Rato Rinpoche, a great Tibetan lama; Kalsang Yeshi, who later became a minister to the 14th Dalai Lama in Dharamsala, India; and Nima Dorjee, a Tibetan historian and the Sanskrit teacher for The Tibet Center. I decided that they were "authentic" Tibetans because of their beaming smiles and because they seemed genuinely interested in knowing why I had come to The Tibet Center. Only in retrospect did I realize that this encounter had changed the direction of my life. I have remained friends with all three, one of whom I married. At that time, I was pursuing a bachelor's degree in Asian religions at Columbia University. Like many of my generation, I was attracted to Zen Buddhism, but this initial interest never gelled.

Within three years, I married Nima Dorjee. He liked being known as "Mr. Tibet," so I knew when marrying Nima that I had to like Tibet because I would hear about it daily. His love of Tibet influenced me tremendously. Eventually I would obtain a doctorate in Tibetan Buddhism from Columbia University. Over the years I have both studied and taught about Tibet, its culture, its history, and, most importantly, Tibetan Buddhism. One word pervasive in Tibetan Buddhist belief is *tashi* (*bkra shis*, "auspicious"). Certain encounters, certain days, certain "coincidences" are deemed auspicious. Another related word is *tendrel* (*rten 'brel*), used less in the philosophical sense of interdependence than to indicate serendipity or disparate things coming together in a favorable way.

Furthermore, when one is in the company of certain Tibetan lamas, one's worldview can be transformed. One's ordinary sense of fixed time and space becomes suspended. At times, an event that was only an hour long can feel as if it lasted many hours because the intensity of the experience is deeply touching. Also one's senses can be sharpened and one's awareness can penetrate barriers that appear impenetrable but that are actually mere flimsy façades. Spaces that seem constrained and limited suddenly disintegrate, and one is in a vast space of freedom.

Now that this book is finished and I reflect on the journey of discovering the female lamas of the Sakya school of Tibetan Buddhism, researching their lives, and finally assembling a book about them, I see how many things came together in auspicious ways. Though I am the author, this book depended on numerous people—each contributing in her/his own capacity to create this homage to the hidden female lamas. First and foremost, I thank Her Eminence Jetsun Kushok and His Holiness the 41st Sakya Trizin for giving me their approval to write about their lives, for endlessly sharing their knowledge and memories of their own lives as well as the lives of the illustrious female lamas, and for constantly encouraging the project over the years. Next, I thank my husband, Nima Dorjee, who is inspired by spiritual biographies as much as I am. His willingness to share his knowledge of Tibetan beliefs, history, language, and idioms—and to help me understand many texts—is as vast as the ocean.

Over the years, I was fortunate to meet many people who knew about the Sakya Khon family. Frequently it was serendipity that led from one chance encounter to another. For example, when I stayed with a Tibetan friend in Rajpur, India, she introduced me to Chiwang Tulku, a lama who performs purification rituals and who is the former director of Sakya Centre in Rajpur. I received a purification ritual, and during this visit I found out that he knew the Sakya Khon family very well. He had even known Dagmo Trinlei Paljor, the aunt who raised both Her Eminence Jetsun Kushok and His Holiness the 41st Sakya Trizin. This occurred right when I was looking for people who had known Dagmo Trinlei Paljor, who played such a pivotal role in Her Eminence and His Holiness' lives. One can say that it was a mere coincidence, but Tibetans would interpret it differently. They would say that the main reason that I met Chiwang Tulku was to hear his memories of Dagmo Trinlei Paljor—that our meeting was a case of conditions coming together. This happened frequently in my research. Many times I felt that I was being "guided" to a person, a place, or a text.

The other people whom I interviewed at length were the late Ani Chime Dolma, younger sister of the 3rd Dezhung Rinpoche; Dagmo Jamyang Sakya, niece of the 3rd Dezhung Rinpoche and wife of the late Jigdal Dagchen Sakya; Jetsunmas Tsegen Wangmo Sakya and Chime Wangmo Sakya, sisters of Jigdal Dagchen Sakya; and Drawupon Rinchen Tsering, with the help his daughter Dagmo Lhanze Sakya. In addition I interviewed Ngaklo Rinpoche, whose previous reincarnation was a teacher of Her Eminence Jetsun Kushok and His Holiness the 41st Sakya Trizin; Gyalyum Tashi Lhakee, the wife of the 41st Sakya Trizin; Kunga Yonten Horchotsang, former director of the Namgyal Institute of Tibetology in Sikkim and first cousin to Gyalyum; Dagmo Kalden Dunkyi, wife of the 42nd Sakya Trizin, Ratna Vajra Rinpoche; Ngor Thartse Lama Kunga Rinpoche, cousin of Her Eminence and His Holiness; Jay Goldberg (Ngawang Samten, now Lama Jay), longtime student of His Holiness; Ga Yudron, the second wife of Tashi Palrab (younger brother of Dagmo Trinlei Paljor); and Aja Dolkar and her son, Tsering Dorje, longtime attendants to the Dolma Palace Sakya family. Moreover, I interviewed Tenzin Dawa, former abbot of Ngor Monastery in Sikkim; the late Dongthong Rinpoche, Tibetan historian of Ngor Monastery and Sakya; and the late Geshe Thuchey Wangchuk, Tibetan historian of Sakya. These interviewees were invaluable in sharing their memories and providing little-known details about historical events. I thank them all.

I appreciate the various organizations that invited me to present my research. The first one was the Tibetan Buddhist Learning Center in Washington, New Jersey, followed by the Lhatse Foundation and Columbia University in New York, and the Société Française d'Études du Monde Tibétain in Paris. Also I was invited to present at the 11th and 13th Seminars of the International Association for Tibetan Studies, held in Bonn, Germany, and Vancouver, Canada, respectively. I thank Nicola Schneider, a Tibetan scholar who focuses on Tibetan women's lives, and Françoise Robin, a scholar of Tibetan language and literature at Inalco, Paris, for inviting me to submit an article about the female lamas. It was published in the *Revue d'Études Tibétaines* 34 (Décembre 2015).

I thank Alex Gardner, director of the terrific website *The Treasury of Lives*, for asking me to publish some of the earlier versions of the lives of the female lamas. With much gratitude I thank Catherine Tsuji, editor of *The Treasury of Lives*, who created the maps for this volume. I encourage everyone to look at this website, which has an extensive collection of Tibetan biographies.

I thank David P. Jackson, a scholar of Sakya history and Tibetan art, for his help over the years and for sharing photos from his collection. Thank you, Jeff Schoening, a Tibetan scholar and translator, for helping me find information and especially in working with Geshe Thuchey Wangchuk. Also we share a common interest in all things Sakya and the Khon families. The late E. Gene Smith, whose extensive labors of digitizing Tibetan texts have preserved invaluable manuscripts, generously shared some crucial works. Cyrus Stearns, a prolific translator of Tibetan biographies, related some of his memories.

The next paragraphs name many *kalyāṇamitras* (Sanskrit for "spiritual friends") who generously cared about this project and helped me at various stages. Foremost is Priya Beverly Moon, whose dedication and tireless work over many years helped me through the most discouraging times. Without her weekly suggestions and encouragement, the book might never have been written. Dear Priya, my gratitude to you is great. Toward the completion of the manuscript, I thank the Khyentse Foundation for providing me with an Ashoka Grant. I thank Victoria R. M. Scott for editing and streamlining my writing, keeping me consistent in names, creating the Major Figures list and Sakya Family Names table to help the reader, and generally making the book more accessible. She is an excellent editor with tremendous patience and boundless energy! Also, when you want a job done, Kurt Schwalbe is your man. Thank you, Kurt, for helping find texts and people. One of those people was Ani-la Dechen Wangmo of the Sakya College for Nuns, who sent me a copy of an important text. Thank you, Ven. Dechen Wangmo.

Throughout this process, friends read portions of the book and offered suggestions. I thank Diana Cutler, Anne Davies, Jay Goldberg, Abby Petty, and Carolyn Swan. I especially thank both Edwina Williams and Jin Yeo for a careful and thoughtful reading of the manuscript. I thank April Dolkar, a wonderful artist, for her idea for the book cover and for providing photos. I was delighted to brainstorm with Jeff and Lara Sanderson about the title. Cate Hunter came to the rescue when I was desperately looking for expertise in producing the five genealogical charts. Graciously she accepted the challenge and created comprehensive family trees as well as helping me streamline some chapters—many thanks to you, Cate. I appreciate tremendously Gopa Campbell's elegant design for both the cover and interior, which allows all the elements of the book to shine in a clear and balanced way that honors its contents.

I am thankful to Chodrung-ma Kunga Chodron of Tsechen Kunchab Ling in Walden, New York, for all her help with this publication. The generous contributions of the Sachen Foundation, Sakya Dechen Ling, the Sapan Fund, Diana Cutler, Lillie Scudder, Michael Wick, and other donors are also deeply appreciated. Since I worked on this book for a long time, please excuse me if I have forgotten to acknowledge you. Thank you to everyone who helped me. Any mistakes are mine alone.

The first printing appeared in early 2021 for free distribution from the Sapan Fund. With demand quickly exceeding supply, the Sapan Fund happily found that Shambhala Publications was interested in producing and distributing the ebook and future printings. It has been a pleasure to work with Shambhala's Nikko Odiseos and Tucker Foley to ensure that *The Sakya Jetsunmas* will remain available to readers everywhere.

Elisabeth Benard
Among the sequoias and the pines
Tacoma, Washington
January 2022

Major Figures by Chapter

CHAPTER 1

Jetsun Kushok (b. 1938), *contemporary Sakya jetsunma (Chapters 8 and 9)*
Jetsunma Tsegen Wangmo (b. 1936), *sister of Jigdal Dagchen Sakya*
Jetsunma Chime Wangmo (b. 1939), *sister of Jigdal Dagchen Sakya**

CHAPTER 2

The Five Founders of the Sakya School:
    Sachen Kunga Nyingpo (1092–1158)
    Lopon Sonam Tsemo (1142–82)
    Jetsun Drakpa Gyaltsen (1147–1216)
    Sakya Pandita Kunga Gyaltsen (1182–1251)
    Chogyal Phakpa (1235–80)

CHAPTER 3

Jetsunma Chime Tenpai Nyima (1756–ca. 1855), *teacher of four Sakya Trizins and many others; first female bestower of the Path with the Result*
31st Sakya Trizin, Sachen Kunga Lodro (1729–83), *her paternal uncle and main teacher*
39th Sakya Trizin, Dragshul Trinlei Rinchen (1871–1935), *author of her brief biography*

---

*Not to be confused with Jetsunma Chime Trinlei Wangmo (1900–ca. 1955), the third daughter of Dragshul Trinlei Rinchen (see major figures for Chapter 6 below)

CHAPTER 4

Jetsunma Tamdrin Wangmo (1836–96), *teacher of her great-niece Kyabgon Pema Trinlei (Chapter 5), three Sakya Trizins, and many others, in Kham and elsewhere; second female bestower of the Path with the Result*
36th Sakya Trizin, Ngawang Kunga Sonam (1842–82), *her younger brother and one of her main disciples*
Chokyi Langpo (1844–66), *her youngest brother, who accompanied her to Kham and later died in an earthquake*
Tulku Nyendrak Tenpai Wangchuk (1854–98), *one of her main disciples*
39th Sakya Trizin, Dragshul Trinlei Rinchen (1871–1935), *her great-nephew, one of her main disciples, and the author of her biography*

CHAPTER 5

Kyabgon Pema Trinlei (1874–ca. 1950), *great-aunt of Jetsun Kushok (Chapters 8 and 9) and teacher to many lamas, including the renowned Chogye Trichen (1920–2007); third female bestower of the Path with the Result; honored by Tibetans with the title Kyabgon (Protector)*
39th Sakya Trizin, Dragshul Trinlei Rinchen (1871–1935), *her older brother; lifelong diarist of the Sakya Khon family (Chapter 6)*
Dagmo Lharitsema Chime (n.d.), *their mother, a devout practitioner, avid reader, and famed as an excellent storyteller*

CHAPTER 6

39th Sakya Trizin, Dragshul Trinlei Rinchen (1871–1935), *lifelong diarist; disciple, brother, and father of Sakya jetsunmas*
Jetsunma Ngodrub Wangmo (1880–1939), *usually referred to as Jetsunma Ngowang, his younger sister, with whom he traveled to Lhasa*
Jetsunma Kunga Wangmo (1896–1929), *his first daughter*
Jetsunma Kalzang Chodron (1898–?), *usually referred to as Jetsunma Kala, his second daughter*
Jetsunma Chime Trinlei Wangmo (1900–ca. 1955), *his third daughter*
Dagchen (earlier Dungsay) Kunga Rinchen (1902–50), *his first son; father of Jetsun Kushok and the 41st Sakya Trizin*
Dungsay Kunga Gyaltsen (1904–ca. 1943), *also known as Ngawang Kunga Gyaltsen, his second son, uncle to Jetsun Kushok and the 41st Sakya Trizin*

Jetsunma Kunga Tenpai Nyima (1914–ca. 1952), usually referred to as Jetsunma Kunten, *his fourth daughter*

Jetsunma Kalzang Chodron (1917–62), usually referred to as Jetsunma Chungwa (Younger One), *his fifth daughter*

Khen Jampal Zangpo (1901–61), *abbot of the South Monastery in Sakya, advisor to the Dolma Palace, and compiler of Dragshul Trinlei Rinchen's diary*

CHAPTER 7

Dagmo Trinlei Paljor (1906–75), *maternal aunt of Jetsun Kushok and the 41st Sakya Trizin*

Dagyum Sonam Dolkar (1918–47), *mother of Jetsun Kushok and the 41st Sakya Trizin; younger sister of, and co-wife with, Dagmo Trinlei Paljor*

Dagchen Kunga Rinchen (1902–50), *father of Jetsun Kushok and the 41st Sakya Trizin*

CHAPTER 8

Jetsun Kushok (b. 1938), *teacher of many disciples worldwide; fourth (and youngest) female bestower of the Path with the Result*

41st Sakya Trizin (b. 1945), Ngawang Kunga Thegchen Palbar Trinlei Samphel Wangyi Gyalpo, *younger brother of Jetsun Kushok*

Dagmo Trinlei Paljor (1906–75), *maternal aunt of Jetsun Kushok and the 41st Sakya Trizin (Chapter 7)*

CHAPTER 9

Jetsun Kushok (b. 1938), *teacher of many disciples worldwide; fourth (and youngest) female bestower of the Path with the Result*

41st Sakya Trizin (b. 1945), *younger brother of Jetsun Kushok*

Gyalyum Tashi Lhakee (b. 1952), *wife of the 41st Sakya Trizin*

Dagmo Jamyang Sakya (b. 1934), *wife of Jigdal Dagchen Sakya*

EPILOGUE

Jetsunma Kunga Trinley (b. 2007), *great-niece of Jetsun Kushok*

Dungsay Akasha Vajra Rinpoche (b. 2010), *great-nephew of Jetsun Kushok*

Jetsunma Kunga Chimey Wangmo (b. 2013), *great-niece of Jetsun Kushok*

Sakya Family Names

SHORT NAME used throughout (followed by dates and full names)	RELATIONSHIPS TO OTHER MAJOR FIGURES
DAGCHEN KUNGA RINCHEN (1902–50) Dagchen Ngawang Kunga Rinchen	co-husband of Dagmo Trinlei Paljor and her sister Dagyum Sonam Dolkar; father of Jetsun Kushok and the 41st Sakya Trizin
DAGMO JAMYANG SAKYA (b. 1934) Dagmo Jamyang Pema Palgyi Butri; birth name Sonam Tsedzom Jamyang Palmo	wife of Jigdal Dagchen Sakya; niece of the 3rd Dezhung Rinpoche
DAGMO LHARITSEMA CHIME (n.d.) Dagmo Lharitsema Chime Rigzin Palha	mother of Kyabgon Pema Trinlei
DAGMO TRINLEI PALJOR (1906–75) Dagmo Trinlei Paljor Zangmo; birth name Dechen Chozom Bonshod	wife of the Dagchen Kunga Rinchen and his brother Ngawang Kunga Gyaltsen (no children), then co-wife with her younger sister Dagyum Sonam Dolkar; maternal aunt who raised Jetsun Kushok and the 41st Sakya Trizin
DAGYUM CHIME KUNGA DOLMA (1878–early 1940s) Sakya Dagyum Chime Kunga Dolma Rigzin Palgye Lhamo; birth name Tseten Dolma, from the Ragashar (or rDo zur) noble family	wife of the 39th Sakya Trizin Dragshul Trinlei Rinchen; mother of five jetsunmas and two dungsays

SHORT NAME used throughout (followed by dates and full names)	RELATIONSHIPS TO OTHER MAJOR FIGURES
DAGYUM SONAM DOLKAR (1918–47)	co-wife, with her older sister Dagmo Trinlei Paljor, of Dagchen Kunga Rinchen and his brother Ngawang Kunga Gyaltsen; mother (who died young) of Jetsun Kushok and the 41st Sakya Trizin
DRAGSHUL TRINLEI RINCHEN (1871–1935)	39th Sakya Trizin (r. 1915–35); lifelong chronicler and diarist of the Sakya Khon family
DUNGSAY KUNGA GYALTSEN: see Ngawang Kunga Gyaltsen	
GYALYUM TASHI LHAKEE (b. 1952) Tashi Lhakee, of the Derge Hochotsang noble family	wife of the 41st Sakya Trizin
JETSUN KUSHOK (b. 1938) H.E. Jetsun Kushok Chimey Luding; birth name Chime Osel Butri Rigzin Trinlei	older sister of the 41st Sakya Trizin; wife of Sey Kushok Rinchen Luding; mother of Luding Khen Rinpoche (b. 1967), three other sons, and a daughter who died young
JETSUNMA CHIME TENPAI NYIMA (1756–ca. 1855)	niece of the 31st Sakya Trizin Sachen Kunga Lodro (1729–83)
JETSUNMA CHIME WANGMO (1900–ca. 1955) Jetsunma Chime Trinlei Wangmo; also known as Jetsunma Chime Tenpai Dronme, Chime Tenpai Nyima	third daughter of the 39th Sakya Trizin Dragshul Trinlei Rinchen; paternal aunt of Jetsun Kushok
JETSUNMA KUNGA TRINLEY (b. 2007) Jetsunma Kunga Trinley Palter	great-niece of Jetsun Kushok
JETSUNMA KUNGA CHIMEY WANGMO (b. 2013)	great-niece of Jetsun Kushok
JETSUNMA NGAWANG TSEJIN LHAMO (b. 2011)	great-niece of Jetsun Kushok

SHORT NAME used throughout (followed by dates and full names)	RELATIONSHIPS TO OTHER MAJOR FIGURES
JETSUNMA NGOWANG (1880–1939) Jetsunma Ngodrub Wangmo	younger sister of Kyabgon Pema Trinlei; younger sister of the 39th Sakya Trizin Dragshul Trinlei Rinchen
JETSUNMA TAMDRIN WANGMO (1836–96) Jetsunma Tamdrin Wangmo Kalzang Chokyi Nyima	great-aunt of Kyabgon Pema Trinlei; great-aunt of the 39th Sakya Trizin Dragshul Trinlei Rinchen
JIGDAL DAGCHEN SAKYA (1929–2016) Jigdal Dagchen Sakya Rinpoche; H.H. Dagchen Rinpoche	eldest son of the Phuntsok Palace; husband of Dagmo Jamyang Sakya
KYABGON PEMA TRINLEI (1874–ca. 1950) Jetsunma Pema Trinlei; in a few sources known as Lharig Khon Dung Jetsunma Pema Trinlei	great-niece of Jetsunma Tamdrin Wangmo; younger sister of the 39th Sakya Trizin Dragshul Trinlei Rinchen
NGAWANG KUNGA GYALTSEN (1904–ca. 1943) Ngawang Kunga Tenpai Gyaltsen; also known as Dungsay Kunga Gyaltsen	younger brother of Dagchen Kunga Rinchen; co-husband of Dagmo Trinlei Paljor and her sister Dagyum Sonam Dolkar; paternal uncle of Jetsun Kushok and the 41st Sakya Trizin
39TH SAKYA TRIZIN: *see* Dragshul Trinlei Rinchen	
41ST SAKYA TRIZIN (b. 1945) known since 2017 as H.H. Gongma Trichen Rinpoche; first birth name Ayu Vajra, second birth name Ngawang Kunga Thegchen Palbar Trinlei Samphel Wangyi Gyalpo	younger brother of Jetsun Kushok; husband of Gyalyum Tashi Lhakee; grandfather of Jetsunma Kunga Trinley
42ND SAKYA TRIZIN (b. 1974) Ratna Vajra Sakya, Ratna Vajra Rinpoche	older son of the 41st Sakya Trizin and Gyalyum Tashi Lhakee; father of Jetsunma Kunga Trinley
43RD SAKYA TRIZIN (b. 1979) Gyana Vajra Sakya, Gyana Vajra Rinpoche	younger son of the 41st Sakya Trizin and Gyalyum Tashi Lhakee

The Sakya Jetsunmas

Introduction

AMONG TIBETAN spiritual biographies there are many life stories of exceptional male wisdom-holders, or *vidyādharas,* such the famous eleventh-century Jetsun Milarepa or the present 14th Dalai Lama (Tenzin Gyatso, b. 1935). These biographies bring to life an intense dedication to spiritual practice, are relevant today as examples of what we are all capable of realizing, and inspire us to strengthen our own practice. Nevertheless, biographies of religious women are few.

When I discovered that for a millennium the Tibetan Sakya Khon family has been raising their daughters to be spiritual adepts, I leapt for joy. This book focuses on the hidden world of the great female spiritual adepts who were born into the Sakya Khon family. It is extraordinary to find an entire family that has been committed for centuries to supporting and guiding its children to become wisdom-holders, not for selfish reasons of fame and power, but to ensure their offspring have the proper means to help others in alleviating their suffering and to guide them on the path to enlightenment, or buddhahood.

THE KHON LINEAGE

The Khon family is one of Tibet's greatest religious families, with the longest continuous line of spiritual leadership. Due to the compassion of Sakya masters throughout the centuries, the teachings of Shakyamuni Buddha have been maintained as methods of spiritual realization in an unbroken line of transmission that continues to this day. His Holiness Gongma Trichen Rinpoche, the 41st Sakya Trizin (b. 1945), has explained, "Buddha gave men and women equal rights to practice. But due to cultural circumstances, there are more male teachers."[1] Padmasambhava,

1. "What Is the Sakya Tradition?," Tibet House, New York, April 2018. https://www.youtube.com/watch?v=GqGLvDUYOug.

the great Indian tantric master who was invited to come to Tibet in the eighth century, echoed the Buddha's view by stating, "The basis for realizing enlightenment is a human body. Male or female—there is no great difference. But if she develops the mind bent on enlightenment, the woman's body is better."[2] Unfortunately, since the early days of Buddhism, women have been required to move beyond cultural prejudices, which tell them they are not as spiritually capable as men.

If a woman has the good karma to be born into the Khon lineage, however, her family provides everything she needs to be able to ripen and become a fully realized yoginī. After delving more deeply into the lives of women born in the Khon family, it became clear that they trained their daughters and gave them the same opportunity and support as their sons. Even so, although there are numerous books about the male throne-holders of the Sakyas, known as the Sakya Trizins, it is very difficult to find any comprehensive information about the illustrious daughters of the Khon family.

THE KHON JETSUNMAS AND THEIR FAMILIES

Historical information about Tibetan female practitioners is sparse, with the exception of major spiritual masters such as Machig Labdron (1055–1149), who is the subject of several lengthy biographies. Most women, including Machig Labdron, had to deal with cultural and religious prejudices. Their lives are rarely discussed in historical literature, except for the briefest of mentions of someone's mother or consort—mentions in which the woman frequently remains nameless. Yet Tibetan Buddhist women continue to strive for liberation, without many stories to relate their own understanding and experiences.

This book unveils "the jetsunma phenomenon": who is a *jetsunma* (a "venerable woman" worthy of worship), how one receives this title, and the unique position that Sakya jetsunmas have among Tibetan Budddhist practitioners. I focus on three historical Sakya jetsunmas—Jetsunma Chime Tenpai Nyima (1756–ca. 1855), Jetsunma Tamdrin Wangmo (1836–96), and her great-niece Kyabgon Pema Trinlei (1874–ca. 1950)—and on one contemporary jetsunma, Jetsun Kushok Chimey Luding (b. 1938), who lives in Canada and teaches throughout the world. In the Epilogue,

2. Dan Martin, "The Woman Illusion?," in Janet Gyatso and Hanna Havnevik, eds., *Women in Tibet* (New York: Columbia University Press, 2005), 79.

I present the young life of Jetsunma Kunga Trinley (b. 2007), the first vegan jetsunma.

Although information is scant for Jetsunma Chime Tenpai Nyima, the earliest jetsunma highlighted here, her life was so remarkable and record-breaking that it can't be ignored. She was the first female lama to bestow the most precious teachings of the Lamdre (Path with the Result), the core of Sakya philosophy and practice. Her spiritual acumen inspired many to become her disciples, including four Sakya Trizins and their wives and children (both daughters and sons). Jetsunma Chime Tenpai Nyima was also the teacher of some of most eminent lamas of Ngor Monastery, a renowned center of Sakya learning restricted to monks. These Ngorpa lamas in turn taught their disciples, who became influential lamas of the next generations.

The next jetsunma profiled here, Jetsunma Tamdrin Wangmo, practiced diligently from a very young age and became a great lama. Fortunately, one of her main disciples—her great-nephew the 39th Sakya Trizin—wrote her biography. In it, he remarked that "[in all of Tibet,] there is no one like her. She is incomparable."[3] One learns from the oral tradition of her ability to appear as the fierce Vajravārāhī, the goddess who has a boar's face on the side of her human head. Although she could seem ferocious when needed, Jetsunma Tamdrin Wangmo is best remembered as a kind lama who never discriminated and who taught anyone who requested teachings. She was also the second female lama to bestow the Lamdre teachings.

The third jetsunma profiled here, Pema Trinlei, received the title Kyabgon (One Who Protects), a prestigious title rarely conferred on female lamas. Although she was powerful and was a great *mahāsiddha*, or spiritual adept, Kyabgon Pema Trinlei encountered some discrimination as a woman. It appears she lost interest in teaching in her later years and chose to live and practice as a yoginī in a cave near Sakya. Kyabgon Pema Trinlei was the third woman to bestow the Lamdre teachings.

The fourth woman to bestow the Lamdre teachings is Jetsun Kushok Chimey Luding, who started her training at the age of six, began teaching at eleven, and became a fully empowered lineage-holder at eighteen. She

3. Dragshul Trinlei Rinchen (Drag shul 'phrin las rin chen), *Supplement to the Genealogy and Biography of Transmission Lineage Masters of the Sakyas (gDung rabs yang skong ngo mtshar kun 'phel sring shi'i dpal 'byor lhun grub mdzad pa po, brtan bshugs tshogs pa)* (India: Long-Life Offering Committee of the Golden Jubilee for the 41st Sakya Trizin, 2009), 416.

received the same teachings and made the same retreats as her younger brother, the 41st Sakya Trizin (b. 1945), who requested she start teaching again after she moved from India to Canada. Jetsun Kushok has founded Dharma centers in Canada, the United States, Germany, and Hungary, and teaches students globally.

An insider's view of the families of two Sakya Trizins is portrayed in this book, including the role of *dagmo* ("female lord"), the title given to wives of the Sakya Khon family. The diary of the 39th Sakya Trizin (1871–1935) reveals the interactions among his four siblings, his wife, their five daughters, their two sons, and their sons' co-wives.[4] Through these family dynamics, we learn how each family member was taught Buddhism and how they served the family, the Sakya people, and the Central Tibetan Government.

The family of the 41st Sakya Trizin is also featured, including his wife Gyalyum Tashi Lhakee (b. 1952), his sister Jetsun Kushok, their mother Dagyum Sonam Dolkar (1918–47), and her sister Dagmo Trinlei Paljor (1906–75). It was Dagmo Trinlei Paljor—their maternal aunt—who raised Sakya Trizin and Jetsun Kushok after the early deaths of their parents. Although Dagyum Sonam Dolkar and her older sister Dagmo Trinlei Paljor were not jetsunmas, they played pivotal roles in saving the family. Dagyum Sonam Dolkar became the third wife of Dagchen Ngawang Kunga Rinchen (1902–50), since her sister Dagmo Trinlei Paljor, his second wife, could not bear any children and his first wife had died tragically in childbirth. Dagmo Trinlei Paljor had the foresight to find the best teachers for her niece and nephew before they and many other Tibetans had to flee to India. She was also an exemplary practitioner, in addition to fulfilling all the duties of running the Dolma Palace household.

An overview of the Khon family and of Sakya ([Land of] Pale Earth) is also presented. From its modest beginnings Sakya evolved to become a major center for study and practice of Tibetan Buddhism, as well as an important pilgrimage destination. Its Lhakhang Chenmo, or Great Temple, one of the largest in Tibet, became famous because of the exceptional lamas of the Sakya Khon family. Over the generations, various sons of the Khon family have become the throne-holder, the Sakya Trizin. Even today, in exile, the tradition of the Sakya Trizin continues to be highly respected by practitioners worldwide.

4. On polyandry in Tibet, see notes 25, 75, and 252 below.

THE HIDDEN WORLD OF JETSUNMAS

Every daughter who is born into the Sakya Khon family is given the title Jetsunma at birth. This title is not exclusive to the Khon family, but it is uncommon for Tibetan infant girls to receive this title at birth because it is usually reserved for women who have become exceptional spiritual practitioners as adults. The great Sakya jetsunmas—profiled here for the first time in English—taught some of the most famous male lamas of their time. In several cases they also taught a great-niece, who in turn became a renowned teacher. To find this transmission of teachings from one female spiritual adept to another is exceptional and rarely documented.

The most eminent jetsunmas are *vidyādharas*, a Sanskrit term for those who realize the true nature of reality. This wisdom is not an intellectual understanding but a direct experience that exposes and ruptures the illusory view of a substantial reality of persons and phenomena. Those holders of wisdom, who can pierce through the seemingly substantial reality that is truly only a veil of powerful illusions, are *vidyādharas*. It requires a great deal of proper training, meditative practice, patience, perseverance, and faith to eventually have the direct experience of reality.

An ordinary person may have a restless mind, in which thoughts dominate with an endless chattering of words, or a mind that is scattered like leaves blowing in the wind. A great lama rests in the spaces between the thoughts, knows the chatter is simply trivial distraction, and does not react to it. The mind remains unflappable.

Jetsun Kushok, one of the most important female lamas alive today, and her younger brother, the 41st Sakya Trizin, were taught together by some of the most realized lamas in Tibet. One of their lamas was the great *rime* (*ris med*, "nonsectarian") master Jamyang Khyentse Chokyi Lodro (1893–1959), who wrote:

> *My Vital Advice*
> Your mind is the source of everything.
> It is skilled in deception and manipulation, and beguiling
>   when unexamined.
> Once you look into it, it is without basis or root.
> It comes from nowhere, stays nowhere and goes nowhere.
> Everything, including samsara and nirvana,

is but a reflection of pure and impure mind;
in reality neither samsara nor nirvana exists.

The source of compassionate awareness
is primordially empty. Though free from characteristics,
it is not just barren nothingness
but is luminous and naturally present.[5]

This is the mind of a wisdom-holder and a great lama. The four jetsun-mas highlighted in this book were taught by wisdom-holders, and although one not does find the title of wisdom-holder (Tib. *rigzin*) in all their names, their lives reflect their direct experiences of wisdom (Skt. *vidyā*; Tib. *rigpa*), or "the source of compassionate awareness" that is "luminous and naturally present."

Having this awareness, these jetsunmas are remembered as great lamas who shaped numerous lives in Tibet, just as Jetsun Kushok trains and guides Buddhist practitioners today throughout the world. When I have been with her, in our conversations there is a seamless transition from secular to sacred. Nothing seems strictly secular or exclusively sacred. These supposed polarities, which appear separate to many people, do not appear this way in Jetsun Kushok's presence. The two flow into each other without any clear edges. In her presence, one feels an expansiveness of concern, caring, and a desire to help. She combines the wonderful qualities of wisdom, power, and kindness.

Although Sakya jetsunmas were trained equally with the sons, not all Tibetans accepted female lamas as teachers. For example, when Kyabgon Pema Trinlei was visiting a nomadic region of northern Tibet to give a long-life initiation, some nuns who were there chided her, saying, "Who are you, a woman, to give us an initiation?" It is said that, in response, she removed her earrings and hung them in space on the sunbeams coming through the smoke-hole in the roof of the tent.[6] The nuns realized their prejudice and felt remorse for their disrespect toward the great jetsunma.

Extensive genealogies of the Sakya Khon family have been compiled beginning with the founding masters in the eleventh century, and these

---

5. https://safricachamtrulrinpoche.wordpress.com/2012/06/26/my-vital-advice.

6. David P. Jackson, *Lama of Lamas: The Life of the Vajra Master Chogye Trichen Rinpoche* (Kath-mandu: Vajra Publications, 2020), 31.

records have then been supplemented over the generations (see Chapter 1 for details). The 39th Sakya Trizin, Dragshul Trinlei Rinchen (1871–1935), wrote the last major update. However, these comprehensive genealogies (available only in Tibetan) focus almost exclusively on the male members of the family. Even though the Sakya Khon family has had many daughters as well as sons, one rarely finds a jetsunma identified by name in the genealogies, much less any recorded details about her life. Even in the case of one of the most eminent lamas, Jetsunma Tamdrin Wangmo, only one genealogical chapter among hundreds is devoted solely to her. As already mentioned, this entry was written by her great-nephew the 39th Sakya Trizin. He not only updated the genealogies but left us another invaluable source—a lifelong diary that he began keeping when he was eight years old (see Chapters 1 and 6).

The proliferation of elaborate and extensive biographies of the sons who become the Sakya Trizins and the dearth of information on the Sakya jetsunmas are characteristic of the gendered logic described by Tibetan historian Carole McGranahan, who remarks that, "As crucial as class is on many grounds, I find gender to make a bigger difference than class in making modes of production or narration."[7] In other words, even though the jetsunmas are part of a prestigious noble family that possesses annals and genealogies about its ancestors, the female family members' lives are rarely documented.

The jetsunmas' lives are thus hidden and difficult to uncover, but should nevertheless be revealed and known. In searching for information about the Sakya jetsunmas, one must determinedly read many biographies of their fathers, uncles, brothers, and teachers to find perhaps a single sentence about a jetsunma. For example, Jetsunma Chime Tenpai Nyima was a lama to four Sakya Trizins, their brothers, wives, sons and daughters, yet there is no chapter in the genealogies dedicated to her life. Instead, what we know of her is found embedded in the biography of one of her paternal first cousins, who is not remembered as a great lama himself. One can now see the difficulties in finding information about the jetsunmas.

In looking for information about the lives of Jetsunma Tamdrin Wangmo and Kyabgon Pema Trinlei, we are fortunate to have the 39th

7. Carole McGranahan, "Narrative Dispossession: Tibet and the Gendered Logics of Historical Possibility," in *Comparative Studies in Society and History* 52, no. 4 (2010): 776.

Sakya Trizin's comprehensive diary, in which he describes events in the lives of his great-aunt and teacher Jetsunma Tamdrin Wangmo and his younger sister Kyabgon Pema Trinlei. For the life of Kyabgon Pema Trinlei, I was also able to interview people in India, Nepal, and Seattle who knew her personally and who described eloquently what it felt like to be in her presence.

For Jetsun Kushok's life story, I interviewed her many times over the course of a decade at her home in Canada. I also interviewed her brother the 41st Sakya Trizin many times at the Dolma Palace in Rajpur, Uttarakhand, India, as well as in Walden, New York, the seat of the Dolma Palace family in the United States. Both Jetsun Kushok and the 41st Sakya Trizin are important teachers with busy schedules. Sometimes I had to wait a year or more for Her Eminence Jetsun Kushok or His Holiness the 41st Sakya Trizin to be free for a few hours. Since they grew up together, I heard many of the same stories from each of them. Sometimes their memories were similar, but occasionally either Jetsun Kushok or the 41st Sakya Trizin provided me with different or new information about a given time, place, or event. Their generosity in recounting their early lives in great detail makes this book unique. It would have been impossible to collect such particulars without their guidance and support.

In addition, I interviewed many people who knew Dagmo Trinlei Paljor, the aunt who raised both Jetsun Kushok and the 41st Sakya Trizin, and many others who know Jetsun Kushok and the 41st Sakya Trizin. For these interviews, I traveled in India, Nepal, Sikkim, Tibet, the United States, Canada, and Europe, frequently feeling that I was only a conduit for relaying the amazing lives of the Sakya jetsunmas and their close relatives.

Written for Buddhist practitioners and for anyone interested in the lives of female spiritual adepts of the illustrious Sakya Khon family, this book celebrates the lives of the Sakya Jetsunmas.

Sarva Mangalam, happiness to all.

CHAPTER ONE

The Sakya Jetsunma Phenomenon

T HE LIVES OF the Tibetan Sakya *jetsunmas* ("venerable women") are concealed, not by intention but simply by omission. Writing an account of a woman's life mattered less than recording the details of a man's life. Most Tibetans are unaware of the Sakya jetsunmas, and no scholar of Tibetan studies has written about them. This is the first book that chronicles their extraordinary lives.[8]

Jetsunma is a Tibetan term reserved primarily for particular women spiritual practitioners.[9] *Jetsun* is the equivalent of the Sanskrit *bhaṭṭārikā*, a word with many meanings, the most appropriate in this context being "venerable," or "person worthy of worship." It is used as a title for both deities and learned people, especially in Buddhism. It is unclear when the title Jetsun became popular in Tibet, but by the eleventh century, the famous yogi Milarepa (1052–1135) was known as Jetsun Milarepa (rJe btsun mi la ras pa). Compared to the many male spiritual masters who carry the title Jetsun, there are far fewer females who have this title. Women's names can be preceded either by Jetsun or by Jetsunma (the feminine form, sometimes translated as Venerable Lady).

Who are the women who receive this title, and why? There are at least two important ways of acquiring the title Jetsunma: by inherited status, and by achieved status—that is, by developing spiritual abilities that are then recognized by the religious and lay communities. The two are interrelated and can also overlap. Daughters born into either the Sakya Khon family or the Nyingma Mindroling Trichen (sMin grol gling khri chen)

---

8. Some of the material for this chapter was published initially in Elisabeth Benard, "Born to Practice: The Sakya Jetsunma Phenomenon," *Revue d'Études Tibétaines*, no. 34 (Décembre 2015): 1–20.

9. In Tibetan, one of the words for a nun is *btsun ma*; but not all jetsunmas are nuns, nor are all nuns jetsunmas.

family automatically receive the title Jetsunma at birth, since Tibetans believe that girls are born into such families only as a result of their meritorious actions and practices in earlier lifetimes. Her Eminence Jetsun Kushok Chime Luding Rinpoche (b. 1938, hereafter Jetsun Kushok, profiled in Chapters 8 and 9) is a jetsunma who received this title at birth. Another inspiring contemporary example is Mindroling Jetsunma Khandro Tsering Paldron Rinpoche (sMin grol gling rje btsun ma mkha' 'gro rtse ring dpal sgron rin po che), born in 1968 in Kalimpong, India.[10] She is the holder of both Nyingma and Kagyu Tibetan Buddhist lineages and has many disciples in both schools.

The second way to receive the title Jetsunma is by developing one's spiritual practice and subsequent accomplishments, thereby achieving the reputation of being an accomplished practitioner. This recognition can be given by the Tibetan community at large, as in the case of the well-known Jetsun Lochen Rinpoche (rJe btsun lo chen rin po che, 1852–1953) from Shuksep, a remarkable yoginī who had numerous disciples and lived for more than a hundred years.[11] Though many of her practices were Nyingma- or Kagyu-based, she considered herself to be a nonsectarian, or *rime* (*ris med*), practitioner and was best known for her *chod* (*gcod*) practices.[12]

Also an eminent lama can recognize a woman and bestow upon her the title of jetsunma. As a recent example, in February 2008, the 12th Gyalwang Rinpoche of the Drukpa Kagyu lineage honored the British-born Bhikṣuṇī Tenzin Palmo (b. 1943), who lived for twelve years in solitary retreat in a cave and undertook many other rigorous spiritual practices, with the title Jetsunma.[13] At an elaborate public ceremony in

---

10. In 1971 the 16th Karmapa recognized Khandro Rinpoche, as she is known, as a reincarnation of the great *ḍākinī* of Tsurphu Monastery, Khandro Orgyan Tsomo (mKha' 'gro O rgyan mtsho mo). See the chapter on Khandro Rinpoche in Michaela Haas, *Dakini Power: Twelve Extraordinary Women Shaping the Transmission of Tibetan Buddhism in the West* (Boston and London: Snow Lion, 2013), 15–40.

11. See Hanna Havnevik, "The Life of Jetsun Lochen Rinpoche (1865–1951) as Told in Her Autobiography," Ph.D dissertation, University of Oslo, 1999. There are different opinions about Jetsun Lochen's birth and death dates.

12. *Chod* ("severing the ego") is a Tibetan Buddhist meditative practice that involves the visualization of cutting up one's body and presenting it as an offering to others. By being able to do this skillfully, one develops generosity, reduces one's self-cherishing, and gains an understanding of absolute reality.

13. See the chapter on Tenzin Palmo in Haas 2013, 68–90.

Kathmandu, Nepal, he said that he was giving her this title "in recognition of her spiritual achievements as a nun and her efforts in promoting the status of female practitioners in Tibetan Buddhism." He stated:

> Men were always given the privilege to do all practices, but it was not given to women. This is very sad. But now it is different. It would be unkind if I would not give the title of Jetsunma to Venerable Tenzin Palmo for the benefit of all females in the world and the Palden Drukpa lineage.[14]

The unusual and almost unique status of Sakya jetsunmas compared to other autonomous religious women in Tibet is all the more significant in light of the life experiences of other jetsunmas and, more generally, a common cultural reluctance to support women and their spiritual practice. Jetsun Lochen is a prime example of a woman who was mistreated even by her own teacher, Pema Gyatso (d. ca. 1889). The following incident is only one of many difficulties she faced:

> Lochen had met her lama in the summer. In winter, he moved from his cave to another small nunnery nearby, where he gave extensive teachings and [they received] their food by begging alms and wherever Lochen went, people showed her great respect and generosity. Close by was a lama who received far fewer alms than Lochen and who highly resented her popularity. Finally, feeling he could bear it no longer, he went to see Pema Gyatso and told him that Lochen received a great deal of offerings. Pema Gyatso asked what was wrong with that, and he replied, "Nothing, but she goes around saying she is an incarnation of Dorje Phagmo [the highest female incarnation in Tibet]." Pema Gyatso said nothing, but when Lochen appeared before him a few days later with offerings she received, instead of accepting her gift, he grew very angry and accused her of lying and pretending she was an incarnation of Dorje Phagmo. As she stared at him in disbelief, he grabbed her offerings, climbed up to the roof of the nunnery, and flung

14. http://tenzinpalmo.com/index.php?option=com_content&task=view&id=18&Itemid=1, June 2008.

them down at her, along with his boots. Though Lochen was hurt, she crouched down to pick up the boots and placed them on her head as a mark of respect. After this incident, Lochen continued to attend her lama's teachings even though he ignored her.[15]

Various texts that discuss Tibetan views of women reiterate that women must endure more suffering than men due to their female bodies and their dependency on their families to support them. Many also stress the basic Tibetan view that due to being born female, women are *skye dman* (of "lesser birth"), meaning that they have produced worse karma than men in their past lives. The possibility of liberation from cyclic existence is therefore considered to be remote because, due to their lesser merit, they will have fewer opportunities to practice the Dharma (Buddhist teachings) in their present lives. Furthermore, women's bodies make them more vulnerable if they choose to live alone in an isolated place. Tibetan spiritual biographies, or *namthar* (*rnam thar*; literally, "stories of liberation from cyclic existence"), frequently recount the difficulties of practice for both women and men. Whereas men are encouraged to be monks and have the monastic community to support them, some women who are spiritually inclined must marry under duress, suffer ignobly under an unsupportive mother-in-law, or sever ties with their families in order to be able to devote their lives to spiritual practice. Comparing the spiritual biographies of female practitioners with those of men, it is rare to find a case where a family provides a daughter with the means and place to pursue concentrated and sustained spiritual practice.

Yet the Sakya jetsunmas do not face these difficulties. Instead, their status is akin to that of the prestigious male *tulkus* (*sprul sku*), or recognized reincarnations. Although Sakya jetsunmas are not considered recognized reincarnations—except for Jetsunma Kunga Trinley (b. 2007; see Epilogue)—the similarities with tulkus are noteworthy. First, it is believed that one is born into the Sakya Khon lineage only if one has already accumulated much merit in past lives; and many sons are considered reincarnations of their grandfathers, uncles, and/or someone

15. https://theyoginiproject.org/wisdom-dakinis/shuksep-jetsunma-chonyi-zangmo, June 2018. In this short biography Jetsun Lochen is referred to as Shuksep Jetsunma Chonyi Zangpo or Shungsep Jetsun.

else.[16] Second, like tulkus, jetsunmas are given opportunities for spiritual study at an early age. Third, everything is provided for the jetsunma, and after she dies her property is saved for future jetsunmas, in much the same way that the property and belongings of a tulku are passed down to his next reincarnation.

The Sakya Khon family has undergone numerous divisions, but ever since the early nineteenth century, there have been two main branches: the Dolma Phodrang (sGrol ma pho brang, Tara Palace), and the Phun-tsok Phodrong (Phun tshogs pho brang, Excellent Palace; see Charts 1–5). Until 1959, both had their main residences in Sakya (see Chapter 2), and both provided residences, or *labrangs* (*bla brang*), reserved exclusively for their daughters. The labrang was a place to live, study, meditate, and per-form religious rituals. Prior to 1959, jetsunmas were encouraged to live as nuns to pursue religious practice, yet they did not live in Sakya nunneries but in their own labrangs.

Jetsun Kushok described the traditional position of jetsunmas as follows:

Q: Why there are so few female lamas?

A: . . . Now, after the revolution (1959), it has changed. Otherwise, tra-ditionally, I could not have married. Once you were born a woman in the Khon family, you would automatically become a nun. It was your choice whether you took the vows and became a nun or not, but you had to wear the robes. Then you would receive empowerments like Hevajra and Chakrasamvara, and on those occasions you would take Vajrayana vows.[17] In the Vajrayana vows there is a kind of nun's vow included. These are serious vows, and therefore you could not marry.

Q: So once you were born as a woman into the Khon family, you could not lead a worldly life?

16. For example, Jetsun Kushok's younger brother the 41st Sakya Trizin (b. 1945) is recog-nized as a reincarnation both of his paternal grandfather and of Nyingma Terton Orgyen Thrinley Lingpa (gTer ston O rgyan phrin las gling pa, 1895–1945), also known as Apam Terton (A pang [or A pong] gter ston).

17. Every Sakya jetsunma receives anuttarayoga empowerments, which is the highest tantric empowerment. When a tantric practitioner takes this kind of empowerment, she is required to keep three vows—prātimokṣa, bodhisattva, and tantric vows.

A: No, you would always be learning, reciting, and meditating. Some nuns were doing handicrafts like sewing, knitting, and beadwork and so on. These rules were not set by the Tibetan government but by our family.[18]

During one of my interviews with Jetsun Kushok,[19] she explained that until their late teens Sakya jetsunmas usually lived in whichever of the two palaces they had been born into, and then they moved to a labrang that was maintained from one generation to the next by their respective palace. Each palace had five labrangs. If there were more than five daughters in one family, some of the daughters would share a labrang. To provide food and an income, the daughters were also given fields cultivated by servants and yaks and 'dri (female yaks) tended by nomads. As Jetsun Kushok explained:

> Everything comes together. It is like being born in the heavenly desire realm where everything comes together—servants, belongings, and so on. As long as [jetsunmas] did their practice and did not misbehave, the family provided everything. When they died, the immediate family could do what they wanted with their personal belongings. But the fields and animals belonged to the labrang; they could not be sold. These must be kept for the future daughters.

Some jetsunmas became great scholars and taught in Sakya and in Kham (southeast Tibet). Others kept a lower profile; they did their practices and chanting quietly and peacefully. Since everything in the labrang was set up for practice, including meditation rooms, some jetsunmas stayed in their labrangs their whole lives. Basically it was a lifelong retreat. Even if a jetsunma did not do serious religious practice but lived a quiet life with occasional outings, such as having picnics in the summer, she could stay in the labrang.

Jetsun Kushok noted that there were some scandals of jetsunmas marrying and leaving the Sakya area. However, these were the exception; most

18. See http://vajrasana.org/chime1.htm May 2009, accessed May 2016.
19. I interviewed Jetsun Kushok numerous times in 2008, 2010, 2013, and 2017, in Richmond, BC, Canada, and in Walden, New York (see Bibliography).

Fig. 1. Jetsunma Tsegen Wangmo and Jetsunma Chime Wangmo in the Phuntsok Palace in Sakya, Tibet.

Sakya jetsunmas had excellent reputations as committed nuns who did sustained spiritual practices. Furthermore, since most jetsunmas are considered to be spiritual adepts and highly realized women, finding a suitable spouse would be difficult. Jetsun Kushok recounted an interesting story:

> Most daughters in the Sakya family do not marry, because they are considered to be daughters of strong practitioners who cannot marry ordinary men. They all became nuns after this unfortunate incident: During the time of Chogyal Phagpa

Lodro Gyaltsen (Chos rgyal 'phags pa blo gros rgyal mtshan, 1235–80), one beautiful jetsunma married into a wealthy family from West Tibet. She never slept with her husband. She warned him that if he slept with her, it would not be beneficial for his family. He ignored her warnings and took her anyway. Shortly after their union, all the members of his family died.

Thus it is believed that few men have the correct compatibility to marry a jetsunma.

Another account of training from an early age comes from the Phuntsok Palace, from the sisters Jetsunma Tsegen Wangmo (Tshe byin dbang mo, b. 1936) and Jetsunma Chime Wangmo ('Chi med dbang mo, b. 1939; Fig. 1). Jetsunma Tsegen related:

We began studying at age six years old. First, we memorized the Tibetan alphabet, and then we learned how to read and write.[20] We had to memorize many texts; one of the first ones that we memorized was *Samantabhadra's Aspiration Prayer* (*bZang spyod smon lam*). At eight years old, we memorized the propitiation ritual to the Buddhist protector Mahākāla (mGon po'i bskang gso). We would study every day from eight in the morning until four in the afternoon, with a short lunch break. Our main holidays were on the eighth, fifteenth, and thirtieth days of the lunar month. Our first teacher was Ponlop Shakya and our second teacher was Ponlop Kunga.

When we became teenagers, we moved into a labrang. When I was fourteen years old, I moved in with my older sister, Thubten Wangmo (Thub bstan dbang mo, 1922–85), who was living in the Tashi Tseg Labrang in the Northern Monastery area. The move was gradual. I would stay for a few days, then return to the palace, then stay longer at the labrang, and do this a few times until I moved in permanently.

I did several retreats in the labrang. My first important one was Vajrapāṇi Bhūtaḍāmara (Phyag na rdo rje 'byung po 'dul byed). I was in retreat for one month together with my teacher,

---

20. In traditional Tibet, girls from noble families were taught how to read and write, but many other children only learned how to read. Tibetans did not deem it necessary to know how to write if one did not have an "official" position or belong to an "official" family.

who was supervising me. I heard that my family was going on a holiday to the hot springs and I yearned to go with them, but I knew that I needed to keep my commitment. My understanding mother gave me many dried fruits after their return.

Later my oldest sister moved to Gyantse and my second elder sister, Kalzang Chodron (sKal bzang chos sgron, 1926–2007), moved in with me. When I was eighteen years old, I did the crucial Hevajra retreat for seven months. At this time, my brother Trinly Rinpoche (Ngag dbang kun dga phrin las bkra shis, 1934–97) stayed at the labrang, too.[21]

The jetsunmas were given equal opportunity to study with all the religious preceptors or lamas who taught their brothers. Jetsun Kushok likes to emphasize that when they lived in Tibet she received the same teachings and did the same retreats as her younger brother, the 41st Sakya Trizin. One of the most important teachings and practices in the Sakya tradition is the *Lamdre* (*lam 'bras*, "Path with the Result"), a complete and gradual system that combines both the sutras (exoteric teachings) and the tantras (esoteric teachings) to provide a guided path to buddhahood. The 41st Sakya Trizin explains the Path with the Result as follows:

> This term indicates that this sacred system encapsulates the core of Sakya philosophy and practices resulting in the realization of the indivisibility of samsara and nirvana. This indivisibility means that the very samsaric appearances that we experience now themselves transform into pure appearances of primordial wisdom . . . the same base is experienced and seen by different beings, therefore it is called the indivisibility of samsara and nirvana.[22]

Elsewhere he puts it as follows:

> The crux to this golden teaching is the inseparability of the worldly existence (Samsara) and enlightenment (Nirvana). It

21. Personal communication at Jetsunma Tsegen Wangmo's home in Seattle, Washington, on August 28, 2007. These two jetsunmas are sisters of Jigdal Dagchen Sakya, the husband of Dagmo Jamyang Sakya (see Chapters 8 and 9).

22. H.H. Sakya Trizin, "Foreword," in Cyrus Stearns, trans. and ed., *Taking the Result as the Path: Core Teachings of the Sakya Lamdré Tradition* (Boston: Wisdom Publications, 2006).

follows that Nirvana is merely a transformation of Samsara. There is no abandoning of Samsara in order to achieve Nirvana, as the mind is the root of Samsara and Nirvana. Realising this inseparability is the key to attaining enlightenment.[23]

Ideally, every son and daughter in the Sakya Khon family should receive the transmissions and learn how to do the accompanying meditations, chants, and rituals explained in the Path with the Result. All sons are expected to become Lamdre lineage-holders and to continue its unbroken transmission to others.

Though daughters were often taught simultaneously with the sons, learned the meditations and rituals, and did the required retreats, few became lineage-holders and transmitted the Path with the Result to others. In 1955, however, at the age of 17, Jetsun Kushok expounded the teachings for three months (see Chapter 8), becoming the fourth woman in Sakya history to confer the Path with the Result.[24]

Though they received the same privileges as their brothers, the jetsunmas did not have the same obligations or responsibilities. Their brothers, especially those who were the oldest son, were expected to marry and produce a male heir; and sometimes two brothers married one wife to ensure an heir.[25] The male family members were also compelled to be knowledgeable about the significant Buddhist texts and to be proficient in the required religious rituals. They rarely had a choice between being a celibate monk, which some preferred, or marrying to continue the family lineage. Each was trained to be the next throne-holder—namely, the next Sakya Trizin. But only one would inherit this position, either from his paternal uncle or his father. In contrast, the daughters of the family had no such obligations to serve the public.

Nevertheless, occasionally an older jetsunma of the Sakya Trizin's family would be in charge while he went on pilgrimage or visited various

23. https://www.sakyatsechenthubtenling.org/lineage-and-teachers/.

24. The four jetsunmas who taught the Path with the Result are all profiled below: Jetsunma Chime Tenpai Nyima (Chapter 3), Jetsunma Tamdrin Wangmo (Chapter 4), Kyabgon Pema Trinlei (Chapter 5), and Jetsun Kushok (Chapter 8).

25. Alice Travers, "Exclusiveness and Openness: A Study of Matrimonial Strategies in the Dga' ldan pho brang Aristocracy (1880–1959)," *Journal of the International Association of Tibetan Studies* 4 (December 2008): 6–7. Fraternal polyandry was not unusual among aristocratic and taxpayer families in pre-1959 Tibet; see Melvyn C. Goldstein, "Stratification, Polyandry, and Family Structure in Central Tibet," *Southwestern Journal of Anthropology* 27, no. 1 (1971): 64–74.

areas of Tibet, Nepal, or India. As the Phuntsok Palace's sisters Jetsunma Tsegen Wangmo and Jetsunma Chime Wangmo underscored, "We were free. We were encouraged to study and practice [religion], but we could enjoy a more worldly life: it was our choice." In other words, the Sakya jetsunmas are wonderful yet exceptional examples of Tibetan women who were encouraged by their families and by society to be religious practitioners—and they were supported, both spiritually and materially, to do so.

THE SAKYA DAGMOS

Another important role fulfilled by women in the Sakya Khon family was that of *dagmo* ("lady," or wife of the *dagchen*, or lord). A woman who marries into the Khon family acquires the title Dagmo, but it is also a title given to many women in other Tibetan noble families, so it is not exclusive to the Khon family.

It is pertinent here that all marriages involving a Khon family son are secret and arranged. Jetsun Kushok explained that Sakya Khon marriages were always secret because each such marriage was first and foremost a spiritual union. The wife is seen as the consort (*yum*, "mother") of her husband (*yab*, "father") in his position as a tantric practitioner.[26] The wife is visualized as a deity, not as an ordinary human. As Jetsun Kushok put it, "Those [lamas] who make elaborate public wedding ceremonies are acting as ordinary people, not spiritual practitioners."

Jetsun Kushok's brother the 41st Sakya Trizin reiterated[27] that the bride is viewed as a *sangyum* ("secret mother," implying a spiritual partner), but that she is always called Dagmo, a higher title than Sangyum, which is a more common title. This is highlighted in the diary of the 39th Sakya Trizin, Dragshul Trinlei Rinchen (Drag shul 'phrin las rin chen, 1871–1935), who wrote: "Today the bride will become the Khon family brothers' wisdom consort (Tib. *rig ma*; Skt. *kulikā*). Union with the wisdom consort is to gain wisdom (Tib. *yeshe*; Skt. *jñāna*) in order to realize enlightenment."[28]

---

26. A spiritual consort in Tibetan Buddhism is an equal partner with her spouse. She is not considered a paramour such as a Japanese geisha or a courtesan in European traditions.

27. I interviewed H.H. the 41st Sakya Trizin in February 2004, December 2007, June 2012, June 2013, and December 2018 at the Dolma Palace in Rajpur, India, and in Walden, New York.

28. Dragshul Trinlei Rinchen, *Autobiographical Reminiscences of Sakya Trizin Dragshul Trinlei*

Thus the Sakya Khon family emphasizes correct compatibility in both secular and spiritual pursuits as essential. A dagmo must not only be able to run an extensive household and take care of many matters for the Sakya people, but must also be spiritually in tune with her husband, a skilled practitioner in tantric practices. As the scholar Miranda Shaw points out, "At this level the partners permeate one another's being and literally merge their karma and blend their spiritual destinies. This is one of the reasons that tantric union is designated as *karmamudrā*."[29] This blending of families and bodies to produce an heir—one who is capable of continuing the Sakya Khon family lineage as a significant spiritual practitioner and who can teach and transmit the Buddhist teachings properly—is the core of the Sakya Khon family's tradition. Selecting the right dagmo is crucial.[30]

Furthermore, if a dagmo's husband becomes the Sakya Trizin—the throne-holder of the Sakya school—she, too, acquires additional responsibilites and obligations. In the past, when the family lived in Tibet, the Sakya Trizin normally visited Lhasa once or twice in his life and paid an official visit to His Holiness the Dalai Lama. Nowadays, the Sakya Trizin must visit many Sakya monasteries, nunneries, and Dharma centers around the world. He must also attend functions of the Tibetan government in exile, such as ceremonies celebrating and protecting the long life of the Dalai Lama and other religious convocations. Furthermore, there are endless groups of dignitaries, officials, and high lamas who request private audiences or special teachings and religious transmissions, plus all his devotees who want to receive a blessing for their new child or for themselves, or a divination to help decide whether they should move, take a new job, have surgery, apply for a visa to go abroad, and so forth.

For example, Jetsun Kushok's sister-in-law Gyalyum Tashi Lhakee,[31]

Rinchen (*Rdo rje 'chang Drag shul phrin las rin chen gyi rtogs brjod*), 2 vols. (Dehra Dun: Sakya Centre, 1974), 2: 87.

29. Miranda Shaw, *Passionate Enlightenment: Women in Tantric Buddhism* (Princeton, NJ: Princeton University Press, 1994), 171. *Karmamudrā* ("action") is a Vajrayana Buddhist practice with a physical or visualized consort.

30. See Chapter 7 below for more details on how a dagmo is selected.

31. When a dagmo bears a child, she becomes known as *dagyum* ("lady mother"), and if her husband becomes the Sakya Trizin, she is referred to as *gyalyum* ("queen mother"). I interviewed Gyalyum Tashi Lhakee in her home, the Dolma Palace in Rajpur, India, in December 2007.

the wife of the 41st Sakya Trizin, who married her husband in 1974 in Puruwala, India, recalled that her father's advice when she married was:

> You have a big role in the Sakya tradition. You must respect His Holiness [the 41st Sakya Trizin] and his Aunt [Dagmo Trinlei Paljor (1906–75); see Chapter 6]. Do whatever service you can. You should not think of His Holiness as your husband: he is your guru. Take him as your root guru.

Gyalyum continued:

> When I became a dagmo, I learned how to deal with many different kinds of people—much more than if I had not married into the Khon family. I learned how to respect and serve lamas. I have to deal with the social and spiritual needs of people. I especially help people who are depressed, and I learned how to give love to people. I try to help them in whatever way I can. I console people. This is all my initiative; His Holiness does not ask me to do this.

This approach is epitomized in how the 41st Sakya Trizin and the Gyalyum welcome each person with warmth, as if that person is the only one they are seeing that day. Carolyn Swan, a longtime student of the 41st Sakya Trizin and Jetsun Kushok, remembered that, when she visited Rajpur, India, where the new Dolma Palace is located, it was clear that "Gyalyum had many responsibilities—overseeing the building of Dolma Palace—all the details from marble floors to plumbing fixtures—an impressive achievement." Gyalyum herself elaborated:

> Also I must take care of all social events in the Dolma Palace. If a high lama comes, I must make all the arrangements—organize the tents for a tea party, decide on the food, and invite the guests. I help with the work of Sakya monasteries in India and Nepal. Nowadays there is no problem in communication as there was in Tibet. Many of the monks approach me, rather than bothering His Holiness. Some have financial problems, and if it is a small amount, I take care of it. If it is a large sum, then I consult His Holiness. I will take care of small things but consult His Holiness about difficult situations.

When I asked Gyalyum to compare being a dagmo in India and in Tibet, she explained:

> I think that it is more difficult here because India is democratic. One does not have the same power as in Tibet. In Tibet, a dagmo could give an order and it was carried out. It was much more systematic. Sakya had many separate offices with different administrators who took care of things. In Tibet, the Dagmo was in charge of the Dolma Palace; she oversaw the entire palace. She had a chief chef, a business manager, the main attendants of His Holiness, the manager who took care of all the goods, one who took care of the kitchen storerooms, a horse and mule overseer, a chief cleaner, one who looked after the farms and the cattle. These were all Palace officials, and the Dagmo was in charge of all them. They reported to her. In India it is the not same; the Dagmo does not have much authority and must ask people for their help.

Gyalyum Tashi Lhakee is clearly a remarkable woman who has long served the 41st Sakya Trizin and the Dolma Palace with humility, grace, and dedication.

SOURCES OF THIS STUDY

The most extensive historical written sources available for the Sakya jetsunmas are the *Genealogies of the Sakya Families* (*Sa skya gdung rabs*).[32] Some of the more famous are the *Extensive Genealogy* (*gDung rabs chen mo*), written by the 27th Sakya Trizin, Jamgon Amezhab ('Jam mgon A mes zhabs, 1597–1659); its continuation by the 31st Sakya Trizin, Sachen Kunga Lodro, or Kunlo (Kun dga' blo gros, 1729–83); and its final supplement, written by the 39th Sakya Trizin, Dragshul Trinlei Rinchen (1871–1935).[33] Within these massive genealogies, one is lucky to find the names

---

32. There are numerous genealogies of the Khon family. Some of the earlier ones, written in the fifteenth century, are by sTag tshang lo tswa ba shes rab rin chen and Mus srad pa rdo rje rgyal mtshan. I thank Cyrus Stearns for this information.

33. Information about the jetsunmas is interspersed throughout Sachen Kunga Lodro's continuation and Dragshul Trinlei Rinchen's final supplement to the Sakya genealogies. See Sachen Kunga Lodro, *Sakya Genealogy* (*rJe btsun Sa-skya-pa'i gdung rabs rin po che'i rnam*

of the jetsunmas, or who their parents were, and possibly their teachers. Occasionally, if a brother or uncle was the Sakya Trizin or a significant scholar, one finds mention of a jetsunma going with him to visit Lhasa, the capital of Tibet, or to attend a teaching given by an important teacher such as the Dalai Lama.

In addition to the genealogies, a vital textual source of information was written by the 39th Sakya Trizin, Dragshul Trinlei Rinchen, who from the time he was eight years old kept diaries, which were compiled by his two sons and one of his main students, Khen Jampal Zangpo (1901–61), into two large volumes (each more than 800 pages) known as the *Auto-biographical Reminiscences of Sakya Trizin Dragshul Trinlei Rinchen (rDo rje 'chang Drag shul phrin las rin chen gyi rtogs brjod*; see Chapter 6). These provide contemporary information, especially about the two exemplary jetsunmas profiled in Chapters 4 and 5 below: Dragshul Trinlei Rinchen's paternal great-aunt, Jetsunma Tamdrin Wangmo (1836–96), who was one of his principal teachers; and his younger sister, Kyabgon Pema Trin-lei (1874–ca. 1950), a major lineage-holder of the important Vajrayoginī teachings and the paternal great-aunt of Jetsun Kushok. Chapter 6 por-trays Dragshul Trinlei Rinchen's family, which include his five daughters.

Alongside these textual sources, this book draws on the oral traditions passed down over the generations by the Sakya Khon family—primarily those of the Dolma Palace branch—as remembered by contemporary members of the family.[34] Having known the 41st Sakya Trizin for more than four decades, I asked for his help in this research, which he offered with enthusiasm and interest. His immediate approval of the project opened many doors for me. Due to his consent and support, everyone I asked for an interview readily accepted. The two people I relied on most were nevertheless His Holiness the 41st Sakya Trizin himself and his

---

par thar pa ngo mtshar rin po che'i bang mdzod dgos 'dod kun 'byung gi kha skong rin chen 'dzad med srid zhi'i dpal 'byor lhun grub) (India: Long-Life Offering Committee of the Golden Jubi-lee for the 41st Sakya Trizin, 2009); and Dragshul Trinlei Rinchen (Drag shul 'phrin las rin chen), *Supplement to the Genealogy and Biography of Transmission Lineage Masters of the Sakyas* (gDung rabs yang skong ngo mtshar kun 'phel sring shi'i dpal 'byor lhun grub mdzad pa po, brtan bshugs tshogs pa) (India: Long-Life Offering Committee of the Golden Jubilee for the 41st Sakya Trizin, 2009).

34. I interviewed Jetsun Kushok and the 41st Sakya Trizin as noted earlier (for details, see Bibliography). I also interviewed members of the Phuntsok Palace family, though not as frequently or extensively (see Bibliography).

older sister, Her Eminence Jetsun Kushok. Their oral information on the topic is invaluable.

When hundreds of thousands of Tibetans fled their beloved country due to the invasion of the Communist Chinese Army in the 1950s, Jetsun Kushok and her brother the 41st Sakya Trizin sought exile in India, just as the 14th Dalai Lama did in 1959. In the 1960s and 1970s, most of the monasteries, temples, and religious buildings in Tibet were systematically destroyed, erasing all traces of Tibetan history and grandeur. These were some of the worst decades in Tibetan history.

In 1983, I visited Sakya for the first time. Seeing most of Sakya destroyed, I was filled with sadness. Fortunately, the Great Temple was still standing. In the 1960s, its assembly halls, chapels, and rooms had been converted into stables, and its valuable artifacts taken to China to be eventually sold. The rest of Sakya was obliterated, including the Dolma Palace. In the past century, some visitors and pilgrims have visited Sakya. I think it is important to present a brief history of Sakya as a sacred area of Tibet, the origins of the Sakya family, and their role in establishing the Sakya school of Tibetan Buddhism. This summary is given below in Chapter 2.

CHAPTER TWO

The Multiple Meanings of Sakya

THE NAME SAKYA refers to a town, a principality, and the Tibetan Buddhist school established by the eminent family that has ruled in this area for a millennium. Sakya literally means "pale earth" (Tib. *sa skya*), because the earth in this area is distinguished by its pale grey color. Located in south Central Tibet, the Sakya principality covers about 2,100 square miles.[35]

THE TOWN AND PRINCIPALITY

The main town where people settled is known as Dan Sa (Seat of Power), but most people refer to it as Sakya. The northern and southern parts of the town are divided by the Grum River, which flows northwesterly into the mighty Tsangpo (Brahmaputra) River that eventually empties into the Sea of Bengal. Though Sakya's latitude is similar to that of Cairo, Egypt, or Jacksonville, Florida,[36] its altitude is above 14,000 feet. The area is so cold in summer that wheat cannot grow. Only barley can thrive.

The illustrious history of Sakya begins with Khon Konchok Gyalpo (Khon dkon mchog rgyal po, 1034–1102), the future patriarch of the Sakya Khon family.[37] One summer, Khon Konchok Gyalpo and his novice students were having a picnic on a mountain. Sitting in an alpine meadow

---

35. C. W. Cassinelli and Robert Ekvall, *A Tibetan Principality: The Political System of Sa sKya* (Ithaca, NY: Cornell University Press, 1969), xv. I recommend this book for a comprehensive explanation of Sakya.

36. The exact location of Sakya is latitude 28 degrees, 54' 18.00" N, and longitude 88 degrees, 01' 4.80" E.

37. For Khon Konchok Gyalpo's life and accomplishments, see Ronald Davidson, *Tibetan Renaissance: Tantric Buddhism in the Rebirth of Tibetan Culture* (New York: Columbia University Press, 2005), 271–74.

overlooking the valley below, he suddenly had an insight about this area of pale earth with its flowing stream, and proclaimed to his students that a temple should be built on this spot on the northern bank of the Grum River. Construction began in 1073. Upon completion this temple was known as Gorum Zimchil Karpo (sGo rum gzim spyil dkar po). From this single structure, the town expanded on both sides of the Grum River. The temple put Sakya on the map, and Dan Sa became the capital of the Sakya principality. The southern side of the river is flat and vast, whereas the northern side, known as Ponpori (dPon po ri), includes a low mountain with rock outcroppings and natural caves. Over the centuries both sides became replete with religious structures, which Khon Konchok Gyalpo's descendants have maintained through constant care and periods of massive restoration.[38] Sakya became a place of traditional learning and a holy site that pilgrims visited from all over Tibet.

THE KHON FAMILY AND ITS IMPORTANCE IN THE SAKYA SCHOOL

The Sakya school of Tibetan Buddhism is closely bound with the Khon family lineage. The family is known by three names: Lha Rig, Khon, and Sakya. In ancient times the family was first known as *lha rig*, which means "celestial lineage or clan." Family records and Tibetan histories emphasize that this noble family descended from the realm of luminous clarity to the Tibetan Plateau. The early ancestors are remembered as highly accomplished; it is said that some could fly and others could hang their robes on sunbeams. These are signs of knowing reality and cutting through appearances.

Later, the family name became Khon, which means "strife" or "feud." An account relates that one of the celestial beings from the lineage of luminous clarity fought with a demon. No reason is given for the fight, but the result was that the celestial being killed the demon and married the demon's wife. The child born from this union was named Khonpar Kye (Born in a Feud). This is the outer meaning of *khon*. But more importantly, since the demon symbolizes ignorance, the inner meaning is "defeating ignorance," the root of all suffering.

38. Jeff Schoening, "The Religious Structures of SA-KYA," in Lawrence Epstein and Richard F. Sherburne, eds., *Reflections on Tibetan Culture: Essays in Memory of Turrell V. Wylie* (Lewiston, NY: E. Mellen Press, 1990), 11–47.

The scholar-lama Migmar Tseten states: "The Khon trace their origin to a class of gods called *wosel lha* ('gods of luminous clarity'). . . . Manjushri [the Bodhisattva of Wisdom] is said to have emitted the three gods of luminous clarity to benefit others."[39] In this brief quote we can see that the Khon family traces its ancestry to a divine origin and consciously decided to come to Tibet with the motivation to help others. This association remains to the present day, and practitioners view many of the Khon family members as highly realized beings. Most of the sons are considered to be embodiments of the Bodhisattvas Mañjuśrī (the embodiment of Buddha's wisdom), Avalokiteśvara (the embodiment of the Buddha's compassion), and/or Vajrapāṇi (the embodiment of the Buddha's power). Some of the daughters are considered to be emanations of the great goddess Vajrayoginī.

Chapter 5 below notes that the jetsunma known as Kyabgon Pema Trinlei (1874–ca. 1950) was listed by her guru as his principal disciple for transmission of the *Compendium of Tantras* (*rGyud sde kun 'dus*) under the name "Lharig Khon Dung Jetsunma Pema Trinlei." *Lha rig* refers to her family's divine origin. During her visit in Kham (southeast Tibet) when she was conferring an empowerment, Kyabgon Pema Trinlei suspended a ritual vase in midair while arranging her robe that had fallen off her shoulder. She did this intentionally because she was aware that some monks had come to disrupt the empowerment, believing that it was inauspicious for a woman to confer an initiation. However, after witnessing this "miracle," some of their ignorance was dispelled and they eagerly sought her blessings after the completion of the initiation.

Though the family traces its origin to a divine ancestry, historically the Sakya Khon family originates with Lui Wangpo. He was one of the first seven Tibetans to be ordained as monks in the late eighth century at Samye Monastery, established in 779 C.E. as the first monastery in Tibet. However, the name Sakya was not associated with the family until the eleventh century, with their ancestor Khon Konchok Gyalpo (1034–1103), originally known as Khon Sakyapa.[40] Today the family continues to use the combined names of Sakya and Khon.

As the family's fame and power increased, one of the sons in each generation became the throne-holder of the Sakyas. His position was

39. Migmar Tseten, *The Treasures of the Sakya Lineage: Teachings from the Masters* (Boston and London: Shambhala, 2008), 229.

40. Tseten 2008, 228–32.

known by various titles, such as Gongma (Superior One), Trichen (Great Throne), and Trizin (Throne-Holder). In this book I use *trizin* in most places. This position is given to one son or nephew at a time, and only male members of the Khon family are eligible to become a Sakya throne-holder.[41]

Thus some of male members must marry to keep the lineage intact, although they are expected to maintain numerous vows similar to those taken by a monk. To show this combination of religious and lay status, they wear a white skirt that symbolizes the lay aspect, along with a red shirt that indicates the spiritual dimension. In contrast, those male family members who become monks wear a full-length red robe (with some saffron cloth as part of the sleeveless shirt).

The five founders of the Sakya school, beginning with Khon Konchok Gyalpo's son, Sachen Kunga Nyingpo (1092–1158), are known as "the three dressed in white and the two dressed in red" because three were laymen and two were monks. The three laymen were Sachen Kunga Nyingpo and two of his three sons, Lopon Sonam Tsemo (1142–82) and Jetsun Drakpa Gyaltsen (1147–1216). The two monks were Sakya Paṇḍita, or Sapan for short (1182–1251), who was a son of Palchen Odpo (1150–1203, the youngest son of Sachen), and Chogyal Phagpa (1235–80), who was a nephew of Sapan.

Over the centuries, divisions occurred in the family. Each division was known as a *labrang* (a residence or house). The last single residence for the Khon family was the Duchod Labrang,[42] after which the family divided into the Dolma Palace and the Phuntsok Palace in the nineteenth century. These two branches continue to thrive today. The Dolma Palace is located in Rajpur, India, and the Phuntsok Palace in Seattle, United States.

THE SAKYA SCHOOL

The Sakya school is one of the four major schools of Buddhism in Tibet. It developed in the late eleventh century, during the second diffusion of Buddhism there. At this time Tibetans went to India to find Indian gurus with whom they could study and receive the precious Buddhist

41. See Appendix C for more information about the position of Sakya Trizin.
42. See the Dudchod Labrang Genealogical Chart in Chapter 3.

teachings. The Tibetan students met different gurus who had distinct teachings. These teachings were distinguished not so much by philosophical differences as by allegiance to the instruction lineages given by specific masters. The Sakya lineage began with Khon Konchok Gyalpo. He was the main disciple of Drogmi Lotsawa Shakya Yeshe (993–1072), an excellent translator who had studied Sanskrit and received the authentic Lamdre (Path with the Result) teachings in India.

This important transmission began in ninth/tenth century with the Indian scholar-yogi Virūpa, who was one of the Eighty-Four Mahāsiddhas. Lamdre is one of the most important teachings of the Sakya tradition (see Chapter 1). It outlines the complete Buddhist path in progressive stages, beginning with the necessary preliminaries and culminating in the highest level of buddhahood. Having received these teachings, Khon Konchok Gyalpo, and his sons and grandsons, continued to practice and transmit the Lamdre teachings. With emphasis on these teachings, the Sakya school was established and has flourished to the present day.

The Sakya school received other exceptional teachings from Tibetan translators who had studied with Indian masters. Mal Lotsawa introduced the Vajrayoginī lineage known as "Naro Khachodma." This continues to be one of the most significant teachings in the Sakya school, and its transmission and cycle of teachings are taught by many lamas up to the present time. Bari Lotsawa (1040–1111) transmitted many tantric practices, the foremost being the cycle of practices known as the "One Hundred Sādhanas."[43]

His Holiness Gongma Trichen Rinpoche, the 41st Sakya Trizin (b. 1945, r. 1959–2017), has explained that the Sakya school has three specialties, prophesies, and visions that helped establish the Khon lineage and ensure that the teachings would flourish:

- In the eighth century Padmasambhava made a prophesy that in the future a large monastery would be built in the Ponpori hills that would provide immense benefit and spread the teachings in all directions. He then blessed the land and built four stupas, one in each direction, where the Sakya monastery would later be built.

43. For the recent inauguration of the Sakya Temple of the Dolma Phodrang in Bodhgaya in November 2019, the beginning of the "One Hundred Sādhanas" was transmitted. This transmission will continue at the Sakya Temple for several years until it is completed.

- When visiting the area, the Indian scholar Atisha had a vision in 1042. After seeing seven Sanskrit letters on the empty, grey earth that would become Sakya, he prophesied that many great Bodhisattva emanations would be born here. In accordance with Atisha's prophecy, the Sakya family lamas are regarded as emanations of Avalokiteśvara, Mañjuśrī, and Vajrapāṇi.

- Sakya Kunga Nyingpo, the son of Khon Konchock Gyalpo, had a vision of Virūpa, the original Indian guru of the Lamdre teachings. Virūpa covered the grey earth across the whole valley of Sakya with his body, blessing it with the proclamation, "This earth belongs to me."[44]

Visionary encounters are recognized as both a mystical phenomenon and a source of important transmission of teachings or instructions in the Tibetan Buddhist tradition.

THE GREAT TEMPLE

The Grum River divided Sakya into two main sections. As the Sakya Khon family and the Sakya school began to attract practitioners and faithful followers, a massive temple complex was constructed on the southern side of the Grum in the thirteenth century.[45] Known as the Lhakhang Chenmo, or Great Temple (Fig. 2), it was one of the largest temples in Tibet.[46] Each of its surrounding outer walls is about 260 feet long.[47] The main temple has an extensive two-story assembly hall, also referred to as the Sutra Hall, which can hold 7,000 monks. It is considered the largest single assembly hall in a temple in Tibet. When it was completed it had 156 pillars, each about 5 to 6 feet thick.

The Great Temple complex dominates the flat and vast southern side of the river. Within its high walls were many sections and buildings hous-

---

44. "What Is the Sakya Tradition?," Tibet House, New York, April 2018. https://www.youtube.com/watch?reload=9&v=GqGLvDUYOug.

45. See Matthew Akester, "The Last Traces of Gyere Lhakhang," *The Tibet Journal* 29, no. 3 (2004): 55–64. The no longer extant Gyere Lhakhang was the inspiration for the Lhakhang Chenmo.

46. Cassinelli and Ekvall 1969, 12.

47. Ibid., 290.

Fig. 2. The Lhakhang Chenmo, or Great Temple, Sakya, 2007.

ing lamas who taught Buddhist philosophy and the monks who studied with them. Nearby was the Tara Temple, one of the Four Wonders of Sakya (see next section). Both the Dolma Palace and Phuntsok Palace were located on the southern side.

The northern side, known as Ponpori, is a low mountain with rock outcroppings and natural caves. Over the centuries the northern side became filled with buildings large and small. Largest was the Zhitog building, with five floors, where Sakya Trizin and his family lived on the upper floors during the winter months. Administrative offices were on the lower floors. Also, there was the large Northern Monastery, where esoteric Buddhism, or tantra, was taught. A few buildings had beautiful golden metal roofs, which gleamed for miles. The famous Namgyal Stupa, another of the Four Wonders, was in the northwest, and temples dedicated to particular deities and protector shrines were found throughout the northern section. Some of the jetsunma labrangs, or residences, were located in the middle section. In the lower sections nearer to the Grum River were many residences of the Sakya people. Pilgrims were awestruck by glorious Sakya.

Fig. 3. Gyalyum Tashi Lhakee's extended family in Gangtok, Sikkim, 1964/65. Kunga Yonten Horchotsang is at top center left, with the young Tashi Lhakee at top center right.

Over the ensuing centuries, thousands of Tibetans came as pilgrims to Sakya to pray, make offerings, and visit the myriad impressive buildings. In 1956, when the future wife of the 41st Sakya Trizin, Gyalyum Tashi Lhakee, was only four years old, her extended family—which included her immediate family and her first cousin Kunga Yonten Horchotsang's family—made a pilgrimage to Sakya from their natal home in Kham (southeast Tibet). She never imagined that, two decades later in India, she would marry the 41st Sakya Trizin. Her family knew the Khon family of the Phuntsok Palace well, and they were welcomed as guests to the palace. Some of the attendants of the Phuntsok Palace were their main guides as they visited the temples. Tashi Lhakee's older cousin Kunga Yonten Horchotsang (Fig. 3) was amazed that Sakya had so many temples. The Great Temple impressed him tremendously. He recalls visiting the temple in 1956:

> The Lhakhang Chenmo was one of the largest temples that I had ever seen. If a man stood at a corner of the temple and if you looked from the other corner, he looked very small. When I entered the main temple, I saw that many larger-than-life-

sized statues filled the rear wall. They were very impressive and enormous.[48]

The Great Temple contained many unusual objects (Fig. 4). For example, the northeast pillar was named the Kublai Khan pillar because it had been a gift from the emperor to Chogyal Phagpa (1235–80), the fifth founder of the Sakya school. Due to his relationship as religious preceptor to Kublai Khan, Chogyal Phagpa was able to amass the funds to build the Great Temple. The story is that the enormous tree trunk "was carried by hand from China and the marks of the iron spikes that held the carrying racks remained visible. This pillar symbolized both a political and spiritual function; it was presented as a gift by the Mongolian emperor of China [Kublai Khan], who recognized the special political status and power of Sakya. Each New Year's day, the chief representative of the Sakya Government hung a white scarf on the pillar and monks hung a scarf on it whenever they received a large donation for the temple."[49]

The Great Temple (which survives today) also houses a special conch said to have belonged to the Buddha himself. Later, the Indian king Dharmapala presented it to the Chinese emperor, and when Kublai Khan became emperor of China, he gave it to Chogyal Phagpa.[50] Pilgrims to Sakya believe that when the conch is touched to their heads, the blessing grants their wishes.

Another major gift from Kublai Khan consisted of Tibetan manuscripts written in gold letters. Kunga Yonten Horchotsang recalls that, in 1956,

> Behind the main altar in another room, there were books everywhere. The expression was that books were piled as high as a rocky mountain. One book was so large that it was the

48. Interview with Kunga Yonten Horchotsang at the Institute of Tibetology on April 23, 2009, in Gangtok, Sikkim. He is the former Director of the Institute of Tibetology.

49. Cassinelli and Ekvall 1969, 291. Among Tibetans, a white scarf is offered to another person in many situations. It may be given as a welcome or farewell, as congratulations or as another honor, and all Tibetans celebrate New Year's by offering white scarfs to each other. The pillar symbolized the relationship between Chogyal Phagpa and Kublai Khan and the special status that the Sakyas have in Tibet due to this relationship.

50. Shoening 1990, 11.

Fig. 4. The main altar in the Great Temple, Sakya.

size of a table. [This manuscript of loose pages was 6 feet long and 1.5 feet wide.] It was bound with an iron hook. The name of the book was *lcags lung ma*. Normally the Prajñāpāramitā manuscript had 16 volumes, but this large book contained all 16 volumes in one volume. It had blue folios that were handwritten in silver, gold, pearl, turquoise, and conch shell. It was a wonder.[51]

Long before, during his visit in early December 1882, the Indian scholar Sarat Chandra Das (1849–1917) had noted:

There are preserved here many volumes written in gold letters; the pages are six feet long by eighteen inches in breadth. On the margin of each page are illuminations and the first four volumes have in them pictures of a thousand Buddhas. These books are bound with iron. They were prepared under the orders of Emperor Kublai and present to [Chogyal] Phagpa on his second visit to Beijing.[52]

In November 1900, the Japanese monk Ekai Kawaguchi (1866–1945) remarked:

Once inside we were lost in a sea of dazzling gold; the splendor was simply beyond description. The ceilings and the pillars are all covered with gold brocade, and the images, more than three hundred in number are emblazoned with very fine gold. In the centre of the room there stands a statue of Shakyamuni Buddha, 35 feet high, which, we are told, is made of mud and covered with gold.[53]

Most buildings in Sakya, with the exception of the Great Temple, have distinctive broad vertical stripes of white, red, and blue against a grey

---

51. Interview with Kunga Yonten Horchotsang on April 23, 2009, in Gangtok, Sikkim.

52. Sarat Chandra Das, *Journey to Lhasa and Central Tibet*, ed. W. W. Rockhill (New York: E.P. Dutton and Company, 1902), 241.

53. Ekai Kawaguchi, *Three Years in Tibet* (Benares and London: Theosophical Publishing Society, 1909), 242.

background. The white stripes are said to represent Avalokiteśvara, the Bodhisattva of Compassion; the red, Mañjuśrī, the Bodhisattva of Wisdom; and the blue stand for Vajrapāṇi, the Bodhisattva of Power.[54] These bodhisattvas are known as the Lords of the Three Families (Rigs gsum mgon po).

In Tibetan Buddhism, the goal is to become enlightened so as to be able to help all sentient beings, who are reborn again and again in cyclic existence due to their ignorance of absolute reality. To help others, one needs the abilities of these three bodhisattvas—compassion, wisdom, and power. Many of the great lamas of the Sakya school are considered to be manifestations of one or more of these three bodhisattvas. As a constant reminder to develop and nurture these three qualities, many buildings of the Sakya school both inside and outside Tibet have this identifying color scheme.

THE FOUR WONDERS OF SAKYA

There were many buildings and sacred artifacts in Sakya, four of which were known as the Four Wonders of Sakya. Pilgrims with limited time in Sakya would try at least to see the Four Wonders. The first is a special statue of the goddess Tara. One of the great lamas who was very influential in establishing Sakya as a place of pilgrimage was Bari Lotsawa Rinchen Drak (1040–1111), known as Bari the Translator. The Sakyas believe that the goddess Tara accompanied him wherever he went. One day Bari the Translator witnessed Tara merging into a white turquoise stone. He picked up the stone, which had become a statue of Tara, and built a temple to enshrine her. It is best known as the Tara Temple, or Dolma Lhakhang. A lesser-known name is the White Turquoise Temple (Yu khar mo), because Bari placed the special small white turquoise statue of Tara inside a larger metal statue of Tara in the temple. The Tara Temple existed for almost a millennium. Sadly, the Communist Chinese destroyed it and everything inside it during the Cultural Revolution. Fortunately, someone was able to hide the precious white turquoise statue, and again it has been placed inside a Tara statue located in the main temple of Sakya. The Tara Temple has not been rebuilt.

54. This is one prevalent explanation, but not the only one. Some say that these three colors represent the face of another important protector deity, Vajrakīlaya.

The second of the Four Wonders is the Namgyal Stupa (or reliquary receptacle) constructed under the orders of Bari the Translator and dedicated to the Goddess of Victory (Namgyal), a goddess associated with long life and purification. After Bari's death, his remains were placed in this stupa. Among Sakya followers, it is believed that this stupa serves as barometer of the well-being of the Sakya Khon family.

Dagmo Jamyang Sakya (b. 1934), who married Jigdal Dagchen Sakya Rinpoche (1929–2016), oldest son of the Phunstok Palace family, lived in Sakya from the late 1940s until 1959. She related the following about the Namgyal Stupa.[55] When she returned to Sakya in 1986 for the first time since 1959, almost everything there had been destroyed. It was difficult for her to accept that temples, monasteries, nunneries, and residences built over the course of a millennium had been reduced to rubble. But this devastation did not crush her hope for a new Sakya. Her uncle, the illustrious 3rd Dezhung Rinpoche (1906–87), had asked her to visit certain places, including the Namgyal Stupa. Dagmo Jamyang Sakya told me:

> When I visited in 1986, the temple was destroyed and the gold was taken from the stupa.[56] So when the Chinese officials asked me what I wanted, I told them, "Please rebuild this stupa." I immediately took off my two gold bracelets as offerings for the rebuilding of the stupa.

When she made a second visit in 1996, she was happy to see that the Namgyal Stupa had been rebuilt very well.[57]

The third of the Four Wonders was unusual in both its manufacture and its history. Known as "the flying black-leather mask" (bse 'bag nag po

---

55. I interviewed Dagmo Jamyang Sakya in June 2007, 2012, and 2018 at her home in Seattle, Washington.

56. When I visited Sakya in 1983, the large Namgyal Stupa had been destroyed. However, the people in Sakya had found the smaller stupa with the Goddess of Victory statue, which had been inside the original larger stupa. The Tibetans were overjoyed to recover this precious stupa and statue, which Bari the Translator had placed in the large stupa.

57. Tibetan Buddhist statues and stupas are filled with precious objects. This stupa contained 300,000 mantras of the Goddess of Victory. Bari had also inserted soil from the sacred land of India, a piece of the Bodhi tree, relics of the Historical Buddha, and the waistcoat (samghati) from the robe of Buddha Kasyapa. See Jeff Schoening, "The Sakya Throne Holder Lineage," master's thesis, University of Washington, 1983, 79.

'phur shes), it represents Pañjaranātha Mahākāla as a potent protector. It is believed that the mask was made from the skin of an Indian king who was antagonistic toward Buddhist teachings. This mask reportedly flew to Tibet to be with the great translator Rinchen Zangpo (958–1055). One of Rinchen Zangpo's disciples, known as Mal the Translator, came into possession of this mask. He gave it to Sachen Kunga Nyingpo (1092–1158), the first founder of the Sakya school, after Sachen had received the empowerment of the great Pañjaranātha Mahākāla. The story continues that Mal the Translator commanded, "Mahākāla, I don't need you here. Run off and be the Dharma Protector of the 'Khon Sa skya pa!'"[58]

The mask followed Sachen back to Sakya, where it obeyed Sachen's and his descendants' instructions. Indeed, Pañjaranātha Mahākāla is considered one of the preeminent protectors of the Sakyas to the present day. The mask is the only one of the Four Wonders that was not recovered after the destruction of Sakya in 1960s and 1970s; no one knows whether it is still extant.

The fourth wonder is a statue of Mañjuśrī that Sakya Pandita Kunga Gyaltsen (or Sapan, 1182–1251) created for one of his main teachers, his paternal uncle Jetsun Dakpa Gyaltsen (1147–1216). It is one of the Four Wonders both because Sapan himself created and blessed it and because it was the main object of meditation (*nang rten*) for his uncle, who was an extraordinary teacher and mystic. Originally it was housed in the Utse Nyingma building, built by Sapan's grandfather Sachen. The building was destroyed in the 1960s by the Communist Chinese army. Fortunately, the statue was found among the ruins of the building and is now in one of the chapels of the Great Temple.[59]

THE PRESENT SAKYA

Thus the glorious Sakya principality evolved from the eleventh to the mid-twentieth century. The two branches of the Khon family had their palaces in Sakya, and the wondrous sights of Sakya shone as beacons of hope and refuge. Unfortunately, in the 1960s and 1970s the Chinese Communist army destroyed almost all the temples, residences, and monas-

---

58. Cyrus Stearns, *Luminous Lives: The Story of the Early Masters of the Lam 'bras Tradition in Tibet* (Boston: Wisdom Publications, 2001), 141.

59. Schoening 1990, 14.

teries; only the Great Temple was spared because of its association with the "Chinese" emperor, the Mongolian Kublai Khan. Beginning in the mid-1980s, when some of the dire restrictions were lifted, Sakya began to rebuild itself, as did the rest of Tibet, and it has become a place of pilgrimage once again. However, the Chinese Communist government has imposed many constraining rules. No one can teach the profound texts of Buddhist philosophy. People pray with wariness and fear of possible reprisal if they are labeled a "splitter of the motherland," which is considered a crime of treason. Some of sons of the Khon family who returned for a visit were allowed to remain in Sakya for only two hours, from 3:00 to 5:00 a.m. They could not see anyone, or give blessings or teachings, but were compelled to leave before dawn, with heavy hearts.

Although it remains difficult to be a Buddhist in Tibet today, the Sakya school and its teachings are thriving in exile. Its extraordinary lamas can freely teach in most parts of the world, and they have many more disciples than they would have had in Tibet. Sakya as a place or principality has diminished in stature, but the importance of the Sakya school and the Khon family has proliferated.

CHAPTER THREE

Emanation of Vajrayoginī:
Jetsunma Chime Tenpai Nyima (1756–ca. 1855)

As DISCUSSED PREVIOUSLY, all daughters born into the Sakya Khon family are known as *jetsunmas*. Though one finds biographies of the sons—or *dungsays* (*gdung sras*)—of the Sakya Khon family, biographies of jetsunmas, even the most eminent ones, do not exist. A glaring example is the inadequate account of Jetsunma Chime Tenpai Nyima's illustrious life, which is embedded in the life story of her first cousin Kunga Phende Gyatso,[60] a son of her renowned paternal uncle and main teacher, Sachen Kunga Lodro (1729–83).[61] This material is found in the 39th Sakya Trizin Dragshul Trinlei Rinchen's final supplement to the Sakya genealogy (see Chapter 1).

Jetsunma Chime Tenpai Nyima (1756–ca. 1855) is remembered as an exemplary practitioner and as a teacher of four Sakya Trizins (the 33rd, 34th, 35th, and 36th), as well as their brothers, wives, sons, daughters, and many of the most respected reincarnations and significant teachers in the Sakya tradition. She is also remembered for three additional important accomplishments: (1) she is the sole woman in the lama transmission lineage of the Sakya Nāropa teachings of the goddess Vajrayoginī, including the accompanying teachings;[62] (2) she is one of only four jetsunmas to

---

60. Kunga Phende Gyatso (Kun dga' phan bde rgya mtsho, 1766–88) was also known as Evam Zangpo. Dragshul Trinlei Rinchen 2009, 342–43.

61. Sachen Kunga Lodro was the 31st Sakya Trizin (r. 1741–83). He was a great practitioner, teacher, and prolific writer. Many illustrious lamas from various Tibetan Buddhist sects studied with him, including the Nyingma Jigme Lingpa (Jigs med gling pa, 1730–98) and the Gelugpa 3rd Tukwan Lobzang Chokyi Nyima (Thu'u bkwan blo bzang chos kyi nyi ma, 1732–1802), who received teachings in Sakya while he was visiting Central Tibet between 1757–61.

62. In the lama (or guru) transmission lineage of these Sakya Nāropa teachings, the 27th guru is Sachen Kunga Lodro (1729–83); the 28th is Ngor Thartse Je Jampa Namkha Chime (Thar tse rje byams pa nam mkha'i 'chi med, 1765–1820); the 29th is Jampa Namkha Lekpai

date to bestow the seminal Sakya teaching of the Lamdre (Path with the Result; see Chapter 1); and (3) she is the sole woman in the lama transmission lineage of the teaching on *Parting from the Four Attachments.*

FAMILY BACKGROUND

Jetsunma Chime Tenpai Nyima was born in Sakya on the twenty-second day of the eleventh month in 1756 (Chart 1). This was considered an auspicious date and a foreshadowing of her own future accomplishments because it is the *parinirvana* date (anniversary of the passing) of her illustrious ancestor Chogyal Phagpa (see Chapter 2). Her birth name was a very common one given to many Tibetan baby girls: Chime Butri (Immortal One Who Brings Forth a Son).[63] Her father was Ngawang Thutob Wangchuk (1734–57), the younger brother of the more renowned Sachen Kunga Lodro (1729–83); and her mother was the Gerpa princess Tashi Yangchen (sGer pa'i sras mo bKra shis dbyang can, d. 1756). Her mother died shortly after giving birth to her, and her father died the following year;[64] she was their only child. Fortunately, her paternal uncle Sachen Kunga Lodro took care of her.

EARLY TEACHINGS AND LAMAS

From a very young age, Jetsunma Chime Tenpai Nyima's main teacher was her uncle Sachen Kunga Lodro. One day, he had a vision of Ngorchen Kunga Zangpo (Ngor chen kun dga' bzang po, 1382–1456), founder of prestigious Ngor Ewam Choden (Ewam chos ldan) Monastery, who prophe-

Lhundrup (Byams pa nam mkha'i legs pa'i lhun grub, n.d.); *the 30th guru is Chime Tenpai Nyima*; and the 31st is Ngawang Rinchen (Ngag dbang rin chen), also known as Tashi Rinchen (bKra shis rin chen, 1824–65), who was the 35th Sakya Trizin (see Chart 3 in Chapter 5 below). Many names in Tibet are unisex, so one would not necessarily know that the name Chime Tenpai Nyima refers to a woman without its being preceded by the title Jetsunma. (Chime Tenpai Nyima is, however, referred to as a nun in a few extant lists of this guru transmission lineage.)

63. 'Chi med bu khrid. Though Butri (Bukhrid) is a name given to daughters in Tibet, it seems odd to choose it for a jetsunma who was expected to be a nun and who would be trained accordingly.

64. See Sachen Kunga Lodro 2009, 738, for the death of Jetsunma Chime Tenpai Nyima's mother, and p. 751 for death of her father. On p. 753, it states that her father stayed in meditation (*thugs dam*) for three days after his death.

sied that he would have four "pillar" and eight "beam" disciples. In fact, Jetsunma Chime Tenpai Nyima became one of her uncle's "pillars," meaning that she was one of his closest disciples and would carry on his teachings. In addition, she had a strong connection to various Ngor Monastery lamas.

Among Tibetan Buddhists, the choice of empowerments to receive can vary according to personal inclination, the availability of a qualified teacher, and the tradition of the family. Since members of the Sakya Khon family are educated to become religious teachers, the empowerments they receive have a predictable pattern. In the Sakya tradition, some of the most important deities are Hevajra (Kye Dorje), Vajrayoginī (Naro Khachod), Vajrakīlaya (Dorje Phurba), and Sarvavid Vairocana (Kunrig).

Various empowerments for each of these deities are preserved by different transmission lineages, and each empowerment is accompanied by particular teachings and related commentaries. Due to the paucity of information about Jetsunma Chime Tenpai Nyima embedded in her first cousin's life story, we have few details about her daily spiritual endeavors, though we can infer some aspects of her major meditative practices.

First, we know from the material in her cousin's biography that her uncle Sachen Kunga Lodro imparted to her all the teachings concerning the goddess Naro Vajrayoginī. Later in life, her association with these teachings propelled her to fame as Vajrayoginī incarnate, a belief that remains a substantial part of her legacy.

These empowerments and teachings of the goddess Vajrayoginī comprise a paramount practice among Tibetan Buddhists, especially among the Sakyas. Many of the great Sakya jetsunmas are considered to be an emanation of Vajrayoginī. Devotees of Vajrayoginī belong to various lineages. For the Sakyas, the most popular lineage originates with the Indian *mahāsiddha* ("great adept") Nāropa (956–1040),[65] a renowned scholar at the prestigious Buddhist university of Nālandā in northern India.

According to one story, Nāropa was proud of his acumen and his understanding of Buddhist philosophy. One night when he went to relieve himself, he encountered an old woman cleaning the urinals. As a great scholar, he was not willing to acknowledge such a low-caste woman. However, the woman started to question him: "Do you know the Buddhist teachings?" Looking at her askance, he answered dismissively,

---

65. There are a variety of dates for Nāropa.

CHART 1. THE DUCHOD LABRANG

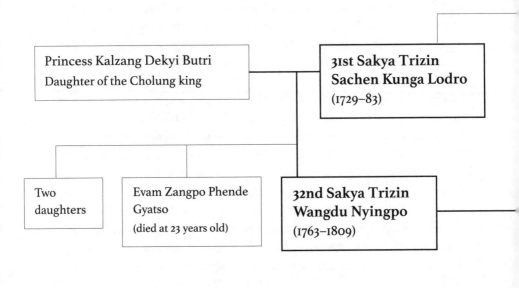

Princess Kalzang Dekyi Butri
Daughter of the Cholung king

**31st Sakya Trizin
Sachen Kunga Lodro**
(1729–83)

Two
daughters

Evam Zangpo Phende
Gyatso
(died at 23 years old)

**32nd Sakya Trizin
Wangdu Nyingpo**
(1763–1809)

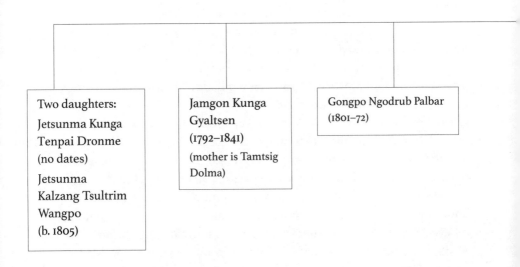

Two daughters:

Jetsunma Kunga
Tenpai Dronme
(no dates)

Jetsunma
Kalzang Tsultrim
Wangpo
(b. 1805)

Jamgon Kunga
Gyaltsen
(1792–1841)
(mother is Tamtsig
Dolma)

Gongpo Ngodrub Palbar
(1801–72)

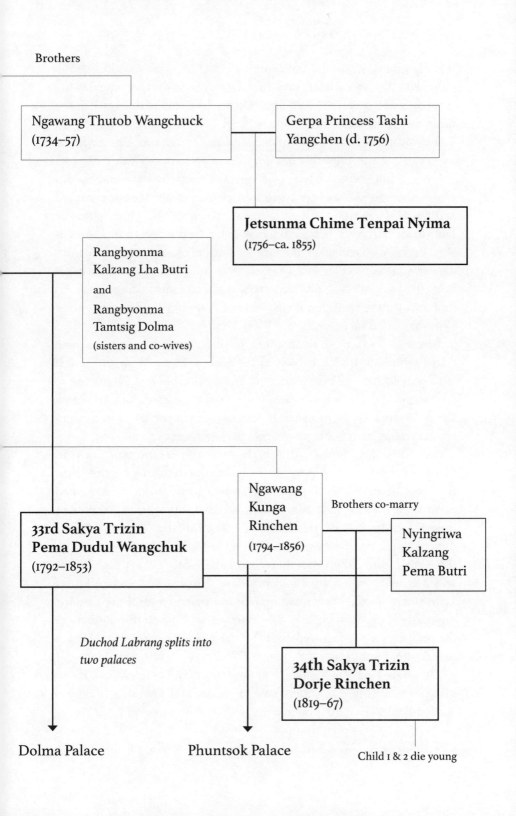

Brothers

Ngawang Thutob Wangchuck
(1734–57)

Gerpa Princess Tashi
Yangchen (d. 1756)

Jetsunma Chime Tenpai Nyima
(1756–ca. 1855)

Rangbyonma
Kalzang Lha Butri
and
Rangbyonma
Tamtsig Dolma
(sisters and co-wives)

Ngawang
Kunga
Rinchen
(1794–1856)

Brothers co-marry

Nyingriwa
Kalzang
Pema Butri

**33rd Sakya Trizin
Pema Dudul Wangchuk**
(1792–1853)

*Duchod Labrang splits into
two palaces*

**34th Sakya Trizin
Dorje Rinchen**
(1819–67)

Dolma Palace

Phuntsok Palace

Child 1 & 2 die young

"I study grammar, ways of knowing, spiritual precepts, and logic." She persisted, "Do you understand them?" In a perfunctory manner, he replied, "Yes." Then she asked him, "Do you understand the words or the meanings of the teachings?" He answered, "The words." She was happy. Then Nāropa added, "I also understand the meanings." She began to weep because she knew this was not true.

Nāropa the great scholar—the one who was in command of his senses, the one who was always in control—suddenly became confused and hesitant. He wondered who this woman might be. How could she interrogate him with such confidence? Later, he discovered that she was Vajrayoginī, who had taken the form of a urinal cleaner, one of the most offensive jobs in Indian society, in order to prod him into realizing that he needed to leave Nālandā University and find a guru who would help him uncover the realizations that were obscured by his own arrogance. Vajrayoginī had succeeded.

Nāropa left extensive instructions for the meditative practices associated with Vajrayoginī, known as the Eleven Yogas of Vajrayoginī. It is these teachings that have been passed down from one generation to the next of the Sakya Khon family for almost a millennium. Jetsunma Chime Tenpai Nyima received this empowerment and its related extensive teachings from her famous uncle Sachen Kunga Lodro.

Second, Sachen Kunga Lodro also bestowed on her the main practices of the Sakya system of Lamdre, the Path with the Result. By hearing these teachings, thinking about them, meditating with a focused mind, and performing the long solitary retreats associated with them, a practitioner can gain realization of the nature of mind. Initially, Jetsunma Chime Tenpai Nyima received the exoteric level (*tshogs bshad*) of the Path with the Result. Later, she privately received the esoteric level (*slob bshad*), which is more experiential and profound. Her teacher Sachen Kunga Lodro was esteemed as a great master and practitioner of the Lamdre, especially of the esoteric level. She practiced both levels throughout her life and became a recognized master of these teachings by giving them to others numerous times.

Although there is no official list, we know that Sachen Kunga Lodro gave her many other major empowerments as well. One that is listed is Sarvavid Vairocana,[66] the main deity with twelve surrounding deities of

66. Some information about Jetsunma Chime Tenpai Nyima, such as her receiving the

the *Sarva Durgati Parishodhana Tantra* (*Elimination of Bad Rebirths*), which is performed when a person dies. In Tibetan Buddhism, a major function of many lamas is to perform funeral rituals and help the recently deceased obtain a good rebirth. Many factors are believed to contribute to gaining a good rebirth. Much depends on one's intentions and actions in one's immediate past life, and also in more distant past lives; this, collectively, is known as karma. Of course, even lamas can't tell exactly where one will be reborn, but a highly realized lama may glean some indications through astrological calculations, dreams, and other signs, and it is thought that practices such as the rite of Sarvavid Vairocana can protect the recently deceased from being reborn in a hell realm, as a hungry ghost, or as an animal.[67]

Third, Jetsunma Chime Tenpai Nyima is the sole female lama in the transmission lineage of the seminal Sakya pith instruction known as *Parting from the Four Attachments* (*Zhen pa bzhi bral*). She immediately follows her teacher Sachen Kunga Lodro in this lineage. Though I was unable to find any commentary by her, many commentaries exist, from early and later Sakya masters alike.[68]

Parting from the Four Attachments continues to be a major teaching among Tibetan Buddhists throughout the world. Jetsunma Chime Tenpai Nyima's inclusion in the lama transmission lineage indicates her erudition and helps us see why she is remembered as a sage. She is well known as belonging to the lama transmission lineage of Nāropa Vajrayoginī, and she is also the only woman in the distinguished lama lineage of *Parting from the Four Attachments*.

Sarvavid Vairocana (Kun rig rnam par snang mdzad) empowerment, was told to me in 2008 at the Dolma Palace in Rajpur, India, by the 41st Sakya Trizin, whose older sister Jetsun Kushok (see Chapter 8) asked him to do research about Jetsunma Chime Tenpai Nyima.

67. For details on these three lower realms of existence in Tibetan Buddhist thought, see Deshung Rinpoche, *The Three Levels of Spiritual Perception* (Boston: Wisdom Publications, 1995, 2nd rev. ed. 2003).

68. For excellent summaries and commentaries on this core teaching, see H.H. Sakya Trizin, *Freeing the Heart and Mind* (Boston: Wisdom Publications, 2011), which includes the transmission lineage on pp. 161–62; Chogye Trichen Rinpoche, *Parting From the Four Attachments: Commentary on Jetsun Drakpa Gyaltsen's Song of Experience on Mind Training and The View* (Ithaca, NY: Snow Lion Press, 2003); and H.H. Sakya Trizin, *A Collection of Instructions on Parting from the Four Attachments: The Basic Mind Training of the Sakya Tradition*, trans. Jay Goldberg (Ngawang Samten) (Singapore: Sakya Tenphel Ling, 1982; 2nd ed. Berkeley: The Sapan Fund, 2018).

LATER ACTIVITIES AND CONNECTION TO VAJRAYOGINĪ

In 1782, when she was 26 years old, Jetsunma Chime Tenpai Nyima took her first monastic vows (Skt. *śrāmaṇera*; Tib. *dge tshul*), administered by Jampa Chokyi Tashi (Byams pa chos kyi bkra shis, n.d.), the 25th abbot of the Sakya Great Temple. He gave her the ordination name Chime Tenpai Nyima (Sun of Immortal Buddhist Teachings).[69]

The following year, 1783, her beloved uncle and teacher Sachen Kunga Lodro died. Part of the funeral rites involved selecting a highly realized lama to recite the meditative prayers of a particular deity as the corpse was being cremated. It is believed that a practitioner who has a daily practice on a meditational deity can generate an "imprint" of that deity in her or his consciousness. This imprint can then be activated during the passage of the subtle but constantly changing consciousness that flows from death to the next rebirth. Having a highly realized lama recite the appropriate prayers during the cremation of the body of such a practitioner may trigger the imprint, which may in turn enable the deceased to be reborn in the heavenly realm of the specific deity concerned, with access to all that is needed to become a buddha. Once the deceased person's main deity is identified, one must therefore find a lama to recite the prayers who is considered to be an "owner" of that deity's meditative practices—in other words, someone eminently qualified and highly respected by others.

One of Sachen Kunga Lodro's main meditative deities was Vajrayoginī. Jetsunma Chime Tenpai Nyima was requested to recite the Vajrayoginī prayers and accompanying offerings for 49 days after her teacher's death. To select a young woman rather than a senior male lama to perform these important rituals indicates her mastery in her practice of the goddess Vajrayoginī. It was a high honor. Many decades later, the famous Sakya and nonsectarian (*ris med*) vajra master Jamyang Khyentse Wangpo ('Jam dbyangs mkhyen brtse'i dbang po, 1820–92) would proclaim that Jetsunma Chime Tenpai Nyima was a veritable Vajrayoginī.[70]

Jetsunma Chime Tenpai Nyima's reputation continued to grow, and her fame as an emanation of Vajrayoginī spread. According to the short account in her cousin's life story, when she was elderly and her eyesight

---

69. Chime = immortal/deathless, Tenpai = teachings of the Buddha, Nyima = the sun.

70. Dragshul Trinlei Rinchen 2009, 342.

was weak, she conferred the Vajrayoginī teachings on one of her main disciples, a great siddha or yogi from Derge (sDe sge sgrub), Drubpon Ngawang Rinchen (sGrub dpon ngag dbang rin chen, n.d.). Suddenly, as she was giving him the teachings, her eyesight improved. Later she told him, "Seeing a lama like you in Tibet restored my eyesight."[71]

In an interview with the 41st Sakya Trizin, he commented that this happened because of their strong lama-disciple relationship. He also mentioned that when she gave Drubpon Ngawang Rinchen the Vajrayoginī inner blessing ritual (nang mchod), which involves a skullcup filled with consecrated liquid, the ambrosia-like liquid in the cup started to boil spontaneously. Numerous bubbles surfaced. As the disciple drank the bubbling liquid, his understanding of the voidness of conventional reality (śūnyatā) expanded.[72] Her reputation spread. Many masters and recognized reincarnations from Kham heard about her extraordinary abilities and spiritual insights. Though they did not have a chance to see her in person, they wanted to receive her lineage teachings of Vajrayoginī and made great efforts to do so. Many lamas praised her highly.

HER DISCIPLES

Jetsunma Chime Tenpai Nyima had numerous disciples all over Tibet. Most of the Sakya Khon family members received the common and uncommon Path with the Result as well as the teachings of Vajrayoginī from her. These included the 33rd Sakya Trizin Pema Dudul Wangchuk (1792–1853), founder of the Dolma Palace in Sakya; his daughter Jetsunma Kalzang Tsultrim Wangmo (1805–?) and his son the 35th Sakya Trizin Tashi Rinchen (1824–65); the 34th Sakya Trizin Dorje Rinchen, also known as Kunga Rinchen (1819–67), founder of the Phuntsok Palace; and his son the 36th Sakya Trizin Ngawang Kunga Sonam (1842–82).

As mentioned earlier, Jetsunma Chime Tenpai Nyima had a strong connection to Ngor Monastery (Fig. 5), which had four monastic houses, or labrangs (bla brang): Luding (kLu sdings), Khangsar (Khang gsar), Thartse (Thar rtse), and Phende (Phan bde). Not only did she instruct many of Ngor's abbots, she also recognized the 53rd Phankhang (or Phende Labrang) abbot, Kunga Tenpai Lodro (1822–84), as the reincarnation of

71. Ibid., 341–42.
72. Interview with H.H. Sakya Trizin, 2008, in Rajpur, India.

Fig. 5. Ngor Monastery, Tsang, Tibet, 1939.

a nephew of the 34th abbot, Palden Chos Kyong (1702–60). In Chapter 4, we will see that Kunga Tenpai Lodro became an important teacher of Jetsunma Tamdrin Wangmo. Jetsunma Chime Tenpai Nyima also bestowed teachings on the 44th abbot of Ngor Thartse, Jampa Namkhai Chime (1765–1820)—whose reincarnation was the renowned nonsectarian master Jamyang Khyentse Wangpo (1820–92) who proclaimed her as an emanation of Vajrayoginī—and on his nephew, the 47th abbot (1811–21), the very eminent and influential Thartse abbot Jampa Kunga Tenzin (1776–1862).

HER DEATH

Jetsunma Chime Tenpai Nyima's last residence was the Rigzin Palace (Rig 'dzin pho brang), which was located in the southeast corner of the Great Temple complex in Sakya (see Chapter 2). Since she lived a long life, at least into her late nineties, people called her Jetsunma Modung Rigzin (Old Noblewoman of Rigzin). It is unclear when she died, but the biography of the 33rd Sakya Trizin Pema Dudul Wangchuk states that after his death in 1853 she was in charge of making *tsa tsa* (relics) deity statues from his pulverized bones.[73] This means that she must have lived until the mid-1850s.

After her death, a memorial silver statue of Vajrayoginī, wearing a beautiful silver crown and ornaments inlaid with precious gems, was made in her honor. Her relics were placed inside the statue, which was placed in the Great Temple of Sakya.

73. Dragshul Trinlei Rinchen 2009, 381, and Sachen Kunga Lodro 2009, 573–74.

As mentioned at the outset, Jetsunma Chime Tenpai Nyima is the sole woman in the lama transmission lineage of the Sakya Nāropa teachings of Vajrayoginī. Yet many practitioners recite the transmission lineage of the Vajrayoginī *sādhana* (meditative manual) each day without knowing that "Chime Tenpai Nyima," the 30th holder of the lineage, was a woman, let alone an accomplished nun-practitioner. The title Jetsunma is not always included in lists of the guru transmission lineage, and many Tibetan names, including hers, are unisex.

Thus "Chime Tenpai Nyima" is simply intoned with the rest of the lamas in the lineage; yet when one investigates her life story, one realizes her mastery and her pervasive influence among the Sakya Trizins, the Ngor Monastery abbots, and other significant lamas. This elite group of her students went on to become the principal teachers of most Sakya monks throughout Tibet. They, in turn, influenced the next generations.

It is an extraordinary discovery that a single woman could have such enormous influence on the legacy of the popular and profound practice of Vajrayoginī from the Nāropa lineage, on the common and uncommon Path with the Result teachings, and on the transmission of *Parting from the Four Attachments*. Jetsunma Chime Tenpai Nyima is remembered today among Tibetan Buddhists as the goddess Vajrayoginī in human form.

CHAPTER FOUR

Lama to All:
Jetsunma Tamdrin Wangmo (1836–96)

ANOTHER OF THE great jetsunmas in the Sakya tradition is the distinguished scholar, teacher, practitioner, and yogi Jetsunma Tamdrin Wangmo Kalzang Chokyi Nyima (1836–96). Her full name means the revered female master (*jetsunma*), an emanation of the horse-necked deity who is a wrathful manifestation of compassion (*tamdrin*), powerful woman (*wangmo*), good fortune (*kalzang*), the one who rejoices in the Buddhist teachings (*chokyi*), and the sun (*nyima*). Tibetans give auspicious names to their children because it is believed that one should begin with the positive in order to ensure a beneficial beginning and, hopefully, a wonderful life. In the case of Jetsunma Tamdrin Wangmo, each name foreshadowed an aspect of her extraordinary life.

EARLY LIFE

In many Tibetan Buddhist biographies of great teachers, one finds stories of unusual circumstances during the pregnancy, foretelling dreams, and easy delivery at birth. None of these is found in the biography of Jetsunma Tamdrin Wangmo written by her great-nephew the 39th Sakya Trizin Dragshul Trinlei Rinchen (1871–1935), who was also one of her main disciples and who regarded her as one of his root gurus.[74] In fact, he records nothing of her early life except who her parents and early teachers were. Her father, Ngawang Kunga Rinchen (Ngag dbang kun dga' rin chen, 1794–1856), had shared a wife[75] with his older brother Pema Dudul

74. Dragshul Trinlei Rinchen 2009, 413–18. Most of the information for this chapter is based on this biography, unless otherwise noted.

75. Polyandry was practiced in many parts of Tibet. Frequently several brothers married a single woman, or in some cases several sisters. This was done primarily for economic rea-

Wangchuk (1792–1853), who reigned as the 33rd Sakya Trizin from 1806 to 1843 (see Chart 1 in Chapter 3). In his early adult life, however, Ngawang Kunga Rinchen decided to remarry and build a new home for this new family in Sakya. This home became known as the Phuntsok Palace (Chart 2). As in most Sakya Khon marriages, the family selected a young woman from a noble family—in this case, Nyima Dawa Wangmo (Nyi ma zla ma dbang mo) from the Samte (bSam lte) noble family. We know virtually nothing about her except that she had three daughters and two sons.

Of the five, Jetsunma Tamdrin Wangmo was the oldest. The second child was Jetsunma Kalzang Tenzin Wangmo (n.d.), and the fifth and youngest was Jetsunma Tsultrim Wangmo (n.d.). Nyima Dawa Wangmo's first son was Ngawang Kunga Sonam (Ngag dbang kun dga' bsod nams, 1842–82), who reigned as the 36th Sakya Trizin from 1866 to 1882, and her second son was Kyabgon Chokyi Langpo (Phyogs kyi glang po, 1844–66). This was Jetsunma Tamdrin Wangmo's immediate family.

HER EARLY TEACHERS

In the Sakya Khon family, it is frequently a father or uncle who chooses the teacher for a child. In Jetsunma Tamdrin Wangmo's case, her paternal uncle, Pema Dudul Wangchuk, appointed the Lopon Loter Zangpo (n.d.) as her main tutor. Lopon Loter Zangpo taught her how to read and chant prayers, laying an excellent foundation for her.

Like every member in the Sakya Khon family, she was given empowerments of important deities whom Tibetan Buddhists believe will help them throughout this life and future lives. In the Sakya tradition, these include Hevajra (Kye Dorje), Vajrayoginī (Naro Khachod), Vajrakīlaya (Dorje Phurba), and Sarvavid Vairocana (Kunrig Nampar Nangdze).[76] Each of these deities has various empowerments according to different

---

sons. When all the brothers married one wife, no land was divided and the brothers' wealth remained intact. Over the generations, a family's wealth and land were thus more likely to increase rather than fragment into small parcels that could not support a family. But in this case the family became divided when Jetsunma Tamdrin Wangmo's father separated from his first wife to marry another woman. Each brother established his separate palace (see the Duchod Labrang Genealogical Chart in Chapter 3).

76. The list of deities for whom Jetsunma Tamdrin Wangmo received the empowerments and teachings and performed the obligatory retreats is an extensive one, and so is not recorded here.

transmission lineages, and each has particular teachings and commentaries. She learned the history of the deity; the meditative practices, or *sādhanas* (*mngon rtog*); how to make appropriate mandalas (*dkyil 'khor*) to represent the residence of the deity in a precise mathematical manner and with decorations; the correct sacrificial offerings (*gtor ma*); daily offering chants (*bskang gso*); and dedication prayers. In addition, she learned all the traditional chants and accompanying music for each practice.[77] This involved a tremendous amount of effort, years of sustained commitment, and a compelling desire to attain enlightenment for the sake of all beings (*bodhicitta*).

THE TEACHINGS

Jetsunma Tamdrin Wangmo had numerous teachers. Her biography relates how her father and his brother, her paternal uncle Pema Dudul Wangchuk, imparted many teachings to her. For instance, she received empowerments and explanations of how to practice and perform the rituals of Vajrakīlaya. Vajrakīlaya is a deity who is portrayed as a wrathful emanation so as to remove obstacles and eliminate forces that are inimical to fostering compassion and wisdom. The Khon family has been following this ancient practice of Vajrakīlaya since the eighth century, when the great Indian yogi Guru Padmasambhava came to Tibet; among his students who received this teaching was Khon Nagendra Raksita, a very early member of the Khon family. The Sakyas celebrated Vajrakīlaya every year throughout the entire seventh lunar month, and despite all the upheavals in 1959, when many Tibetans fled into exile, including the Khon family, these rituals were performed, clearly indicating the paramount importance of Vajrakīlaya in the Sakya tradition.

Jetsunma Tamdrin Wangmo also received the empowerment of the deity Cakrasaṃvara (Tib. 'Khor lo bde mchog) according to the lineage tradition of the Indian adept (*siddha*) Krishnapada.[78] Cakrasaṃvara can be translated as "Wheel of Supreme Bliss"; supreme bliss is a sign that one has attained the realization of reality. Furthermore, Cakrasaṃvara is

77. Dragshul Trinlei Rinchen 2009, 414.

78. Krishnapada (Nag po zhabs) is also known as Kṛṣṇācārya (Tib. Nag po spyod pa). There are three main transmission lineages of Cakrasaṃvara from Indian siddhas. The Sakya Khon family has all three, but at this time in her life, Jetsunma Tamdrin Wangmo was given the transmission lineage that begins with Krishnapada.

CHART 2. THE PHUNTSOK PALACE

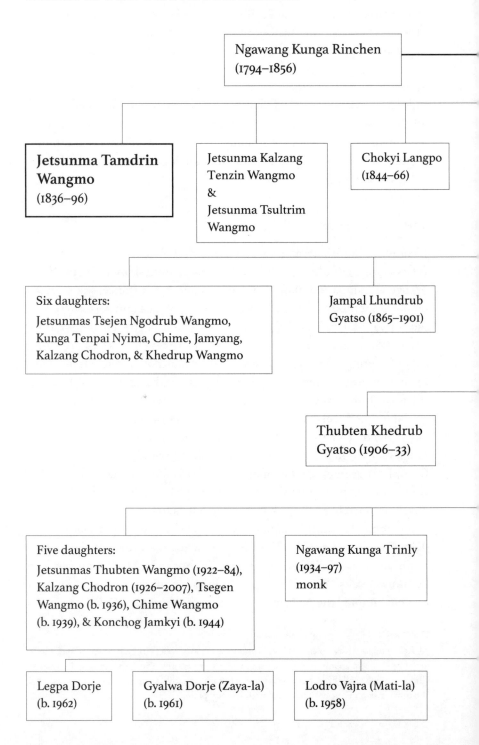

Ngawang Kunga Rinchen
(1794–1856)

Jetsunma Tamdrin
Wangmo
(1836–96)

Jetsunma Kalzang
Tenzin Wangmo
&
Jetsunma Tsultrim
Wangmo

Chokyi Langpo
(1844–66)

Six daughters:
Jetsunmas Tsejen Ngodrub Wangmo,
Kunga Tenpai Nyima, Chime, Jamyang,
Kalzang Chodron, & Khedrup Wangmo

Jampal Lhundrub
Gyatso (1865–1901)

Thubten Khedrub
Gyatso (1906–33)

Five daughters:
Jetsunmas Thubten Wangmo (1922–84),
Kalzang Chodron (1926–2007), Tsegen
Wangmo (b. 1936), Chime Wangmo
(b. 1939), & Konchog Jamkyi (b. 1944)

Ngawang Kunga Trinly
(1934–97)
monk

Legpa Dorje
(b. 1962)

Gyalwa Dorje (Zaya-la)
(b. 1961)

Lodro Vajra (Mati-la)
(b. 1958)

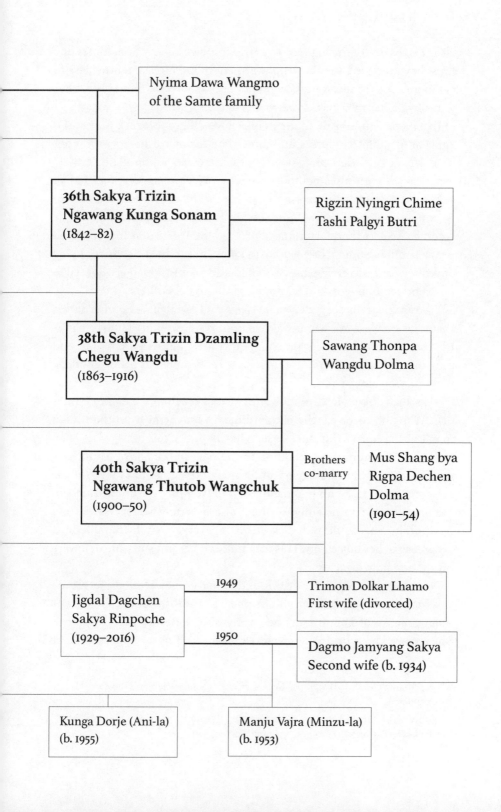

Nyima Dawa Wangmo
of the Samte family

**36th Sakya Trizin
Ngawang Kunga Sonam**
(1842–82)

Rigzin Nyingri Chime
Tashi Palgyi Butri

**38th Sakya Trizin Dzamling
Chegu Wangdu**
(1863–1916)

Sawang Thonpa
Wangdu Dolma

**40th Sakya Trizin
Ngawang Thutob Wangchuk**
(1900–50)

Brothers
co-marry

Mus Shang bya
Rigpa Dechen
Dolma
(1901–54)

Jigdal Dagchen
Sakya Rinpoche
(1929–2016)

1949

Trimon Dolkar Lhamo
First wife (divorced)

1950

Dagmo Jamyang Sakya
Second wife (b. 1934)

Kunga Dorje (Ani-la)
(b. 1955)

Manju Vajra (Minzu-la)
(b. 1953)

classified as one of the highest of tantric empowerments. Sometimes one must have received a major empowerment in the highest tantra classification in order to receive other initiations, so this paved the way for her to receive other major empowerments in the future.

In Tibetan Buddhism, many deities have different forms. Cakrasaṃvara has fifty different forms, and some of his forms are the father/mother or *yab/yum* one, depicting two deities in sexual union. The "father" aspect represents the method—namely, the compassion—needed to sustain a lifelong commitment to striving for the goal of helping all sentient beings. But, of course, compassion is not enough on its own. The "mother" aspect therefore represents wisdom. If one does not have the proper understanding, or wisdom, to know how to help a sentient being effectively, one can create more problems and confusion. It is essential to have both compassion and wisdom in order to help others.

Cakrasaṃvara is seen as a male deity, and his female counterpart is the great goddess known as Vajrayoginī or Vajravārāhī. Though she is his counterpart, for many practitioners Vajrayoginī is paramount, and in many depictions of Vajrayoginī she is represented as a sole goddess, without a visible partner.[79]

This leads us to next empowerment and teachings Jetsunma Tamdrin Wangmo received: the extraordinary Vajrayoginī from the Indian mahāsiddha Nāropa lineage. As seen in Chapter 3, this lineage has been passed down from one generation to the next in the Sakya Khon family for almost a thousand years, and some of the great Sakya jetsunmas are considered to be an emanation of Vajrayoginī.[80] Jetsunma Tamdrin Wangmo received this empowerment and its extensive teachings from her family. She conferred these teaching very often in her lifetime, according to her biography. This teaching and her transmission of it were one of her main legacies.

Now that she had received the foundational empowerments, Jetsunma was instructed by her older half brother, Dorje Rinchen, in the Sakya's main practice of Lamdre, or the Path with the Result (see Chapter 1). She received both the exoteric, more public teaching and the esoteric or

---

79. See Elizabeth English, *Vajrayoginī: Her Visualizations, Rituals and Forms* (Boston: Wisdom Publications, 2002).

80. At times, Jetsunma Tamdrin Wangmo's disciple and biographer, Dragshul Trinlei Rinchen, refers to her as Vajrayoginī in human form.

"uncommon" teaching. She practiced the teachings of both these levels throughout her life and became a recognized master of these teachings by giving them numerous times.

Knowledge concerning these deities and the teachings associated with them may be overwhelming for most people, but for a future teacher, it is imperative to receive as many empowerments and teachings as one is capable of understanding—and also to be able to practice them. Since people have a wide variety of inclinations, temperaments, abilities, and interests, a skillful teacher must have the means to tailor the teachings to each individual student. This does not mean that the teachings are changed, but rather that the teacher's knowledge is vast, so that she or he is well equipped to select the appropriate approach for each disciple. Thus, in Tibetan Buddhism, one encounters a pantheon of deities, both extensive and varied. The forms they assume are numerous: some appear to be very wrathful, for those beings who need to be subdued; others are extremely peaceful, for those who need kindness and love; others are in the father/mother union, to emphasize the importance of the union of compassion and wisdom in attaining enlightenment; and still others are semi-wrathful form, for those who need a jolt to keep them on the spiritual path.

In Tibetan Buddhism, one finds compendiums of meditational deities that can include a hundred deities or more. A popular one among the Sakyas is *One Hundred Methods of Accomplishment* (*Grub thabs rgya rtsa*). Jetsunma received these empowerments from her older half brother Dorje Rinchen. He also gave her the blessings and transmissions of two other important deities, Yamāntaka (Destroyer of Death) and Mahākāla (Great Black One).

RETREATS AND RELIGIOUS COMMITMENTS

One of the obligatory practices for those who undergo these initiations is a solitary retreat for each of the deities from whom one has received a major empowerment. One of the most extensive retreats is the one dedicated to Hevajra, which lasts from seven to eight months. Most others are shorter but still of significant duration, such as the Vajrayoginī retreat, which lasts from three to four months. Some are only a month long, or less. Jetsunma Tamdrin Wangmo did retreats on Hevajra, Vajrayoginī, Vajrakīlaya, Pañjaranātha Mahākāla, the powerful subjugator-goddess

Kurukulle, and Vajrapāṇi Bhutaḍāmara. These many retreats require a considerable amount of time. Only a great practitioner would be able to accomplish so much. Furthermore, she kept her daily commitments, which are known as the Four Unbreakable Practices (Chak mey nam zhi): the practices of Hevajra (Lam dus), the profound path of Guru Yoga (Lam zap), Virūpa protection meditation (Bir sung), and Vajrayoginī (Naljorma). On the eighth, fourteenth, twenty-third, and twenty-ninth day of each lunar month, she made offerings to the beings that protect the Dharma, the Buddhist teachings.

Also, it was standard that all blood members of the Sakya Khon family take the three religious vows—*prātimokṣa*, *bodhisattva*, and *tantra*. The first vow, *prātimokṣa*, is the promise to avoid all nonvirtuous actions that impede individual liberation from cyclic existence.[81] Jetsunma Tamdrin Wangmo received the three vows from the abbot Tashi Chopel of the Great Temple in Sakya. She is remembered as one who kept her vows vigilantly and continuously.

OTHER BUDDHIST ACTIVITIES

In addition to receiving initiations and teachings of various deities and taking vows to follow spiritual practices, Jetsunma Tamdrin Wangmo read spiritual texts. For instance, she managed to read the Kangyur two times completely. For Tibetans, the Kangyur is the sacred canon comprising the "translated words" of the Historical Buddha. Different versions of this sacred canon exist, consisting of between 101 to 120 volumes, with a total of over 70,000 pages. In addition, she read the genealogies of Sakya Khon families, the spiritual biographies of great Sakya masters,[82] and many other biographies of spiritual adepts. When she read these, she often cried. In his biography of Jetsunma Tamdrin Wangmo, her

---

81. The illustrious Nyingmapa master Dudjom Rinpoche succinctly elaborates in his *The Mirror Clearly Showing What to Adopt and Abandon*: (1) To abandon entirely all negative intentions and actions of body, speech, and mind that might cause harm to others is the essence of the prātimokṣa, or vows of individual liberation. (2) To practice wholeheartedly all types of virtue that bring benefit to others is the essence of the bodhisattva's vows. (3) At the root of these two is taming one's own unruly mind by means of mindfulness, vigilance, and conscientiousness, and training oneself to recognize the all-encompassing purity of appearance and existence. This is the essence of the vows of secret mantra. http://www.lotsawahouse .org/tibetan-masters/dudjom-rinpoche/mirror.

82. *sNgags 'chang chen po'i rnam thar ngo mtshor rgya mtsho.*

great-nephew the 39th Sakya Trizin Dragshul Trinlei Rinchen notes that her tears showed that she had a strong faith and the heart of *bodhicitta*.[83] In Buddhism, anyone who aspires to help others needs to develop *bodhicitta*—the compassionate wish to attain enlightenment for the benefit of all beings.

Dragshul Trinlei Rinchen comments further, noting that whoever reads these books and has this kind of feeling is rare, for most people do not have this feeling.[84] Moreover, he writes, "these days" lamas make false claims. They pretend to have clairvoyance, so as to understand past and future lives, but they have none of these powers. Jetsunma Tamdrin Wangmo was the opposite. She never claimed to have such powers. Yet when she practiced the art of divination by using dice, her interpretation of the outcome was accurate and correct.[85]

There is a long tradition of divination in Tibetan Buddhism. A diviner or lama may use dice, a rosary, or a bronze mirror to assess a particular situation and to look into someone's future. There are even people who have the ability to go into a trance and become mediums for oracles. Most lamas carry with them a small circular metal or wooden box that holds dice because their devotees regularly request a divination when they see their lama. After receiving a request, the lama prays to a particular deity, then rolls the dice in the box and interprets the result for the devotee.[86]

Many lamas are trained at an early age to interpret the reading of the dice. Different lamas rely on different deities, depending on their connection to a particular deity. One popular deity is the Bodhisattva of

83. Dragshul Trinlei Rinchen 2009, 415.

84. In Buddhism, to show how sensitive a bodhisattva is, the following example is given: If one puts an eyelash on one's hand, usually one is unaware of the eyelash. Now put it in one's eye, however, and one feels it acutely. This sensitivity toward others' suffering is the difference between the ordinary person who is unaware and the bodhisattva who feels other people's discomfort and pain.

85. Dragshul Trinlei Rinchen 2009, 415.

86. Common reasons for a divination are to ask about making a business deal, selecting a spouse, taking a new job, deciding on a health procedure, or embarking on a journey. The diviner recommends what to do in each case. However, not all divinations are clear. Some reveal that the beginning may appear good but in the end it will be bad, or vice versa. Others indicate that one must wait for a better time, and some state that one must not wait but act immediately. Thus the outcome is unpredictable, and rituals must frequently be performed to remove potential obstacles, negate adverse outcomes, or to enhance a mediocre consequence.

Wisdom, Mañjuśrī. Each die has six sides, and each side corresponds to one of the letters in the mantra of Mañjuśrī. Before throwing the two dice, the lama must visualize Mañjuśrī and feel that Mañjuśrī is revealing the outcome through the dice. Once the dice are thrown, the lama needs to interpret each letter. This can take years of experience. Some lamas are considered much better than others in pronouncing the correct result. Clearly, Jetsunma Tamdrin Wangmo was esteemed as a lama who gave accurate outcomes.

JOURNEY TO KHAM

Sakya is located in south Central Tibet, or Tsang, but many of its followers live in southeast Tibet, or Kham. In Kham, there are many important Sakya monasteries and the Khon family has numerous sponsors who donate goods and money for the support of the Sakya school. Members of the Khon families frequently went to Kham to give empowerments, teachings, and blessings as requested by their practitioners and sponsors. In the late 1850s, Jetsunma Tamdrin Wangmo's younger brother, Ngawang Kunga Sonam, who later became the 36th Sakya Trizin (r. 1866–82), asked her to go to Kham.[87] Following his wishes, she and their youngest brother, Chokyi Langpo, traveled there.

They were sent for several reasons, including to collect donations and to pray for the success of the Central Tibetan Government army against the very powerful Nyarong Gonpo Namgyal, who started an uprising in 1860. For a few years he successfully conquered large areas of Kham and threatened the kingdom of Derge, a traditional seat of the Sakya tradition in Kham. But his success was short-lived, and he was defeated in 1865.[88]

In Dragshul Trinlei Rinchen's biography of Jetsunma Tamdrin Wangmo in the Sakya genealogy, a detailed itinerary is not given, so one can only infer some of the major stops from other accounts. It is definite

87. Dragshul Trinlei Rinchen does not mention any date in the biography. However, p. 7 of a booklet about the history of Black Bull Monastery, Tsering Wangyal and Yama Gonpo (Tshe ring dbang rgyal and Ya ma mgon po), *Crystal Mirror: A History of Lang Nak Monastery* (*gLang nag dgon pa'i lo rgyus mthong gsal shel gyi me long*) (Beijing: Mi rigs dpe skrun khang, 2005), states that Jetsunma Tamdrin Wangmo's youngest brother, Chokyi Langpo, arrived at the monastery in 1860.

88. See Yudru Tsomu, *The Rise of Gonpo Namgyel in Kham: The Blind Warrior of Nyarong* (Lanham, MD: Rowman, 2014).

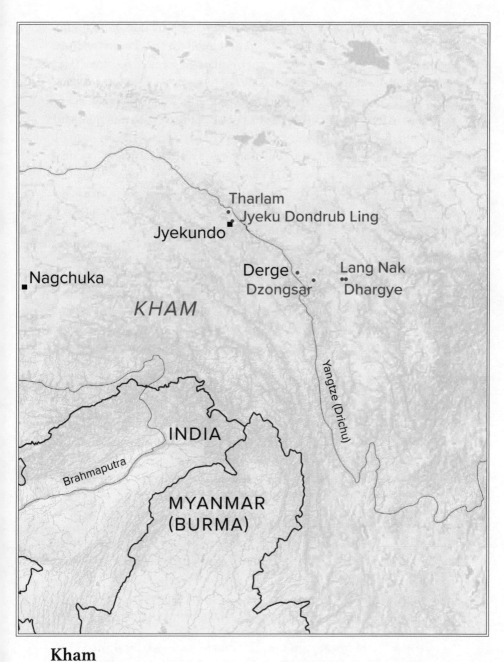

Kham

0   75   150 miles

that Jetsunma visited Jyeku Dondrub Ling (sKye rgu'i don 'grub gling), located in Jyekundo. The eminent Sakya scholar Phakpa Lodro Gyaltsen established it in the thirteenth century, and in the fifteenth century Dagchen Sherab Gyaltsen, the 20th Sakya Trizin (1473–95), expanded it. This monastery, one of the larger Sakya monasteries in Kham, included many buildings in its complex. One was the palace of the wealthy and powerful family of Drawupon Jigme Kunga Wangyal (1893–1952),[89] known until its destruction in the 1990s as the Drawupon's Palace. In 1959, when the Communist Chinese were invading Tibet, Drawupon Jigme Kunga Wangyal's son, Rinchen Tsering (b. 1930; Fig. 6), was one of the main resistance leaders in Kham. The men under his leadership fought valiantly but were forced to flee into exile in India during the early 1960s.

Fig. 6. Drawupon Rinchen Tsering
in Xining, Amdo, 1953/54.

Drawupon Rinchen Tsering recounted some of his family's oral tradition about Jetsunma Tamdrin Wangmo's 1860s visit to Jyekundo to his daughter, Dagmo Lhanze Sakya (b. 1964).[90] He recounted that when Jetsunma Tamdrin Wangmo visited Jyeku Monastery, she resided in the Drawupon's Palace. It was a large red structure reserved solely for religious purposes, such as undertaking a retreat and performing rituals.

89. Drawupon Jigme Kunga Wangyal received his name from the 39th Sakya Trizin, Dragshul Trinlei Rinchen (personal communication from his son, Drawupon Rinchen Tsering). Dagmo Lhanze Sakya email, May 6, 2019.

90. I met Dagmo Lhanze Sakya on August 24, 2016 in Seattle. Since her father lives in India, she recorded her father's account via WeChat and we listened to it together.

Jyeku Monastery had very strict rules. For example, the monks could not speak to each other outside of the monastery, to reduce socializing and potential gossip; and women were not allowed to stay overnight within the monastery complex.[91] Jetsunma Tamdrin Wangmo must have been regarded as a great lama first and foremost because she was permitted to stay in the palace even though she was female. After her long stay, the retreat room where she had resided became a shrine room, due to having been blessed by her presence and practice. Her main ritual instruments—a *damaru* (small ritual drum), bell, and *dorje* (ritual thunderbolt)—were preserved in the shrine. Also, she had made, for her own practice, three masks of protectors. The three masks represented Guju Gonpo (Mahākāla with Stick), Pango Sha (Four-Faced Mahākāla), and Palden Lhamo; each was about 6–7 inches in height. Since Jetsunma made these masks and used them in her practice, they were imbued with her blessings. Thereafter, daily prayers and sacrificial offerings (or *tormas*) were made in this room.[92]

There is another story that Drawupon Rinchen Tsering recalled: In Singdze (Seng dze), the main palace of Pon Jigme Kunga Wangyal (Drawupon Rinchen Tsering's father), Jetsunma Tamdrin Wangmo was invited to the Vajrakīlaya (or Dorje Phurba) ceremony and lama dance.[93] During the visit, she was asked to give a blessing in the palace. In the audience near her was a mother with her five-year-old son. When she was sprinkling tea as part of the blessing ritual, some of the hot tea fell on the young boy's face. His mother became alarmed, but the boy was unfazed and instead of crying, as most children would have, he was very happy. Jetsunma Tamdrin Wangmo observed this reaction and said that he was a special child.

91. When Jigdal Dagchen Sakya Rinpoche, his wife Dagmo Jamyang Sakya, and her mother visited Jyeku Monastery in 1953, Dagmo Jamyang Sakya's mother was not allowed to stay overnight in the palace because it was within the monastery complex, although an exception was made for Dagmo Jamyang Sakya because she was the wife of Jigdal Dagchen Rinpoche. See Jamyang Sakya and Julie Emery, *Princess in the Land of Snows: The Life of Jamyang Sakya in Tibet* (Boston: Shambhala, 1990), 145.

92. All this information is from Drawupon Rinchen Tsering and reflects his pronunciation of names.

93. Dagmo Jamyang Sakya briefly describes Singdze; see Sakya and Emery 1990, 154. She describes the massive stone *mani* wall that is still there and how people come to circumambulate it from all over Kham and beyond.

During this time, a group of monks who had been students of the 3rd Gyanak (rGya nak) Tulku, one of the two main recognized reincarnations (*tulkus*) in Jyeku Monastery, went to Sakya to inquire where their teacher had been reborn. Sakya Gongma (as Tibetans call the head of the Sakya school) told the monks that their tulku had been born in Singdze and was most likely this five-year-old boy. He advised the monks to ask Jetsunma Tamdrin Wangmo since she had been in Jyeku and might know whether or not this boy was their tulku. When the monks asked Jetsunma, she declared without hesitation that this boy sprinkled by the tea offering was the reincarnation. In this manner, the 4th Gyanak Tulku was recognized as the new reincarnation.

Jetsunma Tamdrin Wangmo gave the Drawupon family a small thumbprint-sized mask of Mahākāla that she had made. The family regarded it as very precious and kept it in her shrine room. Later, one of the main tulkus of Jyeku Monastery, Khentrul Meghan (Mai rgan) Rinpoche, resided in this room. He placed the tiny mask in a broken musical clock box for safekeeping. The young Drawupon Rinchen Tsering knew that it was there and wanted it. Hoping to get the mask, he brought in exchange a working musical clock box. This he gave to Khentrul Meghan, asking him if he might have the thumbprint-sized mask. Being kind, the lama gave it to the boy. Drawupon was very happy, but when his uncle found out, he reprimanded him and asked why he wanted the mask. Drawupon immediately told his uncle that he wanted to wear it every day. Later, his father placed the small mask in a broken watch, where it fit perfectly, and Drawupon wore it for protection.

Not too far from Jyekundo is Tharlam Monastery, the main monastery of the 3rd Dezhung Rinpoche (1906–87). Dezhung Rinpoche's younger sister, Ani Chime Dolma (1922–2015), remembered that in the vicinity, near the Yangtze River, there was a white stone throne for Jetsunma Tamdrin Wangmo.[94] From the throne it took about two hours on foot to reach Tharlam Monastery. In the Tibetan countryside, one often finds a smooth white stone with a back that was prepared as a seat for a special lama. Such a throne was usually near a main road. Ani Chime's remark that the throne was quite far away indicates that the people highly

94. Interview with Ani Chime Dolma, Tharlam Monastery, Bodhnath, Nepal, November 14 and 15, 2007.

respected Jetsunma Tamdrin Wangmo, and demonstrated this by walking a great distance from the monastery to the throne to welcome her. Such a throne is set up out of respect for a dignified personage. There the lama is offered tea and given some time to relax before traveling on to the monastery. One seldom hears of thrones for female lamas, however, so this is another indication that Jetsunma Tamdrin Wangmo was a remarkable woman.

While Jetsunma Tamdrin Wangmo and her brother were in Kham, they visited different places. It seems that they stayed for several years in the area of Trehor, especially at the Lang Nak (gLang nag, "Black Bull") Monastery, established by Chogyal Phakpa (1235–80) in 1276, when he was returning to Sakya from his third stay in China as the spiritual preceptor of Emperor Kublai Khan.[95] The authors of *Crystal Mirror: A History of Lang Nak Monastery* state that the third tulku associated with the monastery, Tulku Nyendrak Tenpai Wangchuk (sNyan grags bstan pa'i dbang phyugs, 1854–98), received many empowerments from Jetsunma Tamdrin Wangmo. Due to some disturbances caused by Nyarong Gonpo Namgyal and his men fighting in the area of the Black Bull Monastery, it was decided that the tulku of Black Bull Monastery would travel to the Sakya Sa Kar Hermitage in Denma, Kham. It was at Sa Kar Hermitage that the tulku greeted Jetsunma Tamdrin Wangmo as she arrived there.[96] Also at Sa Kar Hermitage, she gave him a number of empowerments and teachings. These included Ghantapa Cakrasaṃvara, Nāropa Vajrayoginī, Sarvavid Vairocana, and Hevajra.[97] In addition, he received an empowerment of Amitāyus, the Buddha of Long Life, combined with the horse-necked deity, Hayagrīva, who dispels obstacles. This is a very popular empowerment to remove anything that might shorten one's lifespan.

In 1864 at Black Bull Monastery, Jetsunma Tamdrin Wangmo's youngest brother, Chokyi Langpo, gave Tulku Nyendrak Tenpai Wangchuk the three vows (*prātimokṣa*, *bodhisattva*, and *tantra*) as well as the teachings of

95. Tsering Wangyal and Yama Gonpo 2005, 5.

96. Ibid., 21–22.

97. Ibid., 18. Later, when Tulku Nyendak Tenpai Wangchuk was about 17 years old, he visited Sakya, where he received many secret tantric teachings from Jetsunma Tamdrin Wangmo. Tsering Wangyal and Yama Gonpo state that the tulku did not write down these teachings since they were so secret.

Hevajra with oral commentary.[98] Moreover, Chokyi Langpo bestowed on him the seven mandalas of Ngor and other teachings in his retreat cave.[99] The fact that this took place in the tulku's retreat cave implies that these were special teachings conferred on a small and selected group.

Sadly, on the fifteenth day in the third month of 1866, residents of the Trehor area experienced a large earthquake that killed many animals and people, including Tulku Nyendrak's parents and Chokyi Langpo.[100] Chokyi Langpo's death must have been a shock to the Sakya family. He was only about 22 years old. In Sakya, his second sister, Jetsunma Kalzang Tenzin Wangmo, who was living at her residence, Tashi Tseg (bKras shi btsegs) Labrang,[101] was sent immediately to Kham to perform the funeral rites for her brother.[102] Chokyi Langpo's body was cremated and a memorial stupa was erected at Black Bull Monastery, where the 3rd Nyendrak Tulku performed the Sarvavid Vairocana (Kunrig) rituals for all the beings who had died in the earthquake.[103] In *Princess in the Land of Snows*, Dagmo Jamyang Sakya writes that "when the tremor first struck," Chokyi Langpo (whom she calls Kyagon Cholang) "had insisted that his followers leave, saying he would die for the cause of subduing the

98. Ibid., 21–22, states that Tulku Nyendak received these vows when he was 11 years old. I am calculating according to the Tibetan custom of being one year old at birth.

99. Ibid., 22–23. Khyenrab Gephel, the first abbot of Black Bull Monastery, had established the retreat cave, and it was named Increasing Virtue (*dGe 'phel*) in his honor. See Jackson 2020, 31ff., which discusses Gephel Tulku.

100. Tsering Wangyal and Yama Gonpo 2005, 23. There is conflicting information as to when Chokyi Langpo died. According to Dragshul Trinlei Rinchen, 2009, 425, he was 22 years old when he died on the fifteenth day of the third month in the wood mouse year (1864). However, the genealogy also states that he was born when his father was 51 years old. His father was born in 1794, so Chokyi Langpo was born in 1844 (according to the Tibetan calculation of counting from conception, rather than at birth). Thus 1866 seems to be the correct year of his death. Tsering Wangyal and Yama Gonpo 2005, 23, state that the earthquake occurred in the third month of 1866.

101. Dragshul Trinlei Rinchen 2009, 425. In the early 1950s, the Phuntsok Palace Jetsunma Kalzang Chodron (sKal bzang chos sgron, 1926–2007) and Jetsunma Tsegen Wangmo (b. 1935) lived at Tashi Tseg Labrang and did some retreats. Jetsunma Tsegen now lives in Seattle. She is quoted in Chapter 1, where she mentions staying in the labrang with her older sister Jetsunma Kalzang Chodron.

102. Ibid., 418. The phrase in Tibetan is *dgongs rzogs*, literally, "to complete his wishes."

103. In addition, the 3rd Nyendrak Tulku recited 600,000 mantras of Kunrig and did a retreat to help the deceased have a good rebirth.

quakes. He decreed that after his death his body should remain [at Black Bull Monastery] in a stupa, saying this would prevent future quake disasters."[104] Also another stupa of gilded gold and silver was constructed in Tashi Tseg Labrang in Sakya as a memorial.[105]

Jetsunma Tamdrin Wangmo gave many blessings, empowerments, and teachings while she was in Kham. However, she did not forget the words of her brother, the 36th Sakya Trizin Ngawang Kunga Sonam, who had advised her to look for a lama who had the lineage of the esoteric Path with the Result, Vajrāvalī Wangchen, and Marpo Korsum (Three Great Red Ones).[106] Emphasizing that few lamas had received these teachings and that their transmission could be lost for future generations,[107] Ngawang Kunga Sonam had told her, "If you find a lama who is qualified to bestow these teachings, request them and receive them." Fortunately, she did find Kunga Tenpai Lodro, the 53rd Phankhang (or Phende Labrang) abbot of Ngor, who had the lineage and the authority to instruct her in all these teachings.[108] *The Great Collection of the Lamdre Tshogse Teachings* relates that when the abbot was 44 years old (1866), he went to Upper Ga in Kham. When he arrived at Jyeku Monastery, he met Jetsunma Tamdrin Wangmo, who asked him to give the teachings of the esoteric Path with the Result and Vajrāvalī to a select group of lamas and

104. Sakya and Emery 1990, 194.

105. Dragshul Trinlei Rinchen 2009, 425.

106. Among the Sakyas, the Marpo Korsum are Kurukulle, Ganapati, and Takkiraja. The color red signifies power.

107. In Tibetan Buddhism, teachings and practices must be transmitted from lama to disciple in every generation. If a lama holds a rare teaching that perhaps only he, and no one else, had received from his lama, he feels compelled to continue this lineage. But the right disciple must be found who will be able to receive and practice the teachings. When the right disciple does appear, the lama is pleased that he can transmit the teachings. Since these teachings are precious, some lamas and disciples make it their mission to receive and pass on such rare or lesser-known practices. This maintains the guru transmission lineage intact and keeps it viable. In deity meditation manuals, the guru transmission lineage is included to show the authenticity and authority of a given practice.

108. Kunga Tenpai Lodro's (Kun dga' bstan pa'i blo gros, 1822–84) connection with Jetsunma Chime Tenpai Nyima is described at the end of Chapter 3 above. He was appointed the 53rd Ngor abbot by the 36th Sakya Trizin Tashi Rinchen. His tenure as Ngor abbot began in 1849 and ended in 1852. Khenchen Appey Rinpoche, ed., *The Great Collection of the Lamdre Tshogse Teachings* (Kathmandu: Sachen International, 2008–10), vol. 29: 826. For a painting of him, see http://www.himalayanart.org/items/54316.

monks. In total there were 30 people, and the teachings lasted for three months.[109]

Therefore, Jetsunma Tamdrin Wangmo was able to preserve this unbroken lineage. When she returned to Sakya, she conferred these teachings on her surviving brother—the 36th Sakya Trizin Ngawang Kunga Sonam.[110] Thus one of her great legacies was saving the lineage and transmitting these teachings. She also gave the 36th Sakya Trizin many additional teachings, including Hevajra, Vajrakīlaya, Pañjaranātha Mahākāla, and other tutelary deities and protectors, as well as Cakra-saṃvara, Guhyasamāja, and Yamāntaka.[111] He, too, made a strong effort to preserve the transmissions and teachings just as his elder sister and teacher, Jetsunma Tamdrin Wangmo, had.

It is unclear when Jetsunma Tamdrin Wangmo returned to Kham for the second time, but in the autobiographical *Life of Jamyang Khyentse Wangpo* (1820–92), the renowned scholar-yogi states that she was a great tantric practitioner and that he gave her empowerments and teachings at Dzongsar (rDzong sar), Kham, in 1875.[112] Her biography by the 39th Sakya Trizin also specifically states that the renowned Jamyang Khyentse Wangpo gave her the empowerment and transmission of the lion-faced goddess Siṃhamukhā (Senge ge dong chen kha dro).[113]

---

109. Khenchen Appey Rinpoche 2008–10, vol. 29: 841; vol. 27: 439. Among the distinguished group were Khenchen Ngawang Sonam Gyaltsen, Palden Lodro Gyaltsen, Ngawang Tenpai Gyaltsen, and the 45th King of Derge, Palden Chime Dakpa Dorje. The abbot also transmitted the extensive and brief teachings about Mahākāla.

110. The 36th Sakya Trizin did not travel extensively; he went to West Tibet twice, but he stayed mostly in Sakya.

111. Dragshul Trinlei Rinchen 2009, 419. Since her younger brother, the 36th Sakya Trizin Ngawang Kunga Sonam, was one of Jetsunma Tamdrin Wangmo's main disciples, he received many teachings from her. These include Ra Lotsawa's lineage of the thirteen-deity Yamāntaka (the empowerment, reading transmission, and teachings collection); special teachings of Hevajra, including four different lineages (bka babs); four different lineages of Mahākāla; the Thirteen Golden Dharmas; the Khachod Korsum (empowerment, teachings, and commentary of Vajrayoginī); the complete set of the ten-deity Pañjaranātha Mahākāla; the complete teachings of the Six Yogas of Niguma; the five-deity lion-faced ḍākinī; Begtse with cemetery protector deities set; three lineages of Cakrasaṃvara; three lineages of Guhyasamāja; and twelve mandalas of Vairocana (sbyong dkyil wang).

112. Jamgon Kongtrul, *The Life of Jamyang Khyentse Wangpo* (New Delhi: Shechen Publications, 2012), 219 n. 266.

113. Dragshul Trinlei Rinchen 2009, 414. Jamyang Khyentse Wangpo has one of the most extensive commentaries on Siṃhamukhā practice and is well known for his mastery of this

Another story about Jetsunma Tamdrin Wangmo is from the 41st
Sakya Trizin:

> Generally, people greatly respected the Sakya jetsunmas, and
> Jetsunma Tamdrin Wangmo even more so, since she was very
> beautiful. When she was teaching in Trehor, Kham, there was
> a Chinese official who had a reputation of being a womanizer.
> This man heard that Tamdrin Wangmo was attracting many
> people to her teachings because of her beauty. So he decided
> that he must meet her and he asked for an appointment.
> Jetsunma's attendants did not want to grant him an appoint-
> ment because of his reputation. They suggested to Jetsunma
> that they leave from this area quickly and thus avoid a possible
> confrontation with the official. Jetsunma thought otherwise,
> [saying,] "I will meet him."
>
> On the day of the appointment, the official came and offered
> her the customary white scarf (*khatag* or *khata*). Jetsunma's
> attendants expected him to sit down, but suddenly, he fled
> quickly, as if he were frightened. Those present wondered what
> had happened. Later, the official related that, when he entered
> Jetsunma's room, "I saw a human body but the terrifying head
> was not human; it had a wild boar's head with fierce tusks. I
> fled in fear." Everyone was amazed by Jetsunma's power and
> abilities. The official never bothered her again.[114]

Sakya Trizin remarked further, "Indeed she was Vajravārāhī." He was
referring to Vajravārāhī, the goddess who has a boar's face on the side of
her head.[115]

Another time, while she was in Kham, her traveling party came to a
place frequented by bandits. One night some bandits did indeed steal
some horses and mules, which served to carry their luggage. Many were
enraged and wanted revenge. They were eager to track down the bandits

---

practice. See https://www.lotsawahouse.org/tibetan-masters/jamyang-khyentse-wangpo
/history-of-simhamukha.

114. Personal interview with H.H. the 41st Sakya Trizin in Walden, New York, June 5, 2011.

115. On the Great Sakya Women webpage, Jetsunma Tamdrin Wangmo is considered to
be an emanation of Vajrayoginī. Vajrayoginī and Vajravārāhī are interchangeable in some
instances. http://hhsakyatrizin.net/teaching-great-sakya-women/.

and demand that the stolen animals be returned to them. But Jetsunma said, "No, no. This won't be necessary." She knew that there would be bloodshed and possible loss of life. Having her own special means for finding the animals, she performed a Mahākāla (Great Black One) *puja*, or ritual. As she was performing this *puja*, black dogs and birds suddenly appeared and surrounded the bandits' tents. The animals threatened and frightened them. The bandits were so terrified that they immediately brought all the stolen horses and mules back to Jetsunma Tamdrin Wangmo. The people rejoiced and praised her special abilities.

RETURN TO SAKYA

After her lengthy visit in Kham, Jetsunma Tamdrin Wangmo returned to Sakya. Her biography by her great-nephew the 39th Sakya Trizin gives no information about the route she took or holy places she visited. Also, there is no mention of who accompanied her. By the time she arrived in Sakya, her renown had spread. In U, Tsang, and Kham she had innumerable disciples, including many lamas, monks, and laypeople. Having received the transmissions and completed the necessary retreats, she gave many teachings. In his biography of her, the 39th Sakya Trizin Dragshul Trinlei Rinchen emphasizes that for Jetsunma Tamdrin Wangmo, it never made a difference whom she taught: anyone who asked her to teach, she would teach. She bestowed the complete exoteric Path with the Result numerous times, the esoteric level twice, and Vajrāvalī three times. In 1886 Dragshul Trinlei Rinchen himself, his sister Kyabgon Pema Trinlei (see Chapter 5), and three of his other four siblings received both levels of the Path with the Result from her in Sakya.[116]

Regarding the Vajrāvalī instructions, Dragshul Trinlei Rinchen recalls in his diary that in 1882,[117] when he was eleven years old, Gongkar Tulku[118]

116. Dragshul Trinlei Rinchen 1974, vol. 1, 130–34.

117. Ibid., vol. 1, 73. He remarked that in the previous month, (Sakya) Trichen Kunga Sonam died on the fifth day of Sakadawa (the holy month which is the fourth month in the Tibetan calendar) and the previous [8th] Panchen Lama Tenpai Wangchuk also died in the third month of that year.

118. This was Gong dkar sprul sku of the subsect Dzongpa; see http://www.dzongpa.com /promotions.html. In an email of April 7, 2020, Mathias Fermer states that Gongkar Tulku "is Ngag dbang mi pham thub bstan chos kyi sgron me, who is usually considered the 4th rDo rje gdan pa incarnation by the tradition ... although the counting is questionable from a historical perspective."

requested Jetsunma Tamdrin Wangmo to impart the transmission of Vajrāvalī (Dorje Trengwa) from the eleventh-century Bengali Indian scholar-yogi Abhayākaragupta. Accepting this request, she gave these teachings to Gongkar Tulku, Dragshul Trinlei Rinchen, his father Kunga Nyingpo Samphel Norbu (the 37th Sakya Trizin), and others. However, when she finished half the teachings, the family found that some of the participants had a contagious sickness (*'go nad*), so she had to cancel the rest of the teachings.[119] Later, she gave Dragshul Trinlei Rinchen the complete Vajrāvalī great empowerments, as well as the three Vajrayoginīs (Khachod Korsum, also known as Marmo Korsum, the lineages from the Indian masters Indrabhuti, Maitripa, and Nāropa), the three great red deities (Marpo Korsum), and the Thirteen Golden Dharmas.

Whenever Jetsunma Tamdrin Wangmo gave a reading transmission (*lung*) of a text or a commentary, her pace was not too fast or slow, and her voice was exceptionally clear. She was a fast reader who could complete an entire volume in a day. This is a wonderful skill to have when one has to read numerous volumes within a few days or weeks. From the preliminaries to the conclusions of the rituals, all was done in order. She did everything as required in the *sādhanas,* avoiding any additions or omissions. She followed the instructions precisely. For example, when she placed the various ritual instruments (*dbang rdzas*) on the disciples' heads, she stood up and did this to each one individually. Further, she performed all the *mudras* (religious symbolic hand gestures) accurately. As Dragshul Trinlei Rinchen remarked in his biography "In U, Tsang, and Kham, there is no one like her. She is incomparable."[120] He adds that he believed that she was an emanation of Vajra Nairātmyā (Dorje

119. Dragshul Trinlei Rinchen 1974, vol. I, 70ff. Jetsunma Tamdrin Wangmo gave many empowerments numerous times: (1) the three lineages of Vajrayoginī (Khachod Korsum), and the Nāropa Vajrayoginī blessing and commentary many times; (2) the three different lineages of Cakrasaṃvara—Luipa, Krishnapāda (Ngagpopa), and Ghantapāda (Drilbu); (3) the thirteen-deity Vajrabhairava of Ra Lotsawa's lineage from the oral teachings of ḍākinīs, the five-deity red Yamāntaka of the Virūpa lineage, and the reading transmission of Ra Lotsawa's teachings, which consists of many volumes; (4) four kinds of Hevajra special teachings; (5) the five-deity Mahākāla; (6) the twenty-seven-deity Sitātapatrā; (7) the nine-deity Akshobhya; (8) the twelve mandalas of Vairocana; (9) the Shangpa Kagyu's Six Yogas of Niguma teachings—empowerment, blessing and commentary, and reading transmission; (10) Pañjaranātha Mahākāla and Four-Faced Mahākāla; (11) Magzorma (a wrathful manifestation of Saraswatī) and other protector deities; and (12) special instructions and blessings on the fifteen families of wealth deities and other wealth deities.

120. Dragshul Trinlei Rinchen 2009, 416.

Dagmema), the partner of the deity Hevajra, and also of Vajravārāhī (Dorje Phagmo). He asserted that she was inseparable from them.[121]

Dragshul Trinlei Rinchen also recorded in his diary an incident in which Jetsunma Tamdrin Wangmo was a peacekeeper. In 1883, the position of Sakya Trizin was being transferred from Jetsunma Tamdrin Wangmo's brother, the Phuntsok Palace Ngawang Kunga Sonam (the 36th Sakya Trizin, r. 1842–82), to the Dolma Palace Kunga Nyingpo Samphel Norbu (1850–99), who became the 37th Sakya Trizin (r. 1883–99). In this transitional year, the two palaces disagreed about the financial accounts, and this dispute escalated to such an extent that everyone in Sakya seemed to be involved. In his diary Dragshul Trinlei Rinchen describes it as a fight between a raven and an owl. Despite pleas from officials, abbots, and relatives, the argument became so heated that each palace threatened to take the case to the Central Tibetan Government in Lhasa. This would have been a costly and protracted affair for both palaces, possibly remaining unresolved for several years. Finally, Jetsunma Tamdrin Wangmo and the abbot of the Great Temple, Khenpo Tashi Chophel, intervened.[122] Acting as mediators, they asked family members from both palaces to resolve the dispute. Thankfully, they were successful and the dispute was settled in Sakya without the Central Government becoming involved. Thus Jetsunma Tamdrin Wangmo is also remembered as a conciliator as well as a great teacher.[123]

Among her disciples in Sakya were her younger brother Ngawang Kunga Sonam (the 36th Sakya Trizin), his wife (from the sNying-ri ba family), and their daughters, and also the 37th Sakya Trizin Kunga Nyingpo Samphel Norbu, his wife (from the Lha rigs rtse pa family), and their sons and daughters—who included her great-niece Kyabgon Pema Trinlei (the subject of Chapter 5) and her great-nephew and biographer the 39th Sakya Trizin Dragshul Trinlei Rinchen. Many monks, chanting masters, officials, and abbots—including the Great Temple Khenpo Tashi Chopel (who gave her the three vows)—were her disciples as well. Many, including her paternal uncle the 33rd Sakya Trizin Pema Dudul Wangchuk, held her in high regard as a very pure jetsunma.

121. Ibid.

122. Khenpo Tashi Chophel's present reincarnation is Chiwang Tulku, who lives in the Sakya Centre in Rajpur, India (see Fig. 26 below).

123. Dragshul Trinlei Rinchen 1974, vol. I, 106 and III.

Jetsunma Tamdrin Wangmo lived 61 years and died on the twentieth day of the first month in the year of the fire monkey (1896) at her residence, Pelgyi Labrang, in Sakya.[124] Many special signs appeared at the time of her death. Shortly before she died, she declared that she was in Tushita Heaven. To be reborn in this heaven is considered auspicious because the Future Buddha, Maitreya, and bodhisattvas who are close to enlightenment are believed to reside there. Family members of the Phuntsok Palace performed the funeral ceremonies. After cremation her ashes were treated with great honor. The family set up an altar with offerings and recited religious chants many times, just as they did in funerals for the sons (dungsays) of the Khon family. Not all jetsunmas receive this special treatment; Jetsunma Tamdrin Wangmo was so honored because she was the lama of many of the Sakya Trizins and their entire families, and of many other high lamas as well. Indeed, while she was alive, she had received the same prestigious welcoming ceremonies received by the Khon sons. These included the blowing of double-reed horns (gyalings) and holding of a large yellow parasol over her head during processions.

Shortly after her death, a life-sized silver Nāro Vajrayoginī covered with gilded gold and inlaid with precious gems was made as her memorial statue. It was placed in the Orgyen Temple, which is within the larger Great Temple. Over the years, pilgrims showed their respect by coming to see the statue and make offerings. She is remembered as an emanation of Vajra Nairātmyā and Vajravārāhī.

According to Jetsunma Tamdrin Wangmo's paternal uncle, the 33rd Sakya Trizin Pema Dudul Wangchuk, she was a manifestation of a hundred thousand ḍākinīs appearing in one body. He had prophesied that she would excel in spreading the Buddhist teachings. This brings us back to her full name, Jetsunma Tamdrin Wangmo Kalzang Chokyi Nyima, which reveals the abilities she displayed in her life. And as we have seen, in some situations she needed to display a "wrathful form" (tamdrin) in order to frighten someone, such as the lecherous Chinese official and the bandits. Nor can her influence as a "powerful woman" (wangmo) be overstated. She certainly had "good fortune" (kalzang), and, more importantly,

---

124. Dragshul Trinlei Rinchen 2009, 417. Schoening 1990, 26–27. Schoening's diagram shows Pelgyi Labrang ('Phel rgyas bla brang) southeast of the Zhitog Palace on the northern side of Sakya. It is listed as number 29.

she brought good fortune to those blessed by her presence. As both a superlative student and exemplary teacher, she "rejoiced in the Buddhist teachings" (*chokyi*). And just as the sun (*nyima*) does not discriminate against anyone and shines its rays upon the whole world, so Jetsunma Tamdrin Wangmo left her mark as an astonishing Buddhist teacher who taught everyone who sought her out and requested teachings.

CHAPTER FIVE

The Great Yoginī:
Kyabgon Pema Trinlei (1874–ca. 1950)

JETSUNMA PEMA TRINLEI (1874–ca. 1950) was a great yoginī in the Sakya tradition who is remembered first and foremost as an adept (*siddha*) of the Vajrayoginī practices. Like her paternal great-aunt Jetsunma Tamdrin Wangmo (see Chapter 4), she received many important teachings that she transmitted to her disciples, including the exoteric and esoteric levels of the Path with the Result (see Chapter 1).[125] Later in life she was given the title Kyabgon, which is how Tibetans refer to her today.

Kyabgon, a title usually given to a man, means a protector in whom one takes refuge. Pema is the Tibetan word for "lotus," a symbol of the bodhisattva who continues to be reborn in cyclic existence (like a lotus born in the mud but untainted by it) so as to relieve the suffering of others. Trinlei means "enlightened activity." Thus her name can be interpreted as referring to a bodhisattva who works diligently to help others in their efforts toward enlightenment.

Her father was Kunga Nyingpo Samphel Norbu Tashi Dakpa Gyaltsen (1850–99), the 37th Sakya Trizin (r. 1883–99); her mother was Lharitsema Chime Rigzin Palha (n.d., hereafter Dagmo Lharitsema Chime).[126] They resided in the Dolma Palace with their family of two daughters and four sons (Chart 3). The 39th Sakya Trizin Dragshul Trinlei Rinchen (1871–1935) was the oldest son; the second son was Ngawang Lhundrub Gyaltsen (1876–1913), who married the Sikkimese princess Kunsang Wangmo in 1906.[127] The third and fourth sons were Jamyang Thupten

---

125. For the mention of her birth, see Dragshul Trinlei Rinchen 1974, vol. 1, 40.

126. Lha ri rtse ma (or Lha rgya ri) 'Chi med rig' dzin dpal lha; Lha rgya ri was Dagmo Lharitsema Chime's family name.

127. Kunsang Wangmo's father was the ninth king (*chos gyal*) of Sikkim, Thutob Namgyal, and her mother was Lhading Yeshe Ngawang Lhundrup Gyaltsen (Lha ding ngag dbang

Zangpo (1885–1928) and Kunga Dagpa Lodro (1888–1919). The two daughters were Kyabgon Pema Trinlei (1874–ca. 1950) and Jetsunma Ngodrub Wangmo (1880–1939, hereafter Jetsunma Ngowang).[128] As one can see, Kyabgon Pema Trinlei lived much longer than any of her siblings.

HER PARENTS' EXAMPLE

The life of Kyabgon Pema Trinlei's father, the 37th Sakya Trizin Kunga Nyingpo Samphel Norbu, is well documented as that of a fervent and dedicated religious practitioner.[129] Likewise her mother, Dagmo Lharitsema Chime, was known for her sustained commitment to Tibetan Buddhism.[130] As a young girl, Dagmo Lharitsema Chime and her mother had gone to visit the Dalai Lama.[131] During this visit, while chanting to Tara, she had a vision of the goddess Tara, a very popular deity in the Tibetan tradition. In this vision the young Dagmo Lharitsema saw that in Tara's left palm were the letters of the Bodhisattva of Wisdom Mañjuśrī's mantra, *oṃ a ra pa ca na dhīḥ*, and each letter was then transformed into a grain of barley. This vision was interpreted as meaning that she would have many sons who would be emanations of Mañjuśrī, with the barley indicating much prosperity.[132]

Having a vision of Tara was also believed to indicate that Dagmo Lharitsema Chime had a strong connection to the deity and would remain well connected to Tara throughout her life. It is worth noting that, for many wives in the Sakya Khon family, the main spiritual practice focuses on Tara. Later, when she became pregnant with her first son (the future 39th Sakya Trizin Dragshul Trinlei Rinchen), she dreamt of a fresh saffron flower that she put in a vase. As her son the 39th Sakya Trizin recorded

---

lhun grub rgyal mtshan). From Alice Travers, "Women in the Diplomatic Game: Preliminary Notes on the Matrimonial Link of the Sikkim Royal Family with Tibet (13th–20th Centuries)," *Bulletin of Tibetology* 42.1–2 (2006): 101.

128. See Dragshul Trinlei Rinchen 2009, 495. He states that Jetsunma Ngodrub Wangmo was born in autumn after the family returned from a stay at the hot springs.

129. Ibid., 462–512.

130. Dragshul Trinlei Rinchen 1974, vol. 1, 32, where Dagmo Lharitsema Chime appears as Chi med rig'dzin pal lha.

131. Perhaps this was the 12th Dalai Lama, Trinlei Gyatso (1857–75).

132. Dragshul Trinlei Rinchen 1974, vol. 1, 34.

decades later in his diary, at the time a yogi named Zodpa Chung[133] predicted that his mother would receive many boons from Tara.[134]

After marrying into the Khon family, Dagmo Lharitsema Chime received the complete Path with the Result teachings and completed a Vajrapāṇi retreat to prevent obstacles from arising. Part of her daily practice included chanting the Praises to the Twenty-One Taras and offering sustenance to the hungry ghosts.[135]

Dagmo Lharitsema Chime was an avid reader of spiritual biographies. She enjoyed reading about the life of the great Indian yogi Padmasambhava, the Sakya genealogies, and the biographies of the Sakya masters. Famed as an excellent storyteller, she would regale others with stories drawn from these biographies. Together with the 38th Sakya Trizin Dzamling Chegu Wangdu (dZam gling che rgyu dbang sdud, 1863–1916) from the Phuntsok Palace, she enjoyed discussing these books so much that their servants would be seen busily carrying the books back and forth between the two palaces.[136]

Throughout her life, Dagmo Lharitsema Chime kept up constant spiritual practice. When her oldest son, the future 39th Sakya Trizin, became ill, she secretly did a Ganapati[137] retreat to help speed his recovery. In Tibet, when one is sick for a long time, it is believed that rituals for long life and the removal of potential problems can help the sick person heal more quickly. After the recovery of her son, the family performed a thanksgiving ritual in gratitude to the deities.[138]

---

133. The yogi Zodpa Chung was known as a great adept of Four-Faced Mahākāla.

134. Dragshul Trinlei Rinchen 1974, vol. 1, 34.

135. It is thought that one is born into the hungry ghost realm if one has been stingy and avaricious in a previous life. In paintings the hungry ghosts are shown as having a neck as thin as a razor and an enormous stomach, so they can never be satisfied. To help alleviate their sufferings, humans can make offerings of water and food to them. This appeases them and prevents them from creating havoc in the human realm. For more on hungry ghosts, see Deshung Rinpoche 1995.

136. Dragshul Trinlei Rinchen 1974, vol. 1, 35–36.

137. Ganapati (Tsho bdag glang snga) is a very popular god in Hinduism. He has an elephant head and a human body. He is known as the deity who if ignored can create obstacles, but he can remove obstructions if worshipped properly. In Buddhism he has different forms and is not worshipped as pervasively as among Hindus. However, one form of the Buddhist Ganapati is worshipped also to request that obstacles be removed.

138. Dragshul Trinlei Rinchen 1974, vol. 1, 60.

Chart 3. The Dolma Palace, Late 18th to Late 19th Century

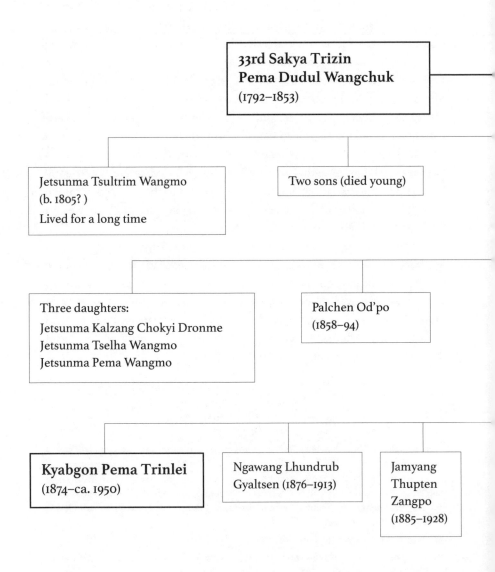

33rd Sakya Trizin
Pema Dudul Wangchuk
(1792–1853)

Jetsunma Tsultrim Wangmo
(b. 1805?)
Lived for a long time

Two sons (died young)

Three daughters:
Jetsunma Kalzang Chokyi Dronme
Jetsunma Tselha Wangmo
Jetsunma Pema Wangmo

Palchen Od'po
(1858–94)

Kyabgon Pema Trinlei
(1874–ca. 1950)

Ngawang Lhundrub
Gyaltsen (1876–1913)

Jamyang
Thupten
Zangpo
(1885–1928)

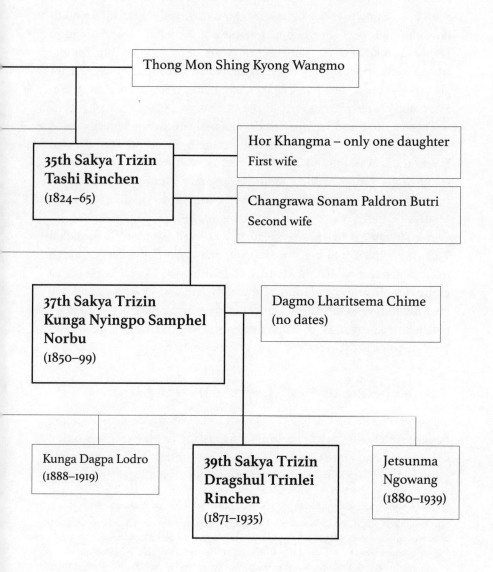

Thong Mon Shing Kyong Wangmo

35th Sakya Trizin
Tashi Rinchen
(1824–65)

Hor Khangma – only one daughter
First wife

Changrawa Sonam Paldron Butri
Second wife

37th Sakya Trizin
Kunga Nyingpo Samphel
Norbu
(1850–99)

Dagmo Lharitsema Chime
(no dates)

Kunga Dagpa Lodro
(1888–1919)

39th Sakya Trizin
Dragshul Trinlei
Rinchen
(1871–1935)

Jetsunma
Ngowang
(1880–1939)

Involved in many religious activities, Dagmo Lharitsema Chime commissioned statues for three of the four famous buildings that contained the Four Wonders of Sakya.[139] In the Utse Nyingma building, she requested the making of life-sized gilded copper statues of the Lords of the Three Families—Avalokiteśvara, Mañjuśrī, and Vajrapāṇi. In addition, she had nine gilded copper statues of Amitāyus, the Buddha of Long Life, made for the Namgyal Stupa. She provided the Tara Temple with gilded copper statues of the eight Taras who protect from the eight great fears (water, fire, lions, snakes, elephants, thieves, false imprisonment, and ghosts).[140]

Thus spiritual and devoted practitioners in her own family surrounded Kyabgon Pema Trinlei when she was young. Later in life she followed her mother's example and commissioned a one-story-high gilded copper statue of the Future Buddha, Maitreya, together with backrest and halo. In the twentieth century, many temples were constructing images of Maitreya Buddha because of the great benefit bestowed on practitioners. Geshe Thuchey Wangchuk (1928–2018), who lived as a monk in the Great Temple complex of Sakya, remembered that it was in the *sambhogakaya* form, which means that the statue was decorated as a royal being with a crown, jewels, and silk clothing. He recalls that it was in the second row near the library of the Great Temple. Also, when he was about 14 years old, he saw Kyabgon Pema Trinlei when she was visiting the Great Temple. She was a short elderly woman dressed in maroon nun's robes.[141]

THE BEGINNING OF HER SPIRITUAL DEVELOPMENT

Although there is no single source giving a dedicated account of Kyabgon Pema Trinlei's life, her older brother Dragshul Trinlei Rinchen kept a voluminous diary (see Chapter 1), and in some entries he recorded some events of her early life. Both he and his sister received teachings from

139. See Chapter 2 for a description of these buildings and the Four Wonders of Sakya.
140. Buddhism originated in India and the possibility of encountering these fearful situations was common for Indians, who needed to walk through jungles and forests frequently. Though some of these fears may be less relevant at the present time, others continue to be of major concern, such as fire, water, robbers, and false imprisonment. Additionally, these can be understood as mental anxieties or negative emotions that prevent one from realizing one's spiritual potential, such as attachment, anger, pride, jealousy, ignorance, false views, greed, and doubt.
141. Interview with Geshe Thuchey Wangchuk in Seattle on November 2, 2016.

their paternal great-aunt, Jetsunma Tamdrin Wangmo (Chapter 4), and their father the 37th Sakya Trizin also gave them extensive teachings. One of the teachings mentioned in the diary concerns their father's instructions about Mahākāla (Great Black One), one of the principal protectors of the Sakyas and, in particular, of the Khon family.

Many Tibetans came to Sakya as pilgrims, including high-ranking lamas. One such lama, Gongkar Tulku,[142] requested a special teaching on Mahākāla from Kyabgon Pema Trinlei's father. This teaching is considered precious and is not given frequently. Her father agreed to bestow the entire teaching—the outer, inner, and secret Pañjaranātha Mahākāla teaching together with an extensive oral commentary—to a small select group. In addition to Gongkar Tulku, who had requested the teaching, the group included Ponlop Lochu (dPon slob blo chos); Kyabgon Pema Trinlei's brother Dragshul Trinlei Rinchen; his teacher Jampa Chok Namgyal (Byams pa phyogs rnam rgyal); and Kyabgon Pema Trinlei herself, who was about 11 years old at the time.[143] After receiving this extensive teaching from their father, Kyabgon Pema Trinlei and Dragshul Trinlei Rinchen underwent a one-month retreat dedicated to the protector Pañjaranātha Mahākāla.[144] Their teacher Ponlop Thuje (dPon slob thugs rje) guided them throughout the retreat to ensure that they performed it correctly and to answer any pertinent questions.

After their retreat was completed, in the tenth month, Kyabgon Pema Trinlei and her brother received the blessings of the Lion's Roar Avalokiteśvara (Siṃhanāda) and many long-life empowerments from the elderly Khenchen Tashi Chopel, abbot of the Great Temple (the same abbot who had bestowed the three vows on their great-aunt, Jetsunma Tamdrin Wangmo, as mentioned in Chapter 4).[145]

Also, Kyabgon Pema Trinlei received the public Path with the Result teachings from her father in the Dechen (Eternal Happiness) room in the Dolma Palace.[146] There were about 50 people who received this teaching, including her brother Dragshul Trinlei Rinchen, some selected monks

142. On Gongkar Tulku, see note 118 above.

143. Dragshul Trinlei Rinchen 1974, vol. 1, 72–73.

144. Ibid., vol. 1, 80. They began the retreat at the end of the eighth month, when Dragshul Trinlei Rinchen was 13 years old.

145. Ibid., vol. 1, 81.

146. After the 41st Sakya Trizin was born (see Chapter 8), he was given this Eternal Happiness room as his bedroom in the Dolma Palace.

from the South and North Monasteries, and some monks who were visiting from Kham.

One of the Khon family's main sponsors, the affluent Khampa business family Pandatsang (sPang mda' tshang), sent their business manager, Sonam Pelgye (bSod nams pal rgyas), to Sakya.[147] He requested long-life empowerments from their father and uncle, but since both were busy with official duties, Dragshul Trinlei Rinchen gave his first long-life empowerment: Tangtong Gyalpo's empowerment of Hayagrīva and Amitāyus. This is a very popular long-life empowerment given by Khon family members because it combines the long-life Buddha Amitāyus and Hayagrīva (the horse-necked deity), who is regarded as a powerful remover of obstacles or dangers to one's life.[148] Dragshul Trinlei Rinchen conferred this initiation on his mother Dagmo Lharitsema Chime; his sister Kyabgon Pema Trinlei; his brother Ngawang Lhundrup; two of his teachers, Ponlop Thuje and Ponlop Lochu; and the main sponsor, Sonam Pelgye. This is an example of the strong relationship between Kyabgon Pema Trinlei and her older brother.

Another example illustrates the special relationship that both Kyabgon Pema Trinlei and Dragshul Trinlei Rinchen had with their great-aunt Jetsunma Tamdrin Wangmo (see Chapter 4). In Dragshul Trinlei Rinchen's diary, he states that, in 1886, Jetsunma Tamdrin Wangmo gave him, his two brothers, and his two sisters—including Kyabgon Pema Trinlei who was 12 years old—very extensive Path with the Result teachings.[149] Jetsunma Tamdrin Wangmo conferred both the exoteric and esoteric Path with the Result with explanations from the great commentators of the tradition, such as Muchen Konchog Gyaltsen (Mus chen dkon mchog rgyal mtshan 1388–1469),[150] who has two commentaries, one more accessible and available to the public and the other considered to be secret and based on his direct experiences of the Path with the Result practices. She also bestowed many empowerments in the context of these teachings, including a major empowerment of the goddess

---

147. Dragshul Trinlei Rinchen 1974, vol. 1, 82. See Carole McGranahan, "*Sa spang mda'gnam spang mda'*: Murder, History and Social Politics in 1920's Lhasa," in Lawrence Epstein, ed., *Khams Pa Histories: Visions of People, Place and Authority* (Leiden: Brill, 2002).

148. See Cyrus Stearns, *King of the Empty Plain: The Tibetan Iron-Bridge Builder Tangtong Gyalpo* (Ithaca, NY: Snow Lion Publications, 2007), 28.

149. Dragshul Trinlei Rinchen 1974, vol. 1, 130.

150. See Stearns 2001, 39–40.

Nairātmyā. This pattern of siblings learning together was repeated many decades later, when the young Jetsun Kushok and her brother the 41st Sakya Trizin jointly received both parts of the Path with the Result (see Chapter 8).

VISIT TO KHAM

Like her great-aunt Jetsunma Tamdrin Wangmo, Kyabgon Pema Trinlei toured Kham when she was in her early twenties (see Map of Kham in Chapter 4).[151] She went to obtain and transmit teachings as well as to receive donations, visiting many of the same places as her great-aunt before her and engaging in similar activities. For example, they both stayed at the Lang Nak (Black Bull) Monastery in Trehor. As mentioned in Chapter 4, Jetsun Tamdrin Wangmo gave many teachings to the 3rd Nyendrak Tulku, Tenpai Wangchuk (1854–98), who later gave teachings to Kyabgon Pema Trinlei.[152] The 3rd Nyendrak Tulku praised his main disciples, lauding them all as scholars and siddhas (*mkhas pa grub pa*), and among them Kyabgon Pema Trinlei heads the list.[153]

One of the main gurus of Kyabgon Pema Trinlei (and also of the 3rd Nyendrak Tulku) was the famous Sakya and nonsectarian (*ris med*) master Jamyang Loter Wangpo (1847–1914). He was a great practitioner who studied widely in the sutras, the monastic code of discipline (Vinaya), the metaphysical treatises or Abhidharma, and the works of major philosophers, in addition to receiving numerous tantras and their commentaries and performing the mandatory retreats and daily recitations. His efforts and abilities surpassed those of many other practitioners. One of his legacies was the compilation of the extensive *Compendium of Tantras* in 30 volumes.[154]

---

151. There is no entry in the diary saying when Kyabgon Pema Trinlei departed for Kham, but we know that she was there in 1897 and that she returned to Sakya in 1898.

152. Tsering Wangyal and Yama Gonpo 2005, 30, refer to Kyabgon Pema Trinlei as Jetsun Rinpoche Pema Trinlei Dud Dul Wangmo (rJe tsun rin po che pad ma phrin las bdud 'dul dwang mo).

153. Ibid.

154. The biography of Jamyang Loter Wangpo states that he traveled from Ngor Monastery in Tsang to Derge in Kham. When he arrived at the well-known Dzongsar Monastery, the great nonsectarian master Jamyang Khyentse Wangpo (1820–92), who was living there, immediately broke his retreat to greet him. This was highly irregular because a retreatant makes a formal commitment to complete a retreat without interruption. However, a lama

This vast repository of tantric transmissions draws from all the great traditions of Buddhist practice in Tibet, including Nyingma, Sakya, Kagyu, Geluk, Bodong, Jonang, Shiche (Zhi byed), Orgyen Nyendrup (O rgyan bsnyen sgrub), and Kālacakra. It takes about six months of daily sessions to bestow all the initiations and instructions contained within it. Jamyang Loter Wangpo's herculean effort to collect and create this compendium was greeted with enormous enthusiasm and appreciation by many admired lamas.[155]

Jamyang Loter Wangpo was able to bestow the entire *Compendium of Tantras* for the first time in 1892. He bestowed it five times in his life—in 1892, 1897, 1901, 1902, and 1909. Fortunately, Kyabgon Pema Trinlei was staying at Dondrub Ling Monastery (also known as Jyeku) in Jyekundo, Kham, in 1897. A Lamdre Lopshe (esoteric Path with the Result) text states that Jamyang Loter Wangpo in his fifty-first year (1897) taught the *Compendium of Tantras* at the famous Dondrub Ling Monastery. He began the transmission in the seventh month, and his principal disciple is listed as "Lharig Khon Dung Jetsunma Pema Trinlei." Many eminent tulkus

---

will break this vow for special reasons. Khyentse asked his personal attendant to invite Jamyang Loter Wangpo to his residence. When he arrived, Khyentse was holding a bundle of incense sticks and showed much delight in meeting him. Khyentse remarked, "You have received many profound teachings, please continue to receive more teachings that you have not yet received. Make the effort to try to understand the essence of each teaching." Khenchen Appey Rinpoche 2008–10, vol. 29: 270.

Khyentse continued, "Ngor Thartse Abbot Jampa Kunga Tenzin Gyaltsen (1829–70) made one collection known as 'Beautiful Rosary of Jewels' (Nor bu phreng mdzas), but he knew that more needed to be collected and organized. He had you in mind to make an extensive collection. You should start collecting these teachings and add to the original collection. You must do this now, before all of this becomes lost. Please make a great effort to accomplish and complete all this. I am asking you because you have the abilities and all the karmic causes are ripened to do this."

In 1882, upon hearing this request from his lama, Jamyang Loter Wangpo began with great eagerness and perseverance. He promised his lama that he would pursue this to the end, regardless of personal deprivations. Knowing that his lama had many teachings that he himself did not possess, he asked him if he might request these from him. Jamyang Khyentse Wangpo was very pleased and said, "I have received more than a hundred special teachings, initiations, and commentaries from great *rime* masters. I am getting old so I will give you as much as I can. Also please ask [the *rime* master] Kongtrul Jamgon Lodro Thaye (1813–99) for other initiations." In the end Jamyang Loter Wangpo collected more than 300 initiations. See ibid., vol. 29: 276–77, and Jackson 2020, 43. In addition to gathering them, he arranged them and published the related liturgies and practical manuals of instructions.

155. Jackson 2020, 157.

were there from all areas of Tibet, but she is the only one listed by name, thereby indicating her special position as a Sakya Khon jetsunma and, more importantly, as one of Jamyang Loter Wangpo's main disciples.

In addition, Jamyang Loter Wangpo transmitted to Kyabgon Pema Trinlei the *Compendium of Sādhanas* (*Grub thabs kun 'dus*), which consists of 14 volumes of empowerments and practices from all four classes of tantra. Jamyang Loter Wangpo was the compiler of this collection of teachings that had initially been gathered by his guru Jamyang Khyentse Wangpo (1820–92). This compendium incorporated three older collections of deity meditation manuals, or *sādhanas*.

In his diary, Dragshul Trinlei Rinchen states that Kyabgon Pema Trinlei returned from Kham in the eleventh month of 1898.[156] Shortly after her arrival in Sakya, there was a large gathering of monks in the assembly hall, where she distributed the goods she had brought back from Kham.[157] The following year, in the tenth month, while Dragshul Trinlei Rinchen was doing a retreat on Four-Faced Mahākāla, Kyabgon Pema Trinlei interrupted his retreat to tell him that their father was ill. On the thirtieth day of the eleventh month of 1899, their father passed away.[158]

For a few years, there is no mention of Kyabgon Pema Trinlei in her brother's diary. But it then notes that in 1907 she was sent to the Northern Plain (Changtang) to give empowerments and collect donations. (As mentioned in Chapter 8, her great-niece Jetsun Kushok was sent to the Northern Plain decades later, for similar reasons.) We are told that Kyabgon Pema Trinlei returned in the tenth month in 1907. Bearing gifts for her older brother, she gave him two horses, a *dzomo* (a hybrid of a cow and yak), much butter, and a nomad delicacy known as *tod* (a mixture of butter, sugar, and cheese).[159]

Kyabgon Pema Trinlei seems to have liked to give gifts to her brother. In the following year, 1908, she brought him an excellent "mattress" from her residence in Tashi Gang, and he appreciated her fine gift.[160] Later

156. Dragshul Trinlei Rinchen 1974, vol. 1, 256–57.

157. Ibid., vol. 1, 257.

158. Ibid., vol. 1, 261–63.

159. Ibid., vol. 1, 302.

160. Ibid., vol. 1, 303. In Tibet, portable mattresses, which are actually large cushions that fold into two parts, have different kinds of stuffing. The most inferior stuffing is straw, and the highest quality is very fine wool similar to cashmere. Most likely Kyabgon Pema Trinlei gave the latter.

in the year, Dragshul Trinlei Rinchen, their younger sister Jetsunma Ngowang, and the manager of Tashi Labrang went to visit Kyabgon Pema Trinlei when she was doing a retreat in the celebrated Mahākāla temple of Khau Drak Dzong (Kha'u brag rdzong).[161]

In 1913, Dragshul Trinlei Rinchen gave a very special empowerment of Mahākāla in the renowned Gorum shrine. Only eight people received it, including his two sons and Kyabgon Pema Trinlei.[162] After the diary entry recording this event, Kyabgon Pema Trinlei is barely mentioned any more in her older brother's diary.

RECOLLECTIONS OF DRAWUPON RINCHEN TSERING

The great Khampa warrior leader Drawupon Rinchen Tsering (b. 1931; see Chapter 4) recalled various encounters with Kyabgon Pema Trinlei in Jyekundo. He mentioned that both she and her great-aunt, Jetsunma Tamdrin Wangmo, stayed in the same room at the Drawupon's Palace there. She, too, left her ritual bell and dorje in the room, which is considered very holy because it was blessed by her presence.

Also, in 1935, when Drawupon Rinchen Tsering was five years old, he went with his parents, uncle, and older sister on a pilgrimage to Sakya. He remembered that Kyabgon Pema Trinlei welcomed the family warmly since she recalled her pleasant time with them in Jyekundo, Kham. She asked many questions about everyone and was happy to see them.

While in Sakya, Drawupon Rinchen Tsering's uncle was eager for his niece to become a nun and for his nephew Drawupon Rinchen Tsering to become a monk. Kyabgon Pema Trinlei showed much concern toward Drawupon Rinchen Tsering's sister, who was only ten years old. She told their uncle that the girl should take the vows of becoming a nun immediately. Repeating "Nyingje, nyingje" (*snying rje*, "Dear sweet one") while holding the girl's hand and patting her head, Kyabgon Pema Trinlei urged her to receive the ordination from Khenpo Lama Gendun (ca. 1880–1939),[163] a famous abbot from Kham who lived in Sakya, was a teacher to many monks, and was one of her own main disciples.

161. Ibid., vol. I, 304. They visited her on the second day of the fifth month.

162. Ibid., vol. I, 398.

163. H.H. the 41st Sakya Trizin related this story (via email, December 12, 2018): Lama Gendun was a strict vegetarian, whereas Kyabgon Pema Trinlei ate meat. One day, after she finished lunch, Lama Gendun finished her meal, which had meat in it. When asked why he

Drawupon Rinchen Tsering recalled, "My sister did become a nun right away."

Once one takes the vows of a nun, one must not violate them. Their uncle asked Kyabgon Pema Trinlei if his niece would break some of her vows in the future. Kyabgon Pema Trinlei was well known for her insight in future events. She reassured him about his niece, saying, "She will be a nun forever." The family was unaware of the future. When they stopped in the holy city of Lhasa on their way home, without warning the girl died. Apparently Kyabgon Pema Trinlei had foreseen her imminent death and wanted her to gain merit by becoming a nun.

TEACHINGS AND EMPOWERMENTS

Unlike her great-aunt Jetsun Tamdrin Wangmo (see Chapter 4), who is well known for transmitting many teachings, Kyabgon Pema Trinlei seems to have been more reserved, and it is more unusual to find instances when she offered public teachings.

His Holiness the 41st Sakya Trizin related an interesting story that reveals some of the challenges faced by women teachers. When Kyabgon Pema Trinlei was in Kham in the 1890s, she gave initiations at Lang Nak (Black Bull) Monastery, which was in the area controlled by the powerful monastery known as Trehor Dhargye Gompa, which housed about 1,900 monks of the Gelugpa tradition. Trehor Dhargye Monastery did not allow lamas from other Tibetan Buddhist traditions to teach in the area without their permission. When the monk-officials there heard that Kyabgon Pema Trinlei was giving empowerments without their permission, they were incensed. In addition, many believed that it was inauspicious for a woman to give initiations. So they sent the monastic "police," the strong and intimidating *dobdobs* (*ldob ldob*), to beat her.

The *dobdobs* arrived as she was giving an empowerment in the temple. Since it was considered uncouth to disrupt an empowerment, the men did not barge in. As they were peeking through the curtains, Kyabgon Pema Trinlei saw them but pretended to be unaware of their presence. She was holding a ritual vase for this part of the empowerment. Her nun's robe was falling off her shoulder, so she suspended her vase in midair

---

would eat meat, he answered that it made no difference whether Kyabgon Pema Trinlei's meal had meat in it or not; the food was blessed because she was a real ḍākinī.

before her, arranged her robe, and then took hold of the floating vase. They were so astonished and impressed by her holiness that when they went in, instead of beating her, they did prostrations and received blessings from her.

Several other reports also provide evidence that she gave teachings. For example, she was one of the few women who gave the Path with the Result teachings. In 2007 in Rajpur, India, the 41st Sakya Trizin stated in an interview that Jetsunma was not the appropriate title for her. She must be addressed as Kyabgon (Protector), since she had conferred the Path with the Result numerous times. Only these vajra masters have this title and are permitted to wear the special red and gold hat.

Furthermore, David Jackson's two-volume biography of the 25th Chogye Trichen (1919–2007)[164] recounts that as Kyabgon Pema Trinlei made her way back to Sakya from Kham in the late 1890s, she stopped at the Sakya Phenpo Nalendra Monastery, north of Lhasa, which belonged to the Tsarpa subsect of the Sakya tradition. It had two famous lama palaces: the Chogye and Zimwok Labrangs. There the the 24th Chogye Trichen (Rinchen Khyentse Wangpo, ca. 1869–1927) and the 5th Zimwok Rinpoche (Jampa Ngawang Kunga Tenzin Trinlei, 1884–1963)[165] asked to receive the transmission of the *Compendium of Sādhanas* from her. She agreed, and gave the extensive teachings not only to these two important lamas, who were the main disciples and recipients of this transmission, but to many monks from Phenpo Nalendra who also attended. Thus it was her tradition that the 25th Chogye Trichen later received from his teacher the 5th Zimwok Rinpoche, and he treasured her lineage of the transmission.[166] Moreover, the biography of Ngaklo Rinpoche (1892–1959) states that "from Sakya's Jetsun Pema Trinlay Dorje Dudul Wangmo, he [Ngaklo Rinpoche] received the blessings and commentaries of *Naropa's Vajrayoginī*."[167] (It doesn't state where the teachings were given, though it may have been at Nalendra Monastery, since Ngaklo Rinpoche was the teacher of the 25th Chogye Trichen.)

164. Chogye Trichen Ngawang Khyenrab Thupten Lekshe Gyatso (bCo brgyad khri chen ngag dbang mkhyen rab thub bstan legs bshad rgya mtsho); see Jackson 2020, 30. Also see ibid., 13. The previous Chogye throne-holder was one of his paternal uncles.

165. For a brief biography of the 5th Zimwok Rinpoche, see ibid., 21–22.

166. See ibid., 30–31.

167. Lama Ngaklo Rinpoche, *Clear Lamp on the Path of Liberation*, translated by Lama Choedak Rinpoche (Canberra, Australia: Gorum Publications, 2019), 59.

Fig. 7. Ven. Dezhung Rinpoche, Seattle, 1962/63.

Kyabgon Pema Trinlei also offered other teachings, as recorded in David Jackson's *A Saint in Seattle: The Life of the Tibetan Mystic Dezhung Rinpoche*. The 3rd Dezhung (sDe gzhung) Rinpoche (1906–87; Fig. 7) was an extraordinary lama who grew up in Kham, fled to India, and in 1960 was invited to immigrate to Seattle as a research scholar at the University of Washington. His memory was phenomenal, and he was a great storyteller. Many of his American students later became Tibetan Buddhist scholars, including David Jackson, Cyrus Stearns, E. Gene Smith, and Jared Rhoton.

His predecessor, the 2nd Dezhung Rinpoche, Lungrik Nyima (Lung rigs nyi ma, ca. 1840s–98), who resided in Kham, had many disciples, including Kyabgon Pema Trinlei. Jackson relates that "she was renowned for having attained siddhis through the practice of Vajrayoginī" and had received that initiation (and commentaries) from the 2nd Dezhung Rinpoche.[168] In late 1949, when the 3rd Dezhung Rinpoche visited Sakya, he was hoping to visit Kyabgon Pema Trinlei. He was told that she was living in the Chogyal Phagpa Cave, owned by the Dolma Palace and near the famous Khau Drak Dzong dedicated to Four-Faced Mahākāla, a few hours east of the town of Sakya. Eager to see her, Dezhung Rinpoche, together with his younger sister Ani Chime Dolma (1922–2015) and his young niece (Dagmo) Jamyang Sakya (who later married Jigdal Dagchen Sakya), climbed the hill and went to the cave. During their first visit, Dezhung Rinpoche requested and received a long-life empowerment and a White Tara initiation.[169] These empowerments are common and could be given by many lamas. This was simply a way to establish a connection with Kyabgon Pema Trinlei. But it is clear that the main purpose of the visit was to request the teachings of Vajrayoginī (Naro Khachod), which she had received from his previous incarnation, Lungrik Nyima. The transmission took a full seven days.

During the transmission of these teachings, they stayed in the nearby Phuntsok Palace cave. It was very pleasant, with a bedroom and kitchen, but no altar. Each day they returned to the spacious Dolma Palace cave. When one entered, there was a simple kitchen on the lower level and the main cave was at a higher level, with a bedroom and a visitor's room. In the rear was a private shrine where Kyabgon Pema Trinlei performed

168. Jackson 2003, 165.
169. Ibid.

Fig. 8. H.E. Jamyang Dagmo Sakya and Ven. Ani Chime Dolma in Seattle, ca. 2003.

her daily practices and retreats. People were not invited into her private shrine. In between the two caves, there was a third cave where her attendants lived, a nun and a young woman of 15 or 16 years old. It was said that this young woman in her previous life had been Kyabgon Pema Trinlei's former manager, Sangye. There were other caves nearby, and nomads were seen frequently in the area.

Both Ani Chime Dolma and Dagmo Jamyang Sakya (Fig. 8) attended these teachings; their memories of the visit provide some insight into Kyabgon Pema Trinlei.[170] Decades later, in November 2007, in her room at Tharlam Monastery in Bodhnath, Nepal, Ani Chime insisted that Jetsunma's correct title was Kyabgon, not Jetsunma—just as the 41st Sakya Trizin also stated that same year (as mentioned above).

Both Ani Chime Dolma and Dagmo Jamyang Sakya remembered Kyabgon Pema Trinlei as a short, plump woman with a round face who was always smiling and showing kindness to others. Constantly repeating mantras, she had grey hair cut short in the typical Sakya jetsunma manner. Jetsunmas normally did not shave their heads as nuns did, but had short hair reaching just below the ears and bangs on their foreheads (similar to the Bhutanese women's traditional hairstyle). Like other jetsunmas, she wore maroon robes and sometimes jewelry, such as a small kidney-shaped amulet (*gau*) and *dzi* beads (unusual agate beads that are black with white ovals and believed to provide spiritual benefits). Ani Chime Dolma recalled that her jewelry was hanging on a wall in the cave.

In contrast to her prosaic description of Kyabgon Pema Trinlei's physical appearance, Ani Chime became very animated in describing the feelings that she evoked. The usually reserved Ani Chime was effusive in her praise. She said that the feeling was very good. She felt happy and had strong faith in her. When she saw her, "All my thoughts ceased." Ani Chime intentionally paused for a minute to make her point about how spiritually powerful Kyabgon Pema Trinlei was. Then she reiterated that she was very pleased when Dezhung Rinpoche and Kyabgon Pema Trinlei met each other; they were so happy to see each other and showed much respect for each other. When she saw this, it made her feel very happy. Indeed, Ani Chime's feeling was palpable, and one felt transported by her joy.

At her home in Seattle, Washington, in June 2007, Dagmo Jamyang Sakya also remembered Kyabgon Pema Trinlei as an extraordinary person. Dagmo Jamyang Sakya herself is a vivacious and very expressive woman. Though she was only 15 years old when she visited Kyabgon Pema Trinlei and did not understand the importance of the transmission of the Vajrayoginī teachings at the time, she said emphatically, "You can

170. Interview with Ani Chime Dolma at Tharlam Monastery, Bodhnath, Nepal, November 14 and 15, 2007.

tell that she is a lady with special powers. Her teachings were very clear."
She elaborated:

> When you see the Dalai Lama, something is there that others
> don't have. Some people have power. When you come into
> their presence, you can feel it. When you were in Kyabgon
> Pema Trinlei's presence, you felt something like "*Oooh!* I can
> feel this." When she said things, it was as if she saw through
> you; she could see inside of you. She was not looking outside.

Ani Chime Dolma recalled that Kyabgon Pema Trinlei and Dezhung
Rinpoche discussed their religious experiences and the appearances
of deities, although Ani Chime didn't understand much of this. When
Kyabgon Pema Trinlei gave the teachings of Vajrayoginī, she put on a
special hat—a red and gold hat like the one the Sakya Trizin wears. Ani
Chime explained that only people who taught the Path with the Result
are permitted to wear this hat.

Also, Ani Chime recalled that Kyabgon Pema Trinlei had a special
thangka (scroll painting) of the protector goddess Magzorma that hung
inside her cave. H.H. the 41st Sakya Trizin explained that during one
of Kyabgon Pema Trinlei's meditative sessions when in retreat, she had
begun to feel dizzy and nauseous. Suddenly she saw an ocean of blood in
front of her. Out of this ocean appeared Magzorma. She was frightened,
but nevertheless noticed that Magzorma appeared in a slight variation
from her usual form.[171] She described this vision to a painter, who created the *thangka* for her.[172]

In this spiritual experience, we can see that Kyabgon Pema Trinlei
had a theophany or a vision of the goddess that evoked fear, but also
awe. It made such an impression on her that she felt it was valuable to
have this vision painted as a reminder of this astonishing experience.
After explaining her vision to Dezhung Rinpoche, he requested that she
bestow the initiation of Magzorma as well. When they returned to the
Dolma Palace and Dagchen Kunga Rinchen (father of Jetsun Kushok
and the 41st Sakya Trizin) heard about Dezhung Rinpoche receiving this

---

171. Magzorma rides a mule. In her vision, the mule had no tail; in place of the tail was an eye.
172. H.H. the 41st Sakya Trizin, via email on December 9, 2018.

initiation, he, too, requested it, and Dezhung Rinpoche transmitted it to him.

Dagmo Jamyang Sakya emphasized that Kyabgon Pema Trinlei was very famous because she was considered by many to be an enlightened person. People sought her blessing, and she blessed them by touching their heads with her hand. Many asked her what to do when someone had died. She would advise them what rituals to perform and what statues should be built to create merit for the deceased person. She was also an excellent prognosticator. At the time of their 1949 visit to her cave, Dagmo Jamyang Sakya asked about their futures. Kyabgon Pema Trinlei prophesied that Ani Chime would have a long life and serve Dezhung Rinpoche well, and that Jamyang Sakya would become a powerful woman and be lucky in her life. Both proved correct. Ani Chime Dolma lived for 93 years. She served her older brother the 3rd Dezhung Rinpoche for many years, and then served his reincarnation the 4th Dezhung Rinpoche (born in Seattle in 1991) by helping financially maintain Tharlam Monastery in Bodhnath, Nepal, which her brother had established for his successor. Dagmo Jamyang Sakya soon married the oldest son of the Phuntsok Palace, Jigdal Dagchen Sakya; later emigrated to Seattle with her husband and young family; and eventually became a respected Buddhist teacher in her own right.

Both Dagmo Jamyang Sakya and Ani Chime Dolma affirmed that Kyabgon Pema Trinlei is regarded as a true emanation of Vajrayoginī. The 3rd Dezhung Rinpoche always spoke highly of her and Tibetans call her Kyabgon Pema Trinlei, an honor usually reserved for men.

JETSUN KUSHOK'S MEMORIES OF HER GREAT-AUNT

In August 2010, in Richmond, BC, Canada, Kyabgon Pema Trinlei's great-niece, Jetsun Kushok (b. 1938),[173] recalled that when she herself was a young girl growing up in the Dolma Palace, her great-aunt would stay in the room next to hers. Her great-aunt's room had one pillar, and on her altar were statues of Vajrayoginī, Green Tara, and Amitāyus. (There may also have been statues of the great Sakya teachers, but Jetsun Kushok is not certain.) Her main residence was Tashi Labrang, but she would come

---

173. Jetsun Kushok was born in 1938 at the Dolma Palace in Sakya. See Chapters 8 and 9 for her biography.

THE GREAT YOGINĪ | 97

to stay in the Dolma Palace to be in charge when the family undertook extended visits or pilgrimages. Later in life, as already mentioned, she lived in the Chogyal Phagpa Cave owned by the Dolma Palace. In the past the Dolma Palace family had used this cave for the presentation of special and secret teachings, but after Kyabgon Pema Trinlei chose to live there, it became her main residence. This was a very pleasant cave that was warm in the winter and cool in the summer. Jetsun Kushok remembers when her great-aunt lived in the cave, she was regarded as a mahāsiddha or great yoginī, a spiritual adept.

Jetsun Kushok recalls that she and her great-aunt treated each other as equals—touching foreheads when they would greet each other. In Tibet, if two people greet each other by touching foreheads, this indicates their high respect for each other. Furthermore, Jetsun Kushok considered the touching of foreheads to be a blessing from her great-aunt. A high lama would rarely greet an ordinary person in this way. Usually the ordinary person would bow low, suck in the breath so as not to "contaminate" the lama, and offer a *khata* (ceremonial scarf) with outstretched hands. The lama would take the *khata* and, by touching it, confer a blessing on it, then place it around the devotee's neck. Touching foreheads is reserved for equals.

"Jetsunma Pema Trinlei loved me very much," Jetsun Kushok declares. "My aunt wanted to give me her jewelry and other precious things, but I regarded myself as a tomboy. I was not interested in jewelry." Her aunt gave her something more valuable: long-life empowerments. Here—as in Chapter 4—we see an example of a jetsunma conferring empowerments on another jetsunma. It is fortunate that we have the actual documentation of three jetsunmas maintaining the Sakya Khon spiritual lineage by the transmission of empowerments from great-aunt to great-niece. One finds numerous such lineages among the males in the Khon family. More commonly, an uncle or father will instruct his nephew or son, but for three women to do this is extraordinary.

THE *BAMO*—A UNIQUE SAKYA PHENOMENON

When pilgrims came to Sakya, they were excited to see all the magnificent temples, statues, and sites that they had heard about from earlier pilgrims. But there was one group of beings that they feared. Many who have visited Sakya will barely whisper their names—the *bamos* ('bar mo, witches). I asked Ani Chime Dolma about her memories of visiting Sakya for the first time. She told me, "When I first arrived in Sakya, I was worried about the *bamos*. They need to be appeased. One would never dare to ignore them." She remembered, "When we visited the Bamo Temple, we were scared. At its entrance, there are paintings of human arms and legs hanging from the ceiling." Continuing her story, she said, "We offered the *bamos* incense and an entire set of clothes and shoes. They like such offerings."

The website Himalayan Art Resources[174] includes an image of a *thangka* depicting the worldly protector Shangmo Bamo. Unique to the Sakya tradition, these *bamos* have a special relationship with the Khon family. They are difficult to control. Usually it is the males of the Khon family who manage to deal with them, but in this case it was Kybagon Pema Trinlei: on the back of the *thangka* is a lengthy inscription signed by her and accompanied by her personal seal. The family who commissioned the painting asked for her help because they had met with a variety of misfortunes. In her inscription, Kyabgon Pema Trinlei writes that the *bamos* must remember their agreement with the Khon family and honor their promises. She exhorts the *bamos* not to harm this family and to quickly remove all obstacles from their lives. This is another situation in which Kyabgon Pema Trinlei was seen as a powerful adept—one who had the ability to control the difficult (and, for most people, frightening) *bamos*.

Since Kyabgon Pema Trinlei had received teachings from her great-aunt Jetsunma Tamdrin Wangmo and later gave her own young great-niece Jetsun Kushok long-life empowerments, there is a spiritual lineage from one jetsunma to another. And just as Jetsunma Tamdrin Wangmo had received teachings from her older brother Dorje Rinchen, so Kyabgon Pema Trinlei received teachings from her older brother, the 39th Sakya Trizin Dragshul Trinlei Rinchen. Her root lamas were her brother the 39th Sakya Trizin and the famous Jamyang Loter Wangpo, while her main lama for the important Vajrayoginī teachings was the 2nd Dezhung Rinpoche, Lungrik Nyima.

174. This *thangka* is listed as #90187 on the Himalayan Art Resources website, https://www.himalayanart.org/.

HER DEATH

It is unclear exactly when Kyabgon Pema Trinlei died (ca. 1950). The 41st Sakya Trizin (b. 1945), though he never met her, remembers that when he was four or five years old an unusual event occurred. His Holiness related this story:

> There is a tradition that when someone dies, clothes of the deceased person are given to the Dagchen [or Lord]. In this case, this was my father [Dagchen Kunga Rinchen]. Usually the clothes of a deceased master would be kept on a low seat, but I noticed some clothes that were placed on a higher seat in the main reception/ceremony room on the third floor of the Dolma Palace. I wondered why it was done this way. The clothes were of a nun. It was unusual because for ordinary people, their clothes are sold. But in the case of the spiritual person, their clothes are saved as relics and at a later date pieces are given to their devotees.[175]

Then His Holiness paused for emphasis. He continued, "Later I found out that the clothes belonged to my great-aunt, Kyabgon Pema Trinlei."

175. Interview with the 41st Sakya Trizin in 2012 at Walden, New York.

CHAPTER SIX

Inveterate Diarist:
Dragshul Trinlei Rinchen (1871–1935),
the 39th Sakya Trizin

THIS CHAPTER highlights the family life of the 39th Sakya Trizin Dragshul Trinlei Rinchen from the time his first daughter was born in 1896 to his death in 1935.[176] By relying on his diary (see Chapter 1), the most extensive extant document to portray the dynamics of an entire Sakya family in Tibet, we can gain a substantial sense of his family's daily life and their interactions among themselves and with Tibetan communities. Dragshul Trinlei Rinchen's family was comprised of his wife, his five daughters, his two sons, and, later, his sons' co-wives (Chart 4). As discussed in Chapter 5, Dragshul Trinlei Rinchen's brothers and sisters lived in the Dolma Palace until they married or moved to their own residences (*labrangs*); some of their activities are included in this chapter.

In the twelfth month of 1895, Dragshul Trinlei Rinchen met his wife Tseten Dolma, who was from the Ragashar (or Dozur, rDo zur) noble family.[177] As in most Khon marriages, the two families arranged the union: the bride was not consulted. After arriving in Sakya, she and her older brother were accompanied by the family to the Dolma Palace, where the marriage ceremony was held. Dragshul Trinlei Rinchen's mother, who wore an elegant *chuba* for the celebration, and his brother Jamyang Zangpo participated in the wedding ceremonies. Dragshul Trinlei Rinchen noted that his father used the family's precious ritual implements made of gold when he bestowed the long-life empowerment of Amitāyus surrounded by the eight-deity mandala, according to the

---

176. Dragshul Trinlei Rinchen's diary clearly states that he died in 1935 (despite it sometimes being given elsewhere as 1936).

177. Dragshul Trinlei Rinchen 1974, vol. 1, 234, writes "Lung Shel" as the family name. Cassinelli and Ekvall 1969, 354, use "Shab rDo Zur."

Indian Mahāsiddha Jetāri lineage, upon the bridal party and the Khon family members. The family served food and drink in their fanciest cups and dishes. The bride received a new name: Sakya Dagyum Chime Kunga Dolma Rigzin Palgye Lhamo (1878–early 1940s, hereafter Dagyum Chime Kunga Dolma).[178]

In 1896, on the twenty-seventh day of the eleventh month, their first child, Jetsunma Kunga Wangmo, was born.[179] Their second daughter, Jetsunma Kalzang Chodron, known simply as Kala, was born in the second month of 1898 (earth dog).[180] Their third daughter, Jetsunma Chime Trinlei Wangmo (hereafter Jetsunma Chime Wangmo), was born in 1900;[181] over the years, she would prove to be an excellent practitioner of Vajrayoginī and a valued advisor for the family.

Dragshul Trinlei Rinchen devoted himself chiefly to making extensive retreats and teaching. During a retreat on Four-Faced Mahākāla, his sister Kyabgon Pema Trinlei (Chapter 5) came to tell him that their father was ill, and the next month, the eleventh month of 1899, he passed away. Now Dragshul Trinlei Rinchen had more responsibilities, especially in transmitting the teachings that he had received from his father and his other root guru, his great-aunt Jetsunma Tamdrin Wangmo (Chapter 4). In 1902, his first son, Dungsay Kunga Rinchen, was born.[182] His second son, Dungsay Kunga Gyaltsen, was born on the third day of the eleventh month in 1904. Following tradition, Dragshul Trinlei Rinchen drew a

---

178. Dragshul Trinlei Rinchen 1974, vol. 1, 233–36.

179. Ibid., vol. 1, 240.

180. Ibid., vol. 1, 255. Jetsun Kushok (see Chapters 8 and 9) stated that Jetsunma Kalzang Chodron had mental problems. This is not mentioned in Dragshul Trinlei Rinchen's diary.

181. Jetsunma Chime Wangmo's birth is not noted in Dragshul Trinlei Rinchen's diary, but her niece, Jetsun Kushok, remembers that she was born in the iron mouse year, which is 1900. Also, her name has many variants in the diary; for example, in ibid., vol. 2, 205, she is called Chime Tenpai Dronme.

182. Ibid., vol. 1, 277. Their full titles were Dungsay Kude (Dung-de [or Dung sras] Kude, "Older Son") Ngawang Kunga Rinchen, and Dungsay Kushung (Dung chung [or Dung sras] Kushung, "Younger Son") Ngawang Kunga Tenpai Gyaltsen, respectively. Dungsay Kunga Rinchen later became known as Dagchen Kunga Rinchen (1902–50) and was the father of Jetsun Kushok and the 41st Sakya Trizin. His younger brother, later known as Ngawang Kunga Gyaltsen, was the co-husband with his older brother of Dagmo Trinlei Paljor and her sister Dagyum Sonam Dolkar. On the practice of polyandry in Tibet, see notes 25 and 75 above and note 252 below.

golden *dhīḥ* on the tongue of his infant son.[183] Since *dhīḥ* is the seed syllable of the Bodhisattva of Wisdom, Mañjuśrī, this ritual creates a propensity to learn and become wise.

Throughout these years, Dragshul Trinlei Rinchen continued his
practice. For example, in 1908 he completed a retreat dedicated to White
Tara, during which he repeated her main mantra a million times. While
on the retreat, he took special note of his dreams. He considered the following dream to be auspicious: he saw a sun and moon rising near a big
river, and blooming flowers were on the north side of a house that he
entered.[184]

Reporting on 1909, Dragshul Trinlei Rinchen writes extensively about
his visit to Central Tibet with his younger sister Jetsunma Ngowang (see
Chart 4).[185] This was a very special year because the Tibetans were hoping
that the 13th Dalai Lama, Thubten Gyatso (1876–1933), would be returning
from his self-imposed exile in Mongolia and China.[186] Members of the
Central Tibetan Government had requested that a representative from
the Sakya Khon family come to Lhasa. When Dragshul Trinlei Rinchen
was selected, he rejoiced that he would see and serve His Holiness the
13th Dalai Lama (Fig. 9).[187]

There was much preparation for such a momentous and lengthy stay
away from Sakya. Before departing, he told his two young sons to study
well and have the root (Hevajra) tantra memorized by the time of his
return. His older son, who was nine years old, expressed concern that
his father would be gone for such a long time and hoped that he would
be fine.[188]

For Dragshul Trinlei Rinchen and Jetsunma Ngowang, the journey
was the opportunity of a lifetime. They left Sakya on the twenty-second

183. Ibid., vol. 1, 289.

184. Ibid., vol. 1, 303. Throughout his diary, he mentions signs that he interprets as auspicious
or inauspicious.

185. Ibid., vol. 1, 308–30. The following material is excerpted from the diary.

186. The reasons for the exile were complicated, but the 13th Dalai Lama initially left in 1904
due to the British invasion of Lhasa and fled to Mongolia. In 1908, he visited various places,
especially holy Buddhist sites in China, and in 1909 he returned to Tibet.

187. Initially, Dragshul Trinlei Rinchen's younger brother Jamyang Thupten Zangpo was
selected to be the representative of the Khon family in Lhasa, but there were some disagreements. In the end, Dragshul Trinlei Rinchen was chosen. See ibid., vol. 1, 309.

188. Ibid., vol. 1, 312.

CHART 4. THE DOLMA PALACE, LATE 19TH TO MID-20TH CENTURY

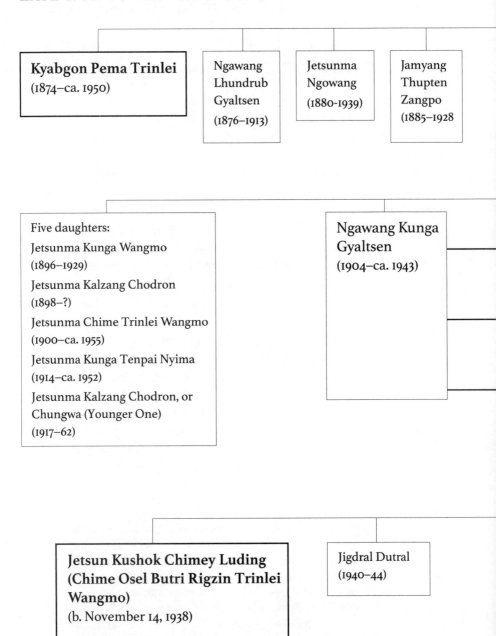

Kyabgon Pema Trinlei
(1874–ca. 1950)

Ngawang Lhundrub Gyaltsen
(1876–1913)

Jetsunma Ngowang
(1880-1939)

Jamyang Thupten Zangpo
(1885–1928

Five daughters:
Jetsunma Kunga Wangmo
(1896–1929)
Jetsunma Kalzang Chodron
(1898–?)
Jetsunma Chime Trinlei Wangmo
(1900–ca. 1955)
Jetsunma Kunga Tenpai Nyima
(1914–ca. 1952)
Jetsunma Kalzang Chodron, or
Chungwa (Younger One)
(1917–62)

Ngawang Kunga Gyaltsen
(1904–ca. 1943)

Jetsun Kushok Chimey Luding
(Chime Osel Butri Rigzin Trinlei Wangmo)
(b. November 14, 1938)

Jigdral Dutral
(1940–44)

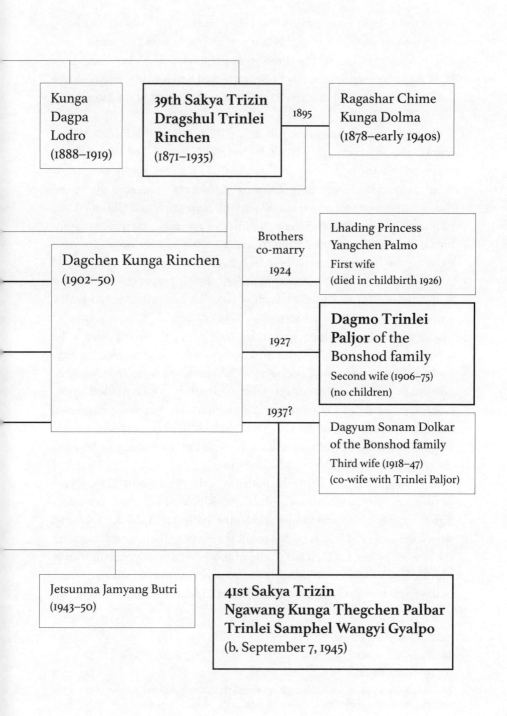

Kunga
Dagpa
Lodro
(1888–1919)

39th Sakya Trizin
Dragshul Trinlei
Rinchen
(1871–1935)

1895

Ragashar Chime
Kunga Dolma
(1878–early 1940s)

Dagchen Kunga Rinchen
(1902–50)

Brothers
co-marry
1924

Lhading Princess
Yangchen Palmo
First wife
(died in childbirth 1926)

1927

Dagmo Trinlei
Paljor of the
Bonshod family
Second wife (1906–75)
(no children)

1937?

Dagyum Sonam Dolkar
of the Bonshod family
Third wife (1918–47)
(co-wife with Trinlei Paljor)

Jetsunma Jamyang Butri
(1943–50)

41st Sakya Trizin
Ngawang Kunga Thegchen Palbar
Trinlei Samphel Wangyi Gyalpo
(b. September 7, 1945)

day of the second lunar month.[189] As they journeyed northeast to Lhasa, they stopped often. One of the first major places was Narthang Monastery, known as one of the three great printing centers in Tibet. After Narthang, they visited the city of Shigatse and had an audience with the 9th Panchen Lama, Thupten Chokyi Nyima (1883–1937), at his monastery, Tashilhunpo.[190]

Beyond Shigatse, they stopped in Tsedong, where the Dolma Palace family had another palace (see Chapter 8); Dragshul Trinlei Rinchen's wife and his younger brother Ngawang Lhundrub warmly welcomed them there. Also, the nearby Tsedong Monastery requested the initiation of the three great protectors Vajrapāṇi, Hayagrīva, and Garuḍa (*Drag po gsum bsgril gyi dbang*). This initiation rite protects practitioners from harm, from obstacles, and from illness. Because all the major preparations for the long journey were to be completed in Tsedong, they stayed there longer than other places they visited. These preparations included readying food for the journey, such as roasting and grinding the barley known as *tsampa*, their main staple, plus packing dried yak meat and dried cheese. In addition, the careful packing of the many gifts to be offered and of the ritual instruments and paraphernalia needed for rituals and empowerments was done here.[191] After their stay in Tsedong, they continued to the famous Rongjamchen Monastery, which housed a two-story-high statue of Maitreya, the Future Buddha. Everyone requested protection cords blessed by Dragshul Trinlei Rinchen, and the monastery asked that he perform a purification puja as well as a consecration of the temple to ensure its continued sanctity.

They reached Lhasa on the thirtieth day of the third month of 1909. Like most Tibetan pilgrims, Dragshul Trinlei Rinchen, his sister Jetsunma Ngowang, and their attendants visited the holiest temple, the Jokhang, where they offered much butter to fill the large golden butterlamps on the altar in front of the sacred statue of Jowo Buddha, an ancient Indian statue of the Historical Buddha.[192] They made many prostrations in front of the Jowo Buddha, and Dragshul Trinlei Rinchen made a wish that all

189. Ibid., vol. 1, 312.

190. Ibid., vol. 1, 313–14.

191. Ibid., vol. 1, 315–16.

192. The Chinese princess Wencheng Konjo brought this statue as part of her dowry when she married the Tibetan king Songtsen Gampo in the seventh century.

Fig. 9. His Holiness the 13th Dalai Lama.

sentient beings would be happy and have all their wishes fulfilled. During their stay in Lhasa, they went numerous times to the Jokhang. Initially they stayed at Shag Ta Wang House, owned by the noble family of Ragashar, who were relatives of Dragshul Trinlei Rinchen's wife.[193]

According to proper protocol, they immediately announced their arrival to the Central Tibetan Government, whose main officials worked in the Potala, the winter residence of the Dalai Lama. On the sixth day of

193. Dragshul Trinlei Rinchen 1974, vol. I, 317. The meaning of "Shag Ta Wang" is unknown.

the holy fourth month, known as Sakadawa,[194] Dragshul Trinlei Rinchen and Jetsunma Ngowang, together with some of their attendants, rode by horse to the Potala. Dragshul Trinlei Rinchen notes in his diary that they received the high honor of being allowed to dismount in the inner rather than the outer courtyard. They were ushered into the shrine room where the stupa of the 9th Dalai Lama, Lungtok Gyatso (1805–15), was located.[195] In this shrine room was the throne of the 13th Dalai Lama, which held his robe (representing the Dalai Lama until his return); everyone prostrated before the throne, and there they offered long silk scarves (khatas). Then the Lord Chamberlain and twelve of his main officials presented them with welcoming scarves. The representative of the Regent and Dragshul Trinlei Rinchen exchanged scarves as equals, and refreshments were served. Later he presented a mandala for the long life of H.H. the Dalai Lama and gifts were exchanged.[196] Eventually the cabinet of the Tibetan government, the Kashag, sent the prince of Rampa to deliver food supplies to them, including tea, tsampa, butter, and dried yak meat, as well as peas and dried grass for their animals. Dragshul Trinlei Rinchen remarks that he was treated with great honor, as if he were already the Sakya Trizin.[197]

Since everyone was waiting to receive word as to when the 13th Dalai Lama would return to Tibet, the government requested Dragshul Trinlei Rinchen to offer many prayers and tormas (sacrificial offerings) on behalf of both the Dalai Lama's safe journey and the continued success of the Tibetan government. Between sessions, Dragshul Trinlei Rinchen and Jetsunma Ngowang visited the major temples, such as the Ramoche and the Jokhang, to pray. Eminent families, such that of the famous business-man Pandatsang (sPom mda' tshang), also requested that Dragshul Trin-lei Rinchen chant prayers to pacify potential negative forces, providing Pandatsang and his relatives with prosperity and a long life.[198]

---

194. Tibetans believe that the Historical Buddha was born, became enlightened, and passed away (parinirvana) in various fourth lunar months of his lifetime, thus the "fourth" is known as Sakadawa, the Buddha (Saka) month (dawa).

195. This shrine room was located in the upper floor of the holy section of the Potala.

196. Dragshul Trinlei Rinchen 1974, vol. 1, 319–20.

197. Ibid., vol. 1, 320. They were staying at Shag rta dbang residence of the rDo zur family, cited in ibid., vol. 1, 317. Dragshul Trinlei Rinchen did not become the 39th Sakya Trizin until several years later, serving in that role from 1915 until his death in 1935.

198. Ibid., vol. 1, 320. Dragshul Trinlei Rinchen provides an extensive list of people who requested prayers.

Later, Dragshul Trinlei Rinchen, his sister, and their entourage moved to the famous Tengyeling (bsTan rgyas gling) Residence, seat of the Demo reincarnation line. Several regents of the Dalai Lama were from this reincarnation line.[199]

Many rumors continued to circulate concerning the arrival of the Dalai Lama. One rumor was that he would be traveling by ship from China to Calcutta, but according to Dragshul Trinlei Rinchen, there was no official letter to confirm this and it was considered mere speculation. Eventually the government officials determined that the Dalai Lama would be traveling overland, so they asked Dragshul Trinlei Rinchen and others to head northeast into the Nagchuka area.[200] On the way he addressed special rituals to the mountain god Nyenchen Tanglha, the well-known protector of the 1,600-km-long Trans-Himalaya mountain range. The highest mountain in this range is known as the Nyenchen Tanglha (7,152 m). Dragshul Trinlei Rinchen and Jetsunma Ngowang camped on this mountain and chanted prayers for five days.[201] From there, they continued to the sacred Namtso Lake to offer more prayers. After arriving in the nomadic region, Dragshul Trinlei Rinchen was asked to bestow various empowerments, including the Garuda and Kurukulle empowerments, as well as to perform a variety of fire ceremonies, incense offerings, and long-life initiations.

While he was in the nomadic region, the Tibetan government instructed Dragshul Trinlei Rinchen to go immediately to Nagchuka. Since he was unable to fulfill all the requests of the nomads, Jetsunma Ngowang and her attendants stayed in the region to satisfy some of these requests. In addition, she was put in charge of the hundreds of yaks and sheep that had been given as gifts to the Khon family.[202]

On the thirteenth day of the eighth month of 1909, Dragshul Trinlei Rinchen arrived in Nagchuka, where he joined many other lamas, such as the 9th Panchen Lama (Chokyi Nyima, 1883–1937) and the 15th Karmapa (Kashab Dorje, 1871–1922), who were waiting to greet His Holiness

---

199. See https://treasuryoflives.org/institution/Tengyeling.

200. Nagchuka is about 200 miles northeast of Lhasa. It is situated in the vast cold and windswept Northern Plain.

201. Dragshul Trinlei Rinchen 1974, vol. I, 324.

202. Ibid., vol. I, 325–26.

the 13th Dalai Lama. Altogether there were 30 head lamas as well as the Phuntsok Palace jetsunma Ani Drung from Tashi Tseg Labrang.[203]

Finally, on the first day of the ninth month, the 13th Dalai Lama arrived in Nagchuka. Those eagerly awaiting an audience with him gathered in the courtyard of the Shabten Monastery, where he was staying overnight. The more elite reincarnations, such as the Panchen Lama, the Karmapa, and Reting Rinpoche, as well as lamas such as Dragshul Trinlei Rinchen and the Phuntsok Palace Ani Drung, stood in line on the right side, while the important lay officials and members of noble families lined up on the left.

Then, when Dragshul Trinlei Rinchen and Ani Drung entered, Dragshul Trinlei Rinchen was escorted to the front, along with Reting Rinpoche and the Karmapa, to sit on a throne with three cushions—a very high honor. In addition, the three had a short private audience with the Dalai Lama. Ani Drung was also treated with respect (although she was considered by some officials to have a lower status than Dragshul Trinlei Rinchen). She was ushered to the area designated for lesser-status reincarnations, such as Mindroling Trichen, each of whom was provided with a cushion to sit on, but not a throne.[204] Dragshul Trinlei Rinchen and Ani Drung were relieved and joyous that His Holiness was back in Tibet. Shortly afterward, the government asked Dragshul Trinlei Rinchen to return to Lhasa and say more prayers for His Holiness there.

Jetsunma Ngowang met him near Rimsar, where he stayed five days to complete certain rituals. As Dragshul Trinlei Rinchen was slowly making his way to Lhasa, monks from the Tsarpa Sakya Monastery of Nalendra were eager for him to visit. The two principal lamas, Chogye Trichen and Zimok Rinpoche (see Chapter 8), had invited him. When Dragshul Trinlei Rinchen and Jetsunma Ngowang arrived at Nalendra Monastery, there was a magnificent welcome with a procession of monks holding incense and playing music. Dragshul Trinlei Rinchen bestowed a long life-empowerment of Buddha Amitāyus and Hayagrīva.[205] He also visited the respective residences (*labrangs*) of Chogye Trichen and Zimok

203. In the diary, Ani Drung is not named. However, Dragshul Trinlei Rinchen 2009, 431, names the sisters of the 38th Sakya Trizin, and only Jetsunma Tsegen Ngodrub Wangmo lived in Tashi Tseg Labrang. Thus Ani Drung must be this jetsunma.

204. Dragshul Trinlei Rinchen 1974, vol. 1, 330.

205. Ibid., vol. 1, 340–41.

Rinpoche. After three days, Dragshul Trinlei Rinchen and Jetsunma Ngowang slowly made their way back to the Tengyeling Residence in Lhasa.

Tibetans were happy that the 13th Dalai Lama was finally back in Tibet. Pilgrims and well-wishers arrived in Lhasa from all corners of Tibet. Prayers and rituals continued to be performed daily and continuously. Finally, on the ninth day of the eleventh month, the Dalai Lama arrived in Lhasa to a grand reception: he was carried in a golden palanquin as everyone lined up on either side to welcome back their beloved leader. Many prayers were chanted everywhere and a ceremony of long-life prayers was held for four days.

On the second day of the twelfth month, Dragshul Trinlei Rinchen and Jetsunma Ngowang as well as Sakya officials and dignitaries had an audience with the Dalai Lama at his summer palace, the Norbulingka. They offered a mandala symbolizing the universe and gifts to His Holiness. Having inquired of Dragshul Trinlei Rinchen concerning what rituals he had performed, the Dalai Lama thanked him and asked him to continue to perform them when he returned to Sakya. Then the Dalai Lama personally placed a long wide silk scarf around Dragshul Trinlei Rinchen's neck—a gesture seldom made by a Dalai Lama.[206]

Dragshul Trinlei Rinchen and Jetsunma Ngowang were then escorted to the guesthouse at the Norbulingka for refreshments and relaxation. Each was seated on a wooden throne; Dragshul Trinlei Rinchen's seat held four cushions, and Jetsunma Ngowang's seat had one cushion. They were offered tea, fruit, cookies, protection cords blessed by the Dalai Lama, six bricks of good quality tea, special tie-dyed woven woolen cloth, and enough brocade to make a *chuba*, the ankle-length robe worn by all Tibetans.

On the thirteenth day of the twelfth month, they left Lhasa. They traveled to numerous places, including Tsedong and Shigatse, where the Panchen Lama offered them refreshments and gifts.[207] Finally, on the first day of the first month of 1910, when they were close to Sakya, Dragshul Trinlei Rinchen's oldest daughter Jetsunma Kunga Wangmo and her attendants came to meet them. A day later, they arrived in Sakya, after a journey of more than nine months. Family members, officials, monks,

206. Ibid., vol. I, 346.
207. Ibid., vol. I, 349–50. Many places and people are listed.

and people from Sakya all welcomed them home. The family then celebrated the New Year together. Dragshul Trinlei Rinchen's two young sons had kept their promise to their father and had passed the exam that involved memorizing the root tantra of Hevajra—a rite of passage for all Khon sons.[208]

Dragshul Trinlei's three daughters were old enough to undertake their first major retreat of Hevajra during the winter of 1912–13.[209] In 1913 he bestowed the Hevajra empowerment on his two sons as well as his three daughters and an abbot.[210] Furthermore, he gave a special Pañjaranātha Mahākāla initiation and secret commentary in the Gorum shrine dedicated to Mahākāla for his two sons, his sister Kyabgon Pema Trinlei (Chapter 5), the Tanak Monastery abbot Ngawang Trinlei, and five selected monks.[211]

On the thirtieth day of the third month of 1914, his fourth daughter, Jetsunma Kunga Tenpai Nyima (usually referred to as Kunten), was born.[212] His fifth daughter and last child, Jetsunma Kalzang Chodron, was born on the twenty-second day of the seventh month of 1917.[213] Although his oldest daughter and youngest daughter have the exact same name, the youngest one was usually referred to as Chungwa (Younger One).

In the second month of 1915, the 38th Sakya Trizin, Zamling Chegu Wangdu (1863–1916), who was from the Phuntsok Palace, invited Dragshul Trinlei Rinchen for a visit.[214] The 38th Sakya Trizin told him secretly that he was not in good health, was relinquishing his position as Sakya Trizin, and wanted Dragshul Trinlei Rinchen to become the next Sakya Trizin. Dragshul Trinlei Rinchen was caught unawares, and he beseeched the 38th Sakya Trizin not to resign. However, the 38th Sakya Trizin had already told the Central Government, which had accepted his resignation. After a meeting with Sakya government officials and monk

---

208. Ibid., vol. 1, 352.

209. Ibid., vol. 1, 388–89. He doesn't provide any other details. (His fourth and fifth daughters were not yet born.)

210. Ibid., vol. 1, 396.

211. Ibid., vol. 1, 398.

212. Ibid., vol. 1, 405.

213. Ibid., vol. 1, 455.

214. Dragshul Trinlei Rinchen 2009, 430. The 38th Sakya Trizin died on the eleventh day of the third month of the fire dragon year.

Fig. 10. H.H. Dragshul Trinlei Rinchen on the throne in Sakya, 1934. On his proper right is his younger son, Ngawang Kunga Gyaltsen, in a brocade jacket.

officials, it was decided that Dragshul Trinlei Rinchen was the best candidate to become the 39th Sakya Trizin.[215]

However, some difficulties arose. In the third month, the 38th Sakya Trizin's wife, referred to as Gyalyum Chenmo, passed away. All the prayers and funeral ceremonies were completed. Then in the seventh month, a father and son—both officials who were disliked by many— were murdered. This created much chaos in Sakya, and the Sakya officials were unable to control people's anger. A few more officials were jailed for their own safety. With the situation escalating, some officials wrote to the Central Tibetan Government for their assistance. This was extremely embarrassing for the Khon family because they preferred to quell such agitation with their own power. Dragshul Trinlei Rinchen and his brother Jamyang Zangpo were sent to Lhasa as the Sakya representatives. The Central Tibetan Government received them cordially, and the matter was resolved with dignity.[216] By the eleventh month of 1915, the

215. Dragshul Trinlei Rinchen 1974, vol. I, 409–11.
216. Ibid., vol. I, 419–23.

enthronement ceremonies could begin. It was a very festive and impressive ceremony. Dragshul Trinlei Rinchen became the 39th Sakya Trizin (Fig. 10).[217]

In 1923, nomads of the Northern Plain (Changtang) made several requests to Jetsunma Kunga Wangmo, Dragshul Trinlei Rinchen's oldest daughter, to come to their areas to give teachings and offer empowerments. To defray some of the costs, the Sakya government asked the Central Tibetan Government to help. In response the Central Tibetan Government issued an official letter (*lam sun*) that required the people of various villages to provide five horses and ten yaks as road transport (*ula*) to Jetsunma Kunga Wangmo and her party as needed. Dragshul Trinlei Rinchen remarks in his diary that this was a special honor, considering that his sons did not receive such help when they traveled.

The party left Sakya on the tenth day of the fourth month of 1924.[218] After visiting the nomads for seven months, they returned on the thirteenth day of the eleventh month. As Jetsunma Kunga Wangmo was approaching home, her younger sister Jetsunma Chime Wangmo, her attendants, and certain Sakya officials rode forth on horseback a long distance from Sakya to show their respect and welcome her. Later, upon her arrival at the Dolma Palace, her mother and other sisters received her at the entrance. Dismounting from her horse, she greeted all of them and then went immediately to see her father to report about her journey. Afterward, the family served her tea as she told them all about her visit to the Northern Plain. Then Jetsunma Kunga Wangmo and her main attendant went to the Gorum Mahākāla shrine to present offerings and say a thanksgiving prayer to the protector Mahākāla for their successful journey and safe return home.[219]

In the meantime, Dragshul Trinlei Richen's two sons had married a co-wife, Princess Yangchen Palmo of the Lhading family (dYang chen dpal mo lha sdings), in the tenth month of 1924.[220] According to tradition (see Chapter 7), this was a secret and private affair; very few family members were present at the ceremony. A month later, on an auspicious

217. Ibid., vol. 1, 427–40.

218. Ibid., vol. 2, 56.

219. Ibid., vol. 2, 102–104.

220. Ibid., vol. 2, 82–84. Also see Elisabeth Benard, "A Secret Affair: The Wedding of a Sakya Dagmo," *Tibetan Studies: An Anthology* (2010): 37–63.

day, the wedding party announced the marriage by means of a public procession in Sakya. This was a special year both because there was a new wife (*dagmo*) and because Jetsunma Kunga Wangmo had returned safely from her long journey. Thus in 1925 the Sakya government decided to hold a bigger New Year's celebration than usual to welcome the new wife and honor Jetsunma Kunga Wangmo. A theater troupe was invited to perform for the people of Sakya. On the first day, they presented the heart-wrenching drama of Nangsa Obum, a woman who had to surmount enormous obstacles to be able to practice the Dharma. In the words of Nangsa Obum:

> Human life is very difficult to find,
> If we do not follow the Dharma at once,
> It will be over, like a flash of lightning.[221]

The drama was so well received by the audience that Jetsunma Chime Wangmo and her two brothers wanted to have it performed again on the second day of the New Year's celebration. This was followed by a philosophical debate showcasing the skills of the monks who had acquired an excellent understanding of Buddhist philosophical tenets. On the third day, the Khon family rewarded the performers with gifts: seven jars of beer (*chang*), seven bundles of barley, two bundles of rice, six bricks of tea, and money (18 *srangs*).[222] Also during this New Year's celebration, the Sakya government welcomed the new bride with a public offering of special white scarves, tea, and ceremonial buttered rice sweetened with tiny sweet potatoes.

Unfortunately, this marriage did not last long. Princess Lhading conceived soon after her wedding; however, she and her infant died in childbirth, at sunset on the sixth day of the eighth month of 1926.[223] The family was devastated. They performed all the funeral ceremonies for a good rebirth for both mother and child.

Due to this sad situation, in 1927 Dragshul Trinlei Rinchen again had to find a new wife for his sons. Bondong Dechen Chozom—later known

221. https://theyoginiproject.org/accomplished-yoginis/nangsa-obum. See Kurtis Schaeffer, *Himalayan Hermitess: The Life of a Tibetan Buddhist Nun* (Oxford University Press, 2004).

222. Dragshul Trinlei Rinchen 1974, vol. 2, 114–15.

223. Ibid., vol. 2, 150–51. In this period a *srang* was usually a coin rather than paper currency; it was equivalent to one ounce of silver or gold.

as Dagmo Trinlei Paljor (1906–75, see Chapter 7)—was selected. As in the case of the previous marriage, it was a secret marriage. Later, on the sixth day of the fourth month, the wedding party announced the marriage in a grand procession as they visited the main temples and shrines of Sakya.[224]

By 1927, Dragshul Trinlei Rinchen's younger son, Ngawang Kunga Gyaltsen, was now competent to teach the Lamdre Lopshe, or esoteric Path with the Result. His two younger sisters, Jetsunma Kunga Tenpai Nyima (Kunten) and Jetsunma Kalzang Chodron (Chungwa, "Younger One"), attended his teachings, along with many monks and lamas.[225] During this same year, on the tenth day of the eleventh month, the two younger jetsunmas expressed the desire to make a retreat of Bhūtaḍāmara Vajrapāṇi. This one-month retreat on Vajrapāṇi is usually the first major retreat because it eliminates potential problems and obstacles that might arise when one is in retreat. Their father gave the empowerment and transmission on Vajrapāṇi, and their teacher Ponlop Dung Rampa Sung-rab supervised their retreat.[226]

Sadly, in 1928 the jetsunmas' uncle Jamyang Zangpo died, on the twenty-second day of the first month. Jamyang Zangpo's younger sister, Jetsunma Ngowang, was in charge of the funeral. Conferring with her older brother, Dragshul Trinlei Rinchen, they compiled notes on which prayers, rituals, and offerings should be made for their brother.[227] Dragshul Trinlei Rinchen wrote a prayer calling for the swift rebirth of his younger brother. The monks in the South and North Monasteries chanted this prayer and many others. In the four main Sakya temples, a thousand butterlamps, offerings of the five senses, and many prayers were performed. In addition, a thousand butterlamps were offered at the sacred Jokhang Temple in Lhasa and also at Samye, the first monastery in Tibet.

Later that year, in accordance with tradition, the family of the Sakya Trizin moved to the Zhitog, their winter residence. Dragshul Trinlei Rinchen, his wife, their two sons, the sons' wife Dagmo Trinlei Paljor (Chapter 7), and the youngest jetsunma (Jetsunma Chungwa) rode on

224. Ibid., vol. 2, 228–34.
225. Ibid., vol. 2, 240.
226. Ibid., vol. 2, 273–74.
227. Ibid., vol. 2, 323–30.

Fig. 11. Most of the Northern Monastery complex in Sakya; the Zhitog is the largest building in the center.

horseback from the Dolma Palace to the Zhitog residence. Sakya women lining each side of the road presented the family with barley beer (*chang*) and tea. It was a festive procession.

Though both buildings were within the town of Sakya, the Dolma Palace was in a more exposed area that is colder in winter. The Zhitog building was located on the other side of the Grum River where there was an extensive group of buildings known as the Northern Monastery complex (Fig. 11). It was more sheltered and one of the most impressive buildings in Sakya. The top floors of the Zhitog were reserved as the winter palace for the reigning Sakya Trizin and his family, who would move from their summer palace to the winter palace every year and stay for three or four months.

Throughout the years, many important lamas, kings, and chieftains had come to pay a visit to the Sakya Khon family. In 1928 the powerful Drawupon chieftain,[228] who was an important sponsor from Kham, and other Khampa leaders came to Sakya. They brought many gifts for the family, including 12 bricks of excellent tea and a monetary offering of 42 *srangs*. One of the reasons for the visit was to offer 50 *srangs* to erect a memorial statue for the recently deceased Jamyang Zangpo. The

228. The Drawupon chieftain isn't named, but most likely it was Jigme Kunga Wangyal (1893–1952).

Drawupon chieftain also requested protection for the people of Kham and long-life rituals for his party.

In 1929, another tragedy occurred: Dragshul Trinlei Rinchen's oldest daughter, Jetsunma Kunga Wangmo, who had taught the nomads on the Northern Plain, died due to gastric problems. Her mother had planned to visit her at her residence, the Shabten Byang Labrang, and was forlorn that she had been unable to reach her daughter before she passed away. The family and numerous monks chanted prayers and placed many butterlamps and other offerings in front of the departed jetsunma's body. By the time the prayers were completed, it was dawn. At this time, one main monk recited the Vajrayoginī sādhana and two other monks recited the Sarvavid Vairocana (Kunrig) sādhana. In addition, four monks from the Great Temple, her mother Dagyum, and the two youngest jetsunmas recited the Vajrayoginī sādhana in the presence of the body. As they were intoning the sādhana, they noticed that the room became warm (an auspicious sign).

On the twenty-seventh day at sunrise, the body was brought down into the courtyard of her residence. The two youngest jetsunmas and their father placed a white scarf on the body. The body was transported from Jetsunma Kunga Wangmo's residence to the Utse building, where people brought offerings to place near her body. Also, two hundred sets of the five sense offerings were offered here. As the cremation fire burned, the Vajrayoginī sādhana and Sarvavid Vairocana sādhana were recited again. After the cremation, the bones and ash were separated. The bones were brought back to Jetsunma Kunga Wangmo's residence and placed near her shrine. Her father recited the Vajrayoginī sādhana once more and provided the special red powder (*sindhura*) offering that is associated with the goddess Vajrayoginī. These symbolic acts were done to help the deceased find her way to Vajrayoginī's paradise, Khecara. All her sisters gave money for the offerings. Meanwhile, in the South and North Monasteries, the monks chanted the Sarvavid Vairocana sādhana.

Jetsunma Kunga Wangmo's father noted that the day of her cremation was sunny and the sky filled with white clouds. The cremated bones were very white. The astrologer who was consulted about the auspicious times and dates to perform the ceremonies reported that everything had gone smoothly. The butterlamps glowed steadily. In the north, all was clear and bright. These were excellent signs indicating that the deceased Jetsunma Kunga Wangmo would have a good rebirth.

After the death of Jetsunma Kunga Wangmo, Dragshul Trinlei Rinchen's third daughter Jetsunma Chime Wangmo had more responsibilities since she was now the oldest jetsunma capable of helping the family.[229] In her father's diary, Jetsunma Chime Wangmo is mentioned more often than the other daughters, especially with respect to receiving religious teachings and performing rituals. For example, in 1924 Dragshul Trinlei Rinchen gave certain very precious teachings about the Marpo Korsum—three important red deities, Ganapati, Takkiraja, and Kurukulle[230]—to his two sons and his third daughter, Jetsunma Chime Wangmo.[231] Later, he bestowed the empowerments and transmissions of Maitri and Indra Vajrayoginīs according to the Ngorchen tradition and Vajravārāhī Korsum according to Jal Lotsawa (dByal lo tsa ba) to his two sons. Though his three oldest daughters had received them previously, they joined their brothers and received them again.[232] In 1929 Dragshul Trinlei Rinchen gave an empowerment of White Tara according to the Tsarpa tradition to his three youngest daughters—Jetsunmas Chime Wangmo, Jetsunma Kunten, and Jetsunma Chungwa. Also, he passed on some of the transmissions from the *Compendium of Sādhanas*. He notes in his diary that from this day on, Jetsunma Chime Wangmo practiced White Tara.[233]

In 1933, when Dragshul Trinlei Rinchen's root guru, the illustrious Ngor abbot Ngawang Lodro Shenpen Nyingpo (1876–1953),[234] was teaching at the Phuntsok Palace in Sakya, Dragshul Trinlei Rinchen invited him to the Dolma Palace. Dragshul Trinlei Rinchen had received the esoteric Path with the Result in 1891 and 1892, but due to prior obligations

229. The second sister, Jetsunma Kalzang Chodron, or Kala, had some mental problems and is rarely mentioned separately in Dragshul Trinlei Rinchen's diary.

230. See www.himalayanart.org for good descriptions of these three deities.

231. Dragshul Trinlei Rinchen 1974, vol. 1, 817.

232. Ibid., vol. 1, 835.

233. Ibid., vol. 2, 393. He gave many teachings and transmissions to his children. See ibid., vol. 2, 535, in which he records giving Ghantapada Cakrasaṃvara to his children; and see vol. 2, 541, where he notes giving the protector Begtse's empowerment and commentary to them. Also, in vol. 2, 544, Jetsunma Chime Wangmo seems to be the only woman who participated in a *tsok* (sacrificial offering) in front of the famous statue of Drakpa Gyaltsen called the Leprosy Skull statue (which was in her father's Eternal Happiness room). For more on the Leprosy Skull, see note 267 below.

234. Later, Ngawang Lodro Shenpen Nyingpo (1876–1953) was also the root guru of Jetsun Kushok and the 41st Sakya Trizin; see Chapter 8.

was unable to receive the entire teaching until 1893. From 1893 on, he did his required practices, but he felt that this was a great opportunity to ask for a "refresher" from the Ngor abbot; in additon, he probably wanted to make a stronger spiritual connection between this great lama and his children as well as with himself. Ngawang Shenpen Nyingpo thus gave a refresher transmission to Dragshul Trinlei Rinchen, his two sons, Jetsunma Chime Wangmo, and others. Jetsunma Chime Wangmo and her two brothers presented thank-you gifts to show their appreciation for receiving teachings from this wonderful lama.[235]

Unlike her older sister Jetsunma Kunga Wangmo, who had moved into her own residence as a young woman, Jetsunma Chime remained at the Dolma Palace for many years, most likely because she had to help her family. She did not move into the Shabten Lho Labrang until 1934, when she was 34 years old. Usually a jetsunma moves to her labrang in her late teens. The move necessitated much planning, so preparations were begun the year before. Clothes were made and the family selected furniture, carpets, and a throne for their daughter's residence. The family presented her with a substantial offering of 300 *srangs*, one rice bundle, three bundles of honey, fifteen bricks of tea, a Chinese carpet, much brocade and cotton cloth, and a quantity of the white scarves needed at all formal occasions.[236] Later, this also became the residence of the youngest daughter, Jetsunma Chungwa.

In 1935, Dragshul Trinlei Rinchen's health was in decline. Beginning the previous summer, many long-life prayers had been recited and rituals to prolong his life performed. The Sakya government sponsored a reading of the 108 volumes of the Buddha's words, known as the Kangyur, to help prolong his life. The prayers to the protectors were offered more often than usual. His own family recited many prayers and entreated their father to remain longer. He replied, "Your motivation is very good, but I don't have the power to extend my life."[237] These prayers seem to have helped extend his life for a month, but sadly, early in the second month, Dragshul Trinlei Rinchen passed away.[238]

235. Dragshul Trinlei Rinchen 1974, vol. 2, 747.

236. Ibid., vol. 2, 817–20.

237. Ibid., vol. 2, 849–51.

238. Ibid., vol. 2, 851. The doctor stated that pulse of the 39th Sakya Trizin was very weak, but fortunately he lived for another month.

Khen Jampal Zangpo (1901–61), who was one of his very devoted students and abbot of the South Monastery, compiled a report of his root lama's final days based on accounts of witnesses in Sakya. The report—included, years later, in Dragshul Trinlei Rinchen's published diary—gives lengthy and precise information about the actual funeral rituals and cremation. Of course, everyone mourned the passing of such an eminent being who had devoted his life to spiritual practice and teaching based on his own realizations and understanding of reality. Though he was highly realized, Dragshul Trinlei Rinchen remained humble, selfless, and devoted to helping all sentient beings—a true bodhisattva.

Khen Jampal Zangpo, who remained devoted to the Dolma Palace and served as advisor to the next two generations of the family (see Chapters 7 and 8), notes in the published diary that Dragshul Trinlei Rinchen's daughter-in-law Dagmo Trinlei Paljor (Chapter 7) had much faith in her father-in-law. It was she who asked Khen Jampal Zangpo to compile Dragshul Trinlei Rinchen's diary. She even provided the paper and ink. Together with Dragshul Trinlei Rinchen's two sons, Khen Jampal Zangpo began the task of compiling all the notes to create a book, which eventually became the diary we have today. He states in the book that Jetsunma Chime Wangmo, who had received numerous teachings from various great lamas and whose spiritual practice was constant, had donated the money to compile the diary and that she requested that it be completed soon. This was accomplished in 1952.[239]

According to Jetsun Kushok, her paternal aunt Jetsunma Chime Wangmo and her maternal aunt Dagmo Trinlei Paljor worked well together. Jetsunma Chime was quiet and reserved; however, she was an excellent advisor and a trusted member of the family. Further, both Jetsun Kushok and her younger brother the 41st Sakya Trizin praise her as an extraordinary practitioner of Vajrayoginī.

From Dragshul Trinlei Rinchen's invaluable diary, we can see how the Sakya Khon family educated his five daughters according to their abilities to understand profound teachings. As a member of a spiritual family, each one was trained to be an excellent spiritual practitioner and given many opportunities to receive important empowerments, transmissions, and explanations directly from lamas. Ultimately, each person needed

239. Ibid., vol. 2, 871. In the published diary, Jampal Zangpo refers to Dagmo Trinlei Paljor as "Dagmo Kusho" and to Jetsunma Chime Wangmo as "Jetsunma Chime Tenpai Dronme."

to practice diligently and continually with faith and perseverance. In addition to practice, each member of the family served the Tibetans, primarily as teachers but also as advisors. Each member needed to help the family: welcoming guests, especially dignitaries; performing necessary rituals for protection, prosperity, long life, and death; and serving the Sakya government and Central Tibetan Government as spiritual guides. Of course, they would enjoy the pleasures of celebrating the New Year together and watching Tibetan dramas and philosophical debates. Occasionally going to the hot springs to ward off the freezing cold of Sakya weather, the family relaxed together there. Moreover, some undertook a long journey to Kham, to the Northern Plain, or to Lhasa. Dragshul Trinlei Rinchen's family did not have to deal with the uncertainty that arose with the loss of Tibet, which had to be faced by those of the next generation: Jetsun Kushok and the 41st Sakya Trizin, the children of Dragshul Trinlei Rinchen's son, Dagchen Kunga Rinchen.

CHAPTER SEVEN

No Time to Sleep:
Dagmo Trinlei Paljor (1906–75)

T HE STORY of the contemporary Jetsun Kushok Chime Luding (b. 1938, profiled in Chapters 8 and 9) is intertwined with those of her younger brother the 41st Sakya Trizin (b. 1945); their maternal aunt Dagmo Trinlei Paljor Zangmo (1906–75), who raised them; and their mother Dagyum[240] Sonam Dolkar (1918–47), who was Dagmo Trinlei Paljor's younger sister. This chapter focuses on the lives of these two sisters and co-wives—Dagmo Trinlei Paljor and Dagyum Sonam Dolkar—as key members of the Sakya Khon family in the Dolma Palace from the early 1900s through 1938, when Jetsun Kushok was born. Jetsun Kushok and the 41st Sakya Trizin's early lives are the subject of Chapter 8.

SOURCES

As mentioned in earlier chapters, one of the most important documents of the Sakya Dolma Palace family is the diary of the 39th Sakya Trizin Dragshul Trinlei Rinchen (1871–1935, Chapter 6), the paternal grandfather of Jetsun Kushok and the 41st Sakya Trizin.[241] This diary contains information about his two sons—Dagchen Kunga Rinchen (1902–50)[242] and Ngawang Kunga Gyaltsen (1904–ca. 1943)—and their joint marriage to Dagmo Trinlei Paljor in 1927 (see Chart 4 in Chapter 6). The diary

240. When a *dagmo* bears a child, she becomes known as *dagyum* (literally, "lady mother"). For more on the dagmos, see Chapter 1.

241. Dragshul Trinlei Rinchen was therefore the father-in-law of Dagmo Trinlei Paljor Zangmo. I refer to some of the entries in Dragshul Trinlei Rinchen's diary later in this chapter.

242. According to Dragshul Trinlei Rinchen 1974, vol. 1, 277, his son Dagchen Kunga Rinchen was born on the fourteenth day of the ninth month of the water tiger year (1902).

Fig. 12. Dagmo Trinlei Paljor being playful.

provides many details on the necessary rituals conducted prior to this joint wedding, as well as on the actual marriage ceremony. Because Dragshul Trinlei Rinchen died nine years later, in 1935, most of the information about subsequent years comes from the numerous, often extensive interviews I conducted with a variety of people who knew Dagmo Trinlei Paljor well—especially her niece Jetsun Kushok and her nephew the 41st Sakya Trizin. In addition, *Biographies of the Great Sachen Kunga Nyingpo and H.H. the 41st Sakya Trizin,* by the 42nd Sakya Trizin, Ratna Vajra Sakya, includes some information about his great-aunt Dagmo Trinlei Paljor.[243]

DAGMO TRINLEI PALJOR (1906–75)

Dagmo Trinlei Paljor (Fig. 12) was born in 1906, in the famous noble family of Bonshod,[244] near Gyantse, Tsang Province. Her mother's maternal

243. Ratna Vajra Sakya, Drolma Lhamo, and Lama Jampa Losel, comps., *Biographies of the Great Sachen Kunga Nyingpo and H.H. the 41st Sakya Trizin* (Rajpur: Sakya Academy, 2003); http://www.buddhanet.net/pdf_file/sakya_bios.pdf. See p. 21 for another photo of Dagmo Trinlei Paljor.

244. The Bon Dong (Bon grong shod pa) or Bonshod family is known by these two names, but Bonshod is the more famous one. See Cassinelli and Ekvall 1969, 110–11. The family is referred to as gZims dPon and was a prominent family in the Khra U area. See Luciano Petech, *Aristocracy and Government in Tibet, 1728–1959* (Roma: Serie Orientale Roma XLV, Instituto Italiano Per Il Medio ED Estremo Oriente, 1973), 122–24, who presents a history of the family and states that it had estates in Rin Spungs and Pa snam. Also, in Dragshul Trin-

family was the Changra family. When she married into the Khon family, her personal name, Dechen Chozom, was changed to Trinlei Paljor Zangmo and she received the title Dagmo (Lady, or wife of a Lord; see Chapter 1). She was the second daughter of seven children who survived to adulthood (three sons and four daughters).[245]

The oldest child was her brother Tseten Dorje (Tshe brtan rdo rje, 1889–1945), who was a famous cabinet minister, known as Kalon Bonshod, from 1934 to 1945 in the Tibetan government.[246] The oldest daughter was her sister Jampal Yangkyi (1894–ca. 1953),[247] who later married into the Chabspel family. Jampal Yangkyi would later help her younger sister during difficult times in Sakya. The second brother was Kelsang Phuntsok (1897–ca. mid-1950s), who married into the Phukhang family. Her youngest brother, known as Tashi Palrab (bKra' shis dpal rab, 1916–84; Fig. 13), was the army general (*depon*) of the Drapchi (Grwa bzhi) Regiment in Lhasa as well as a bodyguard of the Dalai Lama when he escaped to India in 1959.[248] Her second sister was Sonam Dolma (ca. 1915–35), who married into the Gerpa 'Chum Tashi pa family. One of Sonam Dolma's sons, Sho Bo Lozang Dhargey, was a cabinet minister in the Tibetan government and later a judge in the Tibetan Government in Exile

Most importantly for future generations of the Khon family, Dagmo Trinlei Paljor's youngest sister was Sonam Dolkar (1918–47), who later joined Dagmo Trinlei Paljor as a co-wife in Sakya and was the mother of Jetsun Kushok and the 41st Sakya Trizin. In 1959, when many Tibetans fled Tibet, of the seven siblings only Dagmo Trinlei Paljor and her

lei Rinchen 1974, vol. 2, 228, they are known as Shang rJe Bon grong or Shaj rGe Bon grong. Their main residence was in Dranang, Lhoka, near Gyantse.

245. Jetsun Kushok recalls that from 1898–1905 and 1907–13, many of the Bonshod children did not live long. In fact, seven died very early in life.

246. Kalon, or Sawang Chenpo, is a Tibetan title for the cabinet ministers; there were four ministers working together in the Tibetan government. See Melvyn C. Goldstein, *A History of Modern Tibet, 1913–1951: The Demise of the Lamaist State* (Berkeley: University of California Press, 1991), 226.

247. After the death of her first husband, Jampal Yangkyi remarried into the dGa Byang family, whose residence in Lhasa was known as Gabyang House. Their main residence was in Rong Yulha.

248. When Tashi Palrab married in 1935, he changed his natal name of Dorje Damdul to his bride's family name, Palrab. See Kirti Rinpoche, comp., *Gendun Chophel, Portrait of a Great Thinker* (Dharamsala: Library of Tibetan Works and Archives, 2013), 67ff., where he is called Kungo Tashi Palrab.

Fig. 13. Tashi Palrab as a general in the Tibetan army, Lhasa, Tibet, mid-1950s.

brother Tashi Palrab escaped to India, where they remained close for the rest of their lives.[249]

Dagmo Trinlei Paljor was raised near Gyantse (rGyal rtse), a large trading town situated between India and Lhasa. Being one of the older daughters in the family, she learned to read and to write as well as how to run a household. Jetsun Kushok remembers her aunt telling some of her servants that one needs to have skills in order to survive. Recounting her own mother's words, Dagmo Trinlei Paljor said, "My mother told me, 'If you are lucky and marry into a good family, you can supervise well since you have the knowledge. If you marry into a poor family, then you have all the skills needed to run a household.'" She continued, "To teach me, my mother put me in charge, at thirteen years old, of our entire house-

249. Tashi Palrab served in the Tibetan Government in Exile based in Dharamsala, India, and his second wife Ga Yudron opened Gakyi, the first vegetarian restaurant there.

hold in Gyantse. I learned to cook, learned how to manage servants and supervise the dyeing and weaving of cloth."[250]

Dagmo Trinlei Paljor learned these skills well. Jetsun Kushok later emphasized that although her aunt did not have time to weave herself, she did know how to do so. She also stressed that the carpets had to be well made on both sides—front and back—and that the edge is very important.[251]

In the Dolma Palace there were three women who were expert carpet weavers. The oldest was known as Lhachung, the second as Pumchung, and the youngest as Lhadron. Later, in exile, foreign relief organizations recommended that Tibetans make carpets to earn a livelihood. Thus the Tibetan Refugee Self Help Centre near Darjeeling, India, was established on October 2, 1959 and headed by the Dalai Lama's older brother's wife, Ms. Gyalo Thondup (rGyal lo don 'grub), who dedicated herself to the center and helping Tibetan refugees until her death in 1986. At this center these three women became teachers to other Tibetan women who learned how to weave carpets, and Dagmo Trinlei Paljor helped supervise these Tibetans to create high-quality carpets that would be bought by foreigners abroad.

At the Dolma Palace, Dagmo Trinlei Paljor also coordinated the weaving of aprons. In Tibet, women wore a woven apron as a sign of being married. Most Tibetans wore an apron only in front, but in Western Tibet, the women typically wore both a front and back apron. For women who worked in the fields and with animals, the apron was made of sturdy wool. But for noblewomen and on special occasions fancier aprons were worn, sometimes made from delicate silk.

---

250. From http://tibet.prm.ox.ac.uk/photo_1999.23.1.33.2.html (Tibet Album, Oxford). Rich families in the regions of Gyantse and Shigatze sponsored carpet-weaving on their family estates, providing all the materials, such as looms, dyestuffs, etc. Gyantse was well known for the weaving of carpets. There is an excellent photo of the Doring Manor House taken by the British physician Harry Staunton. On the top floor are numerous weavers, and on the floor below are many women carding and spinning the wool in preparation for weaving it.

251. Jetsun Kushok liked to play at weaving when she was young. She was forbidden to go near the actual weavers since she was a jetsunma; a nun should concentrate on her studies and practices. Nevertheless, she enjoyed weaving. She never actually made anything when she was in Tibet. But later, in Canada, she worked as a weaver for designer Zonda Nellis. She said that the weaving there was easy because there was no complicated pattern compared to Tibetan carpets or aprons. It was only color combinations. In her humble manner, she made it sound as if it was simple and not demanding in any way.

From India came orange and pink dyes, which weren't produced in Tibet. Dagmo Trinlei Paljor made some of her own dyes. For example, yellow and green were dervived from rhubarb leaves and roots. Indigo, a dark blue color, came from *ramtso*—tiny roots found near the Indian border. Jetsun Kushok explained that, to set indigo, one used cow urine. She grimaced and said, "It had a terrible smell." She elaborated that anything sour could be a fixative, such as the whey from milk or leftover beer (*chang*) water. The fixative made the color stay longer. The silk—especially the silk used in women's fancy aprons—came from China, India, or Japan. Also, there was very fine wool from the long hair of the sheep that was spun into thin thread, from which robes for the family and shawls for monks were made. This was exceptionally high-quality wool.

Jetsun Kushok further recalled that her aunt's mind turned toward the teachings of the Buddha at a young age. In many wealthy Tibetan families, each daughter was given a piece of land. The income from the sale of crops grown on this property was available as pocket money. Most young women used their discretionary income to buy jewelry or fine silks and brocades, but Dagmo Trinlei Paljor bought butter for offering lamps as soon as the barley from her property was sold each year.

Not much is known about Dagmo Trinlei Paljor's youth prior to her marriage into the Khon family at the age of 21 in 1927. The 39th Sakya Trizin Dragshul Trinlei Rinchen writes in his diary that everything that had been done for the first wife of the two Khon sons[252] was also done for their second wife, Dagmo Trinlei Paljor. The two brothers had wed their first wife, Princess Yangchen Dolkar from the Lhading (Lha sding) family, in the tenth month of the wood mouse year (1924–25), but tragically, she died in childbirth in 1926 (see Chapter 6).

DAGMO TRINLEI PALJOR'S MARRIAGE

The following information from Dragshul Trinlei Rinchen's diary explains the selection of the bride and some of the marriage rituals. The Sakya family selected wives by considering many factors. Of course, com-

---

252. Polyandry was practiced in many parts of Tibet. Frequently several brothers married a single woman, or in some cases several sisters. In the Khon family, this was a way to keep the lineage intact. Offspring were considered to be the sons and daughters of the older of the two brothers who were co-husbands to a single wife. The older brother was called Father, and the younger brother was called Uncle.

ing from a noble family that had a good reputation was important, but there were other more esoteric signs as well, such as auspicious dreams and divinations. One kind of divination (*zan ril*) involved writing the names of three selected candidates on a sheet of paper and then cutting it into three thin strips with one name on each strip. Each strip was then folded and carefully inserted into a ball of roasted barley flour, making sure the three balls were of equal weight. The balls were then put into a bowl that was spun quickly until one of them fell out. Dragshul Trinlei Rinchen himself—the future father-in-law of the bride—did such a divination for the most suitable bride for his two sons in the first month of the fire rabbit year (1927).[253] When the ball that contained Dagmo Trinlei Paljor's maiden name, "Dechen Chozom," fell out, her life suddenly changed dramatically.

Prior to the marriage ceremony, many rituals were peformed and various *sūtras* (Buddhist texts) chanted to repel potentially harmful forces and invite beneficial ones. Just before dawn on the twenty-third day of the second month of 1927—without Dagmo Trinlei Paljor knowing what was afoot—she and a small entourage were brought secretly before dawn to the Dolma Palace, the main residence of the Dolma branch of the Khon family in Sakya. The small group was brought up to the third floor, to what was called the Big Glass-Window Room (see next section). Here she met her future husbands—the two sons of the 39th Sakya Trizin, Dagchen Kunga Rinchen and Ngawang Kunga Gyaltsen—for the first time.[254]

Alhough Dragshul Trinlei Rinchen's diary does not describe the behavior of the new dagmo, Jetsun Kushok explained that a proper bride must keep her eyes downcast and not look directly at her husbands. She should not show any emotion. Since this was the first meeting between Dagmo Trinlei Paljor and her two husbands, being discreet and demure would have displayed her proper upbringing and reflected well on her family.

On the day of their wedding, the Big Glass-Window Room was decorated with fourteen rare *thangkas* (scroll paintings) selected from the collection of the family's illustrious ancestor Sakya Chogyal Phagpa (1235–80), including one depicting Amitāyus surrounded by eight deities (*Tshe dpag med lha dgu*) in a mandala. Amitāyus literally means

253. Dragshul Trinlei Rinchen 1974, vol. 2, 223.
254. Ibid., vol. 2, 228.

"Boundless Life," and he is one of the major Buddhas who protects (and may even increase) one's lifespan. The nine-deity Amitāyus initiation was one of the empowerments given to the future bride and her entourage to foster a long life for everyone. Her father-in-law Dragshul Trinlei Rinchen performed the marriage rituals according to the *White Lapis Lazuli (Vaidurya dkar po)* texts written by the 5th Dalai Lama's regent, Desi Sange Gyatso (1653–1705).

On the altar in front of the *thangkas* were precious offering objects that had belonged to Chogyal Phagpa. These *thangkas* and offering objects, which were more than six hundred years old, were displayed and used only on very special occasions. The bridal party—consisting of the bride, her father and paternal uncle, and the two grooms and their parents— was served roasted wheat coated with honey and *shemar* (a mixture of roasted ground barley and butter) while auspicious verses were chanted: "May you always have good luck and be surrounded by good fortune. May there be abundance and may your work spread throughout the three realms." At the end of verses, everyone took a pinch of *shemar*, raising it up to respectfully offer it to the deities before eating it.

Dagmo Trinlei Paljor's new father-in-law Dragshul Trinlei Rinchen then proclaimed that she, the Bonshod princess (*sras mo*), had become a dagmo in the Khon family by marrying his two sons and becoming their wisdom consort (*rig ma*). This union with a wisdom consort is to gain wisdom to realize enlightenment. Dragshul Trinlei Rinchen then bestowed on her the new name Tsewang Rigzin Trinlei Chime Paljor Zangmo ("powerful life, awareness-holder, Buddha activity, immortal, prosperity, kindhearted"). When a lama gives someone a new name, he sometimes includes one of his own names. In this case, Dragshul Trinlei Rinchen chose Trinlei, which can be translated as "to do the activities of the Buddha," thus foreshadowing Dagmo Trinlei Paljor's future role in preserving the Sakya Buddhist teachings.

After the ceremony, Dagmo Trinlei Paljor's first food consisted of the three dairy products (milk, yogurt, and butter) together with *shemar*. These are regarded as auspicious food. The group chanted verses such as "May this excellent food give you a long life. May you be the mother of the Khon family (*rigs ma dge legs*). May you have good fortune as vast as the ocean and be the cause of good luck." Chanting continued with praises offered to the lamas, Buddhas, tutelary deities, protectors, and gods of wealth. Then Dragshul Trinlei Rinchen bestowed the empowerment of the three long-life deities from the lineage of Mahāsiddha Khyungpo for long life and to create an auspicious beginning to their union. In accord with tradition, in thanksgiving to their lama (who in this case was also their father) for the empowerments, the Dungsays (the two husbands) and Dagmo Trinlei Paljor held a long scarf and offered him a golden mandala, a statue of the Buddha, a Buddhist text and *stupa* (a symbol of enlightenment), and an envelope containing 5 *srangs*.[255]

According to the signs, all went smoothly, but more rituals were needed. It was advised that the older son should visit the holy Gorum shrine of the protector deity Mahākāla and make various offerings for seven days. At the conclusion of the seven days, the older son dreamed of Mahākāla, which augured well for the marriage.

Not only is such a detailed account of a marriage rare, but when people in Tibet married or received empowerments, the father-in-law or the husband(s) rarely presided. In Dagmo Trinlei Paljor's case, she received various empowerments from her father-in-law the 39th Sakya Trizin, and later she also received empowerments and teachings from her husbands. Still later, she would receive empowerments and teachings from her nephew the 41st Sakya Trizin, whom she raised as her own son. In each case, she viewed the male relative as her lama.

For a month, the people of Sakya were unaware that the two sons had married. Then, on the sixth day of the fourth month, an auspicious day according to astrological calculations,[255] the bridal party announced the marriage in a procession accompanied by ceremonial umbrellas and musicians. The newlyweds paid their respects to the most important sacred edifices and objects of Sakya, including the Four Wonders.[256]

The procession lasted all day. Dagmo Trinlei Paljor and her two husbands stopped at many holy places in Sakya and were served auspicious refreshments to celebrate the marriage. Many monasteries, officials, and families presented gifts. For example, the Sakya government presented them with a large bundle of tea, a rice bundle, the dried carcass of a large sheep, and beer; Tsedong Monastery, which has a strong connection to the Dolma Palace family, gave 50 *khe* (*khal*) of barley.[257] The 39th Sakya Trizin notes in his diary that there was no wind or inclement weather,

255. Ibid., vol. 2, 234.
256. See Chapter 2 for the Four Wonders of Sakya.
257. One *khal* is approximately 30 pounds.

and interprets this as a good sign that everything went well. When they returned home, the bride and grooms offered a long-life ceremony to the 39th Sakya Trizin in gratitude.

THE DOLMA PALACE

The Dolma Palace (Fig. 14) was a large building of approximately 80 rooms and was taken care for by 20 to 25 live-in servants. In the front it had only two stories, but in the back there were three. The two lower stories were painted white, like many Tibetan homes, but the third floor was painted a burgundy color, which indicated that this floor had religious significance. In fact the third floor was reserved for the Dolma Palace family.[258] Made of rammed earth, the palace had walls more than 3 feet wide at the base; like many houses in Tibet, the exterior walls sloped inward, creating an illusion of greater height.[259] The roof was flat, with parapets adorned with religious symbols at the corners.

The main entrance faced east, an influence from the Indian cultural belief that the east, where the sun rises, is an auspicious direction. Its large entryway was flat, and wide enough for a truck to drive through. In this courtyard one dismounted from one's horse. After this broad entrance, the inner gate, which faced south, went up four or five steps to a smaller inner courtyard. As one entered the inner courtyard, one saw a small staircase leading farther up, to what looked like a large temple door. Around the door were paintings of the guardian kings of the four cardinal directions.

These images are typical for the front of a temple. But Jetsun Kushok smiled as she describes the building. She remarked, "It was amusing to see people climb the steps and expect to enter a temple, but it actually was a large storeroom for goods bought in India." She explained that every year a horse and mule caravan traveled to India carrying wool to be exchanged for brown sugar, batteries for flashlights, wax candles, radios, soap, Darjeeling tea,[260] oranges, toothpaste, cotton cloth for prayer flags,

258. Males of the Khon family have a similar color combination in their clothes. They wear a white skirt to indicate their lay status, but above it they wear a monastic red sleeveless top that signifies their religious status.

259. The area of walls framing the windows was painted black in a trapezoid shape that was narrower at the top and wider at the bottom. This created an illusion of larger windows as well as enhancing the exterior look of the palace.

260. The British, who owned many Darjeeling tea estates, were trying to encourage the

Fig. 14. The Dolma Palace, Sakya.

peacock feathers, kusha grass needed in religious rituals and processions, and other items. The monks' quarters surrounded the storeroom
on the first floor. A side staircase led to the second and third floors.

In Tibet, the size of a room was determined by how many pillars were
needed to support the ceiling or roof. A one- or two-pillar room was a
good size for a bedroom or for entertaining a few guests. A six-pillar
room was a large main room that could hold 20 or more people for a
party or a private empowerment ritual.

Since the Khon family is foremost a spiritual one, each family member had their own "practice room" in which to do their daily spiritual
practice and necessary rituals. Moreover, each practice/bedroom apartment had a name. Dagmo Trinlei Paljor's bedroom, the Green Tara Cave
(sGrol ma phug), was 1.5 pillars in size. A large shrine took up half of one
wall. It included *thangkas* of the goddess Tara, the red goddess Kurukulle
(Rig byed ma), and others that were covered with yellow silk cloth, as
well as a large Vajrayoginī statue and several smaller statues. Also prevalent were *tormas*—special offerings molded of roasted barley flour, butter, and brown sugar into triangle or cone shapes and painted red on top
with natural dyes. Some are elaborately decorated with molded butter in
shapes of flat flowers. *Tormas* are often offered every two weeks or once

---

Tibetan aristocracy to drink Darjeeling tea. Thus it became fashionable among the Tibetan
elite to drink it, especially in the afternoon. The main tea in Tibet was the Chinese black
brick tea, churned with boiling water, salt, and butter.

a month to particular deities. Dagmo Trinlei Paljor did all her practices in this room. Later in life, when she took care of Jetsun Kushok and the 41st Sakya Trizin, they went there to play and relax. Jetsun Kushok and the other children slept mostly with their aunt and their mother in this room.

In Tibetan Buddhism, a person does not reveal the details of her or his daily practice as long as she or he is alive. To do so would be seen as boasting and as a deterrent to authentic realizations because one would be reinforcing a strong sense of ego. A brief biography of the 41st Sakya Trizin, however, recounts Dagmo Trinlei Paljor's practice as follows:

> Besides having great devotion and pure insight, she was extremely compassionate toward living beings. She was a great practitioner who had accomplished many great spiritual practices such as: 600,000 prostrations along with recitation of the Refuge Verses; 10 million Guru Yoga verses; about 5 million Mandala offerings; 20 million mantras of a Tara deity and many other similar practices. Her meditative attainment exceeded that of many who spend their lives in solitary retreat.[261]

Dedicated meditators frequently built a square wooden meditation box slightly larger than the size of a person when one sits crosslegged. The box is of such a size that it is not possible to lie down in it. The back is as high as the middle of one's back. But one should not lean on the meditation box; instead one's body should be erect to do meditation correctly. Dagmo Trineli Paljor always stayed in her meditation box throughout the night. She never slept on a bed, but would only take occasional naps while sitting in her meditation box. She began this habit in the Dolma Palace and continued it in India.[262]

Later, in India, Ga Yudron, the wife of Tashi Palrab (Dagmo Trinlei Paljor's younger brother), remembered Dagmo as an amazing practitioner.

261. Ratna Vajra Sakya et al. 2003, 31.

262. The 41st Sakya Trizin showed me a photo of Dagmo's room in the Dolma Palace in India. I expected a pristine room with spare furniture. Contrary to my expectations, her room was filled with all kinds of possessions, almost in a chaotic manner, and her meditation box was next to the small bed of the longtime Sakya attendant Aja Dolkar's young son, Tsering Dorje (see Appendices A and B for interviews with Aja Dolkar and Tsering Dorje).

She frequently referred to Dagmo as a *khandro* (or *ḍākinī*).[263] For instance, she remarked, "Khandro [Dagmo Trinlei Paljor] was constantly practicing. She never took off her belt [a sign of a great meditator]. She would meditate all night long. The only time she took off her belt was when she needed to change her clothes." She continued, "She had a wonderful heart/mind. *Sempa yabo, sem chung wa.*"

Dagmo Trinlei Paljor ate regular Tibetan food daily, but on the new moon, the eighth day, and full moon days of each month she did strict *sojong* practice, which involved fasting and performing full-length prostrations. Many Tibetans try to do many thousands of prostrations in their lifetime to develop humility, show devotion to the Lama and the Three Jewels (the Buddha, Dharma, and Sangha), and accumulate merit. Dagmo did hundreds of these on the *sojong* days. Her daily practice was extensive and extraordinary.[264]

Furthermore, she received the Path with the Result from three great lamas: her father-in-law, Dragshul Trinlei Rinchen; the abbot of the South Monastery, Khen Jampal Zangpo (see Chapter 6); and the great Ngor Khangsar abbot Ngawang Lodro Shenpen Nyingpo (also known as Dampa Rinpoche). Later, the 41st Sakya Trizin and Jetsun Kushok also received the teachings of the Path with the Result from Dampa Rinpoche.[265] Dagmo Trinlei Paljor also did retreats, among them Kurukulle (one of the Marpo Korsum, or Three Great Red Ones), Hevajra, and the

263. The Sanskrit term *ḍākinī* is translated in Tibetan as *khandro* ("sky-goer"). This implies a female who has insight into ultimate reality. Just as the sky is free of constraints and is vast in its expanse, so a ḍākinī is not blocked by conceptualizations, which impede one's understanding of the voidness of intrinsic reality.

264. Dagmo Trinlei Paljor's daily practice was as follows. *In the morning:* the Hevajra, Vajrayoginī, Guru Yoga, and Virūpa sādhanas (the Four Unbreakable Practices of all Sakya practitioners of the Path with the Result); the Guru Rinpoche seven-line prayer; prayers to the Great Sakya Lamas; White Tara prayers; Green Tara prayers (with mandala offerings); Red Tara prayers; 100 *torma* offerings (actually the 21 pills offering to the hungry ghosts; one can't eat meat before doing this ritual, so this must be concluded before lunch); the water ritual to the deity of prosperity, Jambala; and 50 butterlamp offerings (which she prepared by herself with a red sandalwood wick when she lived in India). She usually ate lunch at about 2 or 3 p.m. due to all these commitments. *In the evening:* Marmo Korsum (three kinds of Vajrayoginī), using a red sandalwood disc for the mandala offering; Palden Lhamo, protector of the Tibetan nation; and the three Sakya protectors (Guru Mahākāla, Four-Faced Mahākāla, and Begtse).

265. Personal communication with Geshe Thuchey Wangchuk, November 2016. Jeff Schoening translated.

Thirteen Golden Dharmas. She kept her shrine very clean and did every-thing in a proper manner. As the 41st Sakya Trizin remarked, "Dagmo Trinlei Paljor was an extraordinary practitioner and her practices sur-passed those of others who lived their entire lives in solitary retreat."

Returning to the Dolma Palace layout, on the third floor was Jetsun Kushok and the 41st Sakya Trizin's father's practice/retreat room, known as Hevajra Cave (Kye rdor phug), which was the size of 1.5 pillars. The 41st Sakya Trizin's apartment, where his grandfather Dragshul Trinlei Rinchen had lived, was named Eternal Happiness ('Chi med bde ldan). One first entered his study room, then had to go up three steps to enter the main room, which had two pillars and an elaborately carved and painted wooden shrine that covered an entire wall. On the top rows were sacred statues of various deities. Tibetan Buddhist statues are made in strict proportions, which must be followed by the artist. The size can vary from tiny to enormous, but the proportions of the head, body, arms, feet, and so forth must remain constant. Statues can be made of various mate-rials, the most common being either clay or a combination of metals, such as copper or brass gilded with gold, or silver alloy. One might think that a clay statue would be less precious than a metal one, but the clay is frequently mixed with many holy substances.[266]

On the 41st Sakya Trizin's shrine was an exceptional statue of Jetsun Drakpa Gyaltsen, the great mystic and one of the founding fathers of the Khon family. It was a human-sized painted clay statue of Jetsun Drakpa Gyaltsen seated in the lotus position. Because it was regarded as espe-cially precious, a large glass pane protected it and it filled one side of the shrine.[267]

266. For example, in *My Life and Lives*, 57, Khyongla Rato describes the main statue in his monastery of Rato: "The principal image on the chapel altar was the Lord Buddha in a lotus position, made of colored clay mixed with medicinal herbs and powdered precious stones together with sanctified earth and holy water from Buddhist places of pilgrimage in India."

267. The 41st Sakya Trizin stated that this statue was known as the "Leprosy Skull." He thought that this was an odd name for one of the founding fathers and was determined to find out why it was known by this name. He related, "When Jetsun Dakpa Gyaltsen was alive, he told his disciples that each one of them should make a statue of him. But to one disciple, he told him to wait because something special was missing. Later, Jetsun Drakpa Gyaltsen told this disciple to go to Gyantse where an old crazy beggar who had leprosy had recently died. Jetsun said that this beggar was actually a very holy hidden yogi and that his skull should be put in the statue." The disciple went to Gyantse and searched for this hidden yogi. After much searching, he discovered the body in a cave. The disciple found the skull, and to his amazement, the entire mandala of Sri Cakrasaṃvara was visible on it.

NO TIME TO SLEEP | 137

Having a room named Hevajra Cave or Green Tara Cave reinforced the focus on spiritual practice. Throughout Tibet, great meditators retreated to caves to perform sustained practice. Though the Khon family members were not in actual caves, their rooms served the same purpose—to perform the meditations on Hevajra, Tara, and so forth. Furthermore, to show the importance of the Sakya Trizin, one literally had to ascend several steps into his room.

Also on the third floor was the West Side Room (Zim chung nub). Jetsun Kushok's mother stayed there briefly, but it was primarily reserved for visitors. Jetsun Kushok remembers that their aunt would have the room prepared whenever relatives or officials came to visit. It was a traditional Tibetan-style room with long, bed-like couches covered with handwoven carpets adorned with designs of flowers, dragons, and other intricate patterns. As guests sat crossed-legged on the couches, they would drink endless cups of Tibetan tea and eat homemade cookies, dried fruit, and perhaps some oranges from India served on small carved, gaily painted wooden tables. From the early 1910s to 1950s, the primary foreign guests were British Indian political officers. In the 1950s the room had to be converted into a more Western-style room because the Chinese officials demanded tables and chairs.

The largest room, with six pillars, was the Big Glass-Window Room (Shel ling chenmo). Its south wall, lined with glass (*shel*) windowpanes, faced the inner courtyard below, providing warmth in cold Sakya. It must have been impressive to have so many glass windows, which had to be carried from India over the Himalayan mountains by yaks.

This room had a large shrine that held a very special statue of Shakyamuni Buddha. The 41st Sakya Trizin said that the Buddha had blessed it himself, and fortunately the family was able to bring this precious statue with them when they later fled to India. It is presently in His Holiness' shrine room in Rajpur, India.[268] Their father and other lamas performed or received empowerments and gave or heard Buddhist teachings in this room. It was the all-purpose room where guests were received and where the family gathered for celebrations. As already mentioned, it was in this room that Dagmo Trinlei Paljor married her two husbands.

The disciple brought back this astonishing skull and put it in the statue that he made of his lama. This statue, the "Leprosy Skull," was one of the treasures of the Sakya Khon family.

268. H.H. the 41st Sakya Trizin email, December 14, 2018.

There were also other rooms on the third floor, such as another shrine room on the east side that had a larger-than-life-sized statue of Padmasambhava, given to Dragshul Trinlei Rinchen by some of his Mongolian followers. This floor was the family's private area, so the only people who had access to it were those invited by the family.

On the second floor were bedrooms, the kitchen, and servants' rooms. When Jetsun Kushok was a young girl, she was given her own apartment on the second floor for her spiritual practices and studies. It was called Tashi Palkye (Auspicious Circle). The three-room apartment was on the south side of the palace, which faced the main inner courtyard below. Entering from the hallway, one walked through her servant's one-pillar room to enter Jetsun Kushok's main two-pillar room, where she did some of her practices and where her teacher taught her. This room had two small shrines, each with a set of statues of White Tārā, Amitāyus, and Uṣṇīṣavijayā on top. This triad is very popular for use in longevity rites. Further, each shrine had a set of smaller statues of the five Sakya founders. One shrine included a special statue of Sapan (Sakya Pandita) that had originally been made for the deceased tiny infant son of Princess Yangchen Dolkar as a memorial statue.[269]

Her main room had a large window that faced the courtyard below, so when she heard that a visitor had arrived, she would peek through her window to see who it was. Adjacent to her main room was a one-pillar room with a tiny window where she did her obligatory retreats. In this room there were only *tormas*, or special sacrificial offerings, and no statues. Jetsun Kushok emphasized that even though the children had their own rooms, "When we were children, we all slept in our auntie's [Dagmo Trinlei Paljor's] room together [on the third floor]." Next to Jetsun Kushok's servant's room was the room of her paternal great-aunt,

269. According to Tibetan Buddhist belief, after one's death a lama is consulted and advises the family to make a specific statue or *thangka* to help the recently deceased person have a good rebirth (*skyes rtags*). The statue should be completed before the forty-ninth day, when one's subtle consciousness enters a new birth. For the good rebirth of Princess Yangchen Dolkar (the first wife of Jetsun Kushok's father), a 2-foot-tall clay statue of Tara, decorated with some of her own jewelry, was made and placed in the Tara Temple. For her infant son, a 1.5-foot-tall clay statue of Sapan covered with gold paint was made. Jetsun Kushok said that their aunt gave her the Sapan statue because Sapan is recognized as a brilliant scholar who represents wisdom. This statue was a good reminder to practice with determination and effort to attain wisdom.

Kyabgon Pema Trinlei (Chapter 5). Later her great-aunt moved to her labrang.

In the southeast corner of the second floor of the Dolma Palace was an enormous kitchen with a brick hearth on which the fire was kept stoked to provide food and drink for over a hundred people each day. The main cook and kitchen helpers lived near the kitchen. All the meals were brought to the family in their rooms. They never ate in the kitchen. In addition, there were many storerooms on the first and second floors. These included numerous storerooms for food, one for all kinds of herbs to make medicines, a room that held horse tack, and storerooms for religious articles. Unlike most homes in Tibet, there was no storeroom for weapons.

On the first floor, below the 41st Sakya Trizin's rooms on the third floor, were the rooms of the protector deities. These rooms were perpendicular to each other. The west-to-east section was the room for the protector Mahākāla, and the north-to-south section was the room for Tsiu Marpo, the Dolma Palace family's protector. The Mahākāla room contained many protector statues and a main statue that was a life-sized two-armed Mahākāla. The Tsiu Marpo shrine room was smaller and had only two pillars.

In this shrine there was a Hayagrīva statue plus one of Tsiu Marpo with his retinue. More than a hundred Cham meditative dance masks were stored in this shrine room. The 41st Sakya Trizin related, "The Tsiu Marpo statue was made of clay and it was about a foot high. It would move at times, facing different directions, and its countenance would change." His Holiness witnessed this change only once: "When we were deciding if we should leave Tibet and go to India, Tsiu Marpo's face was shining and his hand was in a wrathful *mudra*. When my auntie [Dagmo Trinlei Paljor] saw this, she remarked, 'Now I know that we will be safe in India, that all will go well.'"[270]

Both rooms had their own shrine-keepers who performed the daily rituals. But on special occasions, such as when the *tormas* needed to be changed, a Khon family member would perform the pujas in the shrines.

North of and adjacent to the main palace was a pleasure garden with tall trees and potted flowers. Within its grounds was a lovely four-room house called the Relaxation House (To khang), where the family had

270. H.H. the 41st Sakya Trizin email, December 14, 2018.

picnics, visiting lamas occasionally resided, and in the summer teachings were bestowed. Later, Jetsun Kushok and the 41st Sakya Trizin's mother, Dagyum Sonam Dolkar, moved to this house because it was so pleasant.

In the two vegetable gardens were cold-resistant crops, such as potatoes, Chinese cabbage, large white radishes or daikon, mustard greens, scallions, chives, and sweet turnips. In the surrounding fields grew barley (the main grain for Tibetans), black peas, and mustard plants. It is too cold in Sakya for wheat to grow.

Sadly, the Chinese Communists destroyed the Dolma Palace in the 1960s; not even the foundation remains. Everything of value was carted away and disappeared forever. Some of the more important artifacts began to appear for sale in Hong Kong and abroad in the 1970s. This was the fate of most Tibetans' homes. Houses were stripped of anything of value. Tibetans suffered, and many died of starvation as all their belongings, any means to make a living, and any stored food were taken to China.

Administrative Duties of Dagmo Trinlei Paljor

Typically, a new dagmo was trained by her mother-in-law to run the Dolma Palace so that when the mother-in-law became elderly, the younger dagmo knew how to manage everything well. Dagmo Trinlei Paljor and the older of the two Khon brothers, Dagchen Kunga Rinchen, would confer together on many aspects of the administration of the Dolma Palace and the estates. They would appoint all the managers and assign duties according to the abilities of individual persons. In addition, they were both involved in supervising the hiring of the servants. Dagmo Trinlei Paljor had under her direct supervision the chief chef, the head business manager, the main attendant of her father-in-law the 39th Sakya Trizin, the manager of general merchandise, the main manager of the kitchen storeroom and food, the chief cleaner, and the horse and mule overseer. She also personally supervised the main servants who took care of the individual family members.

Because she was kind and caring, Dagmo Trinlei Paljor felt strongly that all servants needed to learn a trade or skill. Some young women were taught how to sew, weave carpets, or dye cloth and wool. She taught young men how to write in case they later worked with officials who needed secretaries. Jetsun Kushok remembers her aunt telling the servants, "In case you need to leave the Dolma Phodrang [Palace], I want to be certain that you have a skill. We will not 'cut off your hands' [i.e., leave you unskilled], and you will have a useful skill. You won't die from hunger because you will know how to do something." Sometimes Dagmo Trinlei Paljor would get mad when the girls were lazy and would remind them of the importance of having skills. Furthermore, since she was an excellent cook, she taught some monks how to cook. Later, in India, she was well known for her special New Year (Losar) cookies, and learned how to make mango jam. Sometimes a guest would be given a jar of jam as a parting gift.

Whenever Dagmo Trinlei Paljor felt that Jetsun Kushok was becoming lazy, she recounted her own mother's insistence that she needed to be able to take care of herself in any kind of circumstances. She emphasized, "It is important to have survival skills." Sometimes she added, "Since you are a Khon jetsunma, you will not need to worry about such things." But indeed, all these skills proved essential when many Tibetans, including the Khon family, became refugees in India in 1959.

The Dolma Palace had thirteen farms, or estates, each with a manager. Dagmo Trineli Paljor and her older husband Dagchen Kunga Rinchen were in charge of meeting and discussing matters with the managers who reported on the fields, crops, and harvest. The family also had businesses that sold the crops and distributed the goods. Once a year, at harvest time, each tenant farmer reported to Dagchen Kunga Rinchen and Dagmo Trinlei Paljor on the yield of the crops, lining up according to the size of the harvest. The person with the best yield was first in line and received the best present. This continued in succession until the person with the least yield received the smallest present. Jetsun Kushok remembers seeing some people receiving a set of clothes. This usually consisted of an overcoat (*chuba*) made of wool or brocade, depending on the status of the person receiving it, plus shoes and a hat. Sometimes some money was given, but Jetsun Kushok doesn't remember the amount.

People asked the Dolma Palace for help: "I need tea; I need butter." Dagmo Trinlei Paljor gave the needy family some provisions. Some requested loans, and occasionally Dagmo would lend them money. If a dispute arose within a family, they sometimes asked for her intervention. But this was rare. A common dispute between a wife and husband happened when a husband was drunk too often or had a girlfriend. Dagmo Trinlei Paljor would then talk to them, first separately and then together, to decide who was at fault. The guilty party then needed to make amends and present a *khata* (ceremonial scarf) to the innocent one.

Much later, in India in the mid-1960s, the 41st Sakya Trizin had some American students. One of these was Jay Goldberg (Ngawang Samten), who related the following:

> I remember Dagmo Kusho [Dagmo Trinlei Paljor] was a very generous person. One time I was in her presence and happened to be holding my rosary. Dagmo Kusho noticed that it was a simple rosary of only wooden beads and had no orange-colored agate beads that many Tibetans included in their rosaries. She reached into a drawer and found three very lovely, round agate beads and gave them to me. Dagmo told me that it would be auspicious for me to add them to my rosary.[271]

Despite all the demands on her time, Dagmo Trinlei Paljor in her spare time enjoyed making some money for purchasing butter and offering butterlamps in the temples. She did not want to use the family's money for these offerings, so she found another means. She bought silk thread and had the silk woven into lovely Tibetan aprons like those worn by all married women in Tibet. She had them sold in Lhasa. From this personal income, she bought butter and made many butterlamp offerings. It gave her great pleasure to offer butterlamps in temples and in her own shrine room.

A constant concern was to produce an heir. Though she was an excellent administrator and religious practitioner, Dagmo Trinlei Paljor could not conceive a child. For ten years she failed to become pregnant. In 1936, Pandit Rahul Sankrityayan, an intrepid Indian traveler and prolific scholar-writer who visited Tibet three times, described his stay in Sakya:

> The younger Dagmo (princess) of the Dolma Phodrang was ... intelligent in conversation. When I [Rahul] had my camera, she looked at it carefully and asked about the whole mechanism. I found she had more intimacy with the younger husband, because I saw her with him most of the time. The Dagmo did not have a child.[272]

271. Jay Goldberg email, March 16, 2016.

272. Rahul Sankrityayan, *My Third Expedition to Tibet* (1936), translated by Sonam Gyatso

The family did many pujas, performed a special empowerment to the goddess So Sor 'Brang Ma (Skt. Mahāpratisarā), who helps in pregnancy and childbirth, and conducted Vajrayoginī empowerments. But these rituals did not produce the desired result. In Dragshul Trinlei Rinchen's diary, he writes that in 1933 his two sons also went to the Four-Faced Mahākāla shrine in Khau Drak Dzong, where they prayed for a week and gave many offerings because they had the problem of having no heir.[273]

DAGYUM SONAM DOLKAR (1918–47)

Some people doubted the initial divination that had selected Dagmo Trinlei Paljor, arguing that it must have been incorrect since the main reason for the marriage was to produce an heir. As later events unfolded, Dagmo Trinlei Paljor proved invaluable to the well-being of the Dolma Palace family. After ten years of trying to have a child, however, her husband Dagchen Kunga Rinchen decided that he and his younger brother needed to find another wife. Being an ardent practitioner, Dagmo Trinlei Paljor wanted to relinquish her marriage and become a nun since she was unable to produce an heir. She encouraged Dagchen Kunga Rinchen by saying, "Please find a new wife."[274]

The family insisted that Dagmo Trinlei Paljor remain married to the two brothers, but Dagchen Kunga Rinchen did go to Lhasa to find a second wife. This was a delicate situation. Dagmo Trinlei Paljor was loyal to the Sakya family, and they did not want her to leave. However, a spiritual heir was crucial to the family. One of the paternal grandmother's relatives from the Ragashar noble family advised Dagchen Kunga Rinchen, "Your wife has a younger unmarried sister, Sonam Dolkar. Why don't

---

(Dharamsala: Library of Tibetan Works and Archives, 2014), 26–27. I presume that Sankrit-yayan's phrase "the younger Dagmo" refers to Dagmo Trinlei Paljor and not Sonam Dolkar, who did not marry the two Khon brothers before Dragshul Trinlei Rinchen's death in 1935. Dragshul does mention in his diary that an Indian pandit discovered a commentary of the *Pramāṇavārttika* at Sakya when he visited in 1934. Dragshul Trinlei Rinchen 1974, vol. 2, 838. On p. 21 of his work, Sankrityayan mentions that it was the *Vārtikālaṁkāra* (Prajñākaragup-ta's commentary).

273. Dragshul Trinlei Rinchen 1974, vol. 2, 669.

274. There is no record of Dagchen Kunga Rinchen's younger brother and co-husband Nga-wang Kunga Gyaltsen being involved in these decisions or actions.

you ask for her as your second wife?"[275] Dagchen Kunga Rinchen thought this was sound advice. Sonam Dolkar, a younger sister by twelve years, became his second wife. Like his first two brides, however, she was not consulted in this decision.

What happened was this. One day Dagmo Trinlei Paljor visited her natal home and asked Sonam Dolkar to come help her at the Dolma Palace. When she arrived there, Dagmo Trinlei Paljor informed her sister that she would be marrying her two husbands: "Now that you will be their wife, I will leave and become a nun." Sonam Dolkar replied, "If you leave, then I will not stay here." So Dagmo Trinlei Paljor stayed with her younger sister and they became co-wives of the two brothers.[276]

In accord with Sakya Khon family tradition, Sonam Dolkar's marriage to the two brothers was a secret one, just as her older sister's had been. For the actual ceremony, no one from Sonam Dolkar's family was present except her older sister, Dagmo Trinlei Paljor.

Jetsun Kushok explains, "There were no formal invitations, but slowly as people heard the news, people kept coming. It was more as if it was an 'open house'—not like in the West where everyone comes together for one day. After a month the husband and wife travel to the bride's home 'to get permission from the family's spiritual protectors.'" Since Sonam Dolkar was departing her natal home, she had to ask her natal family's protector deity for permission to leave. Now the Dolma Palace's protectors would protect her. "The bride's family gives a party and relatives come," Jetsun Kushok says, to congratulate them and celebrate this joyous marriage.

The bride receives a complete set of jewelry, which includes an elaborate headdress, a necklace, earrings, and other ornaments, which are passed down from generation to generation from one dagmo to another.[277] Jetsun Kushok elaborates, "My paternal grandmother's set was given

275. In parts of Tibet, especially in Kham, two brothers often married two sisters. Ideally this minimized friction between the two wives, and it helped keep the family intact.

276. The 39th Sakya Trizin Dragshul Trinlei Rinchen died in early 1935, and there is no mention of the marriage in his diary, so Sonam Dolkar must have married after his death.

277. Dagmo Kalden Dunkyi (wife of the 42nd Sakya Trizin Ratna Vajra Sakya) described the jewelry as follows in an email (July 20, 2012): "The top of the headwear is a red silk thread hat. Those portions that are white in color are made of strands of pearls. The two sides just beneath the red silk hat are called *padim* or *pasi*. In the center portion, with an X-like design, is the double dorje. The bottom tips of the double dorje are the earrings, made of turquoise with gold lining/trimmings. Just above the earrings, the two rows of big round

to my aunt [Dagmo Trinlei Paljor] and to my mother, Sonam Dolkar. We still have this set now and will not sell it." Furthermore, each dagmo who marries into the Sakya family has her own family jewelry. For example, when Dagmo Trinlei Paljor married, her family gave her valuable turquoises, coral beads, and pearls, a precious *gau* (pendant and necklace set) with expensive *dzi* beads, and a silver set comprising a wallet and a needle case.[278] These belonged to Dagmo Trinlei Paljor, not the Khon family. A bride's natal family decides what to do with these possessions after her death. Her natal family may keep them, give them to someone else, or give them to a monastery to accumulate merit for her. It is the prerogative of the bride's family.

As with previous brides, shortly after the marriage ceremony Sonam Dolkar received the two-day Hevajra empowerment. Since all wives must be spiritual practitioners and maintain a daily practice associated with deities significant in the Sakya tradition, the practice of Hevajra is paramount. He is one of the most important deities in the Sakya sect and is especially connected to the Khon family. The members of the Khon family should also do a daily practice of the Path with the Result. The Khon family has maintained this commitment, which began in the eleventh century, for more than a millennium. Sonam Dolkar also received the long-life empowerment of the nine-deity Amitāyus (one in each of the eight directions and a ninth in the center) from her husband, Dagchen Kunga Rinchen.

About a month later, monks formed a procession and played cymbals, drums, and banners to announce the marriage. The bride and her grooms went around a prescribed circuit, or *lingkor*, which included

---

balls are actually made of turquoise and coral, alternating to make the design interesting. The back of the head ornament is the *kyabdu*, which consists of loose strands of pearls with the free ends decorated with gold the size of pennies. For the ornament that is worn over the dress, the white part is the *yandan* (pearls). The four rows are called *tarkak*, made in gold with ruby, diamond, and turquoise decorations. The breast ornaments are known as *morkor*, made of gold with turquoise, diamond, and ruby inserts. There is a big *mala* that she wears, *kyedak*, with seven big amber balls decorating that. [On] the outer part of the breast ornaments you see another two pieces of ornaments, as well as a third piece just around/below the waist area. Those are the three *ka-u sumdrom*. They are made of gold, but with only turquoise inserts. Strands of turquoise and coral connect the three *ka-u* [or *g'au*]. She holds two strings of a *mala*, one strand is made with amber called *kasha*, and the other is made with coral, called *masha*."

278. Dragshul Trinlei Rinchen 1974, vol. 2, 230.

visits to the Four Wonders of Sakya and the Great Temple. When they returned home, the bride offered a long-life ceremony on behalf of her husbands.

Now there were three dagmos in the Dolma Palace: (1) the co-wives' mother-in-law Dagyum Chime Kunga Dolma (the wife of Dragshul Trinlei Rinchen), (2) Dagmo Trinlei Paljor, and (3) her younger sister and co-wife Dagyum Sonam Dolkar (a dagyum is a dagmo who has become a mother). About his visit of 1936, Pandit Rahul Sankrityayan writes:

> The aged Dagmo of the Dolma Phodrang [Dagyum Chime Kunga Dolma] always engaged in prayers and recitations. She took much care of me, and she often summoned me and prepared the best Tibetan meals. She used to present fresh fruits and dried fruits from Kham, Amdo, Lhadak and Nepal. I gladly consumed sweets made of molasses fried in butter. She used to serve them fresh. Her knowledge however was limited, so I could not talk with her on wider topics.[279]

Jetsun Kushok does not remember her paternal grandmother Chime Kunga Dolma well, because she died when Jetsun Kushok was young. She thinks that it was in the early 1940s—perhaps 1941 or 1942.[280] Jetsun Kushok did hear from the family that their grandmother told them that she thought that Jetsun Kushok was a very special child. Their grandmother rejoiced, "I am happy to have a Jetsunma and a Dungsay," after the first son was born in 1940. She did much Green Tara practice. Her main duties were to be in charge of the Dolma Palace, and Dagmo Trinlei Paljor had been helping her.

The sisters complemented and helped each other in different ways. Dagmo Trinlei Paljor was in charge of running the Dolma Palace after the death of their mother-in-law, and Dagyum Sonam Dolkar's main responsibility was to have heirs and be a companion to her husbands. Though Dagyum Sonam Dolkar did not have robust health, she did give birth to four children. The two sisters raised the children together, but it

279. Sankrityayan 2014, 26.

280. Dragshul Trinlei Rinchen 1974, vol. 2, 222. Dagyum Chime Kunga Dolma was 49 years old in 1927, so she was born in 1878. Her engagement and marriage are described briefly in the first volume of Dragshul's diary; see ibid., vol. 1, 234–37. Her full name was Sakya Dagyum Chime Kunga Dolma Rigzin Palgye Lhamo.

was Dagmo Trinlei Paljor who had most of the responsibility for taking care of them. In addition she shared with their older husband Dagchen Kunga Rinchen the running of the palace and supervision of the estates owned by the family.

Jetsun Kushok describes her aunt Dagmo Trinlei Paljor's personality as very strong and wise; she was very knowledgeable about both religion and politics. She made astute decisions. In hindsight, it is clear that many of her decisions saved the Sakya lineage from coming to an end, especially in India, where Tibetans had to cope with dire problems as refugees. As Jetsun Kushok recalls:

> My aunt [Dagmo Trinlei Paljor] was a big risk-taker; she was very direct, as many Khampas are. Also, if one was loyal to her, she was loyal to them. She had much compassion. However, if someone wanted to compete with her, she was tough and wouldn't give up. If someone wanted to hurt her or put her down, she fought back. My aunt was a formidable woman.[281]

Jetsun Kushok further recalls: "They had quite different looks and personality. My aunt was short and stout; perhaps she was 4 feet 11. She never wore makeup. She was very talkative, whereas my mother was so quiet that she rarely even ordered the servants. Physically my mother was the more attractive of the two. She was over 5 feet 6, slim, and enjoyed wearing makeup."

Both were known to be kind to others. In the mid-1940s, a Ngor Monastery lama, Dongthong Rinpoche Tenpai Gyaltsen (1933–2015), visited Sakya. He remembers meeting Dagyum Sonam Dolkar. She was tall and slim; perhaps she was in her late twenties. Both sisters wore *chubas* (ankle-length robes tied at the waist with a long sash) with long sleeves made of imported wool (*tema*). Dongthong Rinpoche remembered that Dagyum Sonam Dolkar was very kind to him. She gave him a very large

---

281. Tibet was divided into four main regions: Ngari, or West Tibet; Ü-Tsang, or south Central Tibet; Kham, or southeast Tibet; and Amdo, or northeast Tibet. Tibetans from the different regions differentiated themselves by comparing each other. Among the four regions, the Khampas were considered the most direct; and for Central Tibetan sensibility, they were too forward. Since Dagmo Trinlei Paljor grew up in Gyantse, Tsang, it was expected that she would be more soft-spoken, like her contemporaries in Central Tibet, rather than being as forthright as many Khampas.

blessing pill that had been blessed by the 39th Sakya Trizin Dragshul Trinlei Rinchen. Dongthong Rinpoche considered this pill very precious. When he fled to India and could only carry a few things, he took an old bell and dorje and this precious blessing pill.

When interviewing him at his home in Shoreline, Washington, I asked him if he still had the pill, and he told me that, in 2000, Jetsun Kushok had requested her brother the 41st Sakya Trizin to give the esoteric Path with the Result in Vancouver, Canada. Dongthong Rinpoche attended this extensive teaching. After completing it, he asked the 41st Sakya Trizin to give the Vajrakīlaya empowerment in Seattle. Having received it, he invited the 41st Sakya Trizin to his home, and in his great appreciation for receiving these teachings and empowerments, he presented him with this precious pill that had been blessed by Sakya Trizin's own grandfather. H.H. Sakya Trizin was very pleased and surprised.[282]

Jetsun Kushok also mentioned, "Both my mother and my aunt were adept at sewing. In fact, in 1944 on the pilgrimage to Nepal, my mother brought back to Sakya a manually operated sewing machine. She taught my aunt and the Sakya tailors how to use it. Thus the family had the first sewing machine in Sakya. She insisted that the tailors cut material in front of her and then take the cloth to sew in their rooms. She also loved to crochet and knit."[283]

JETSUN KUSHOK'S MEMORIES OF HER PATERNAL AUNTS

Though her mother and her maternal aunt were the central women in Jetsun Kushok's early life, she also remembers her five paternal aunts (Chapter 6), three of whom were older than her father. The oldest was Jetsunma Kunga Wangmo (1896–1929). The second was Jetsunma Kala, whose full name was Kalzang Chodron (1898–?), who had some mental problems. The third was Jetsunma Chime Trinlei Wangmo (1900–ca. 1955), who worked well with Dagmo Trinlei Paljor, especially after the death of Jetsun Kushok's father. The two were considered to be a good team and helped the family very much. Jetsunma Chime Wangmo died of breast cancer in the mid-1950s. Jetsun Kushok remarks that no one

---

282. Interview with Dongthong Rinpoche in Shoreline, Washington, February 11, 2005.

283. Jetsun Kushok observed her mother's facility and learned to crochet and knit as well. Even today Jetsun Kushok continues to crochet blankets and other items for her family.

spoke of breast cancer but simply said that something had happened to her breast.

Then came the two sons (Jetsun Kushok's father Dagchen Kunga Rinchen and his younger brother) who were co-married to the two sisters (Jetsun Kushok's mother and aunt). After the sons, there was Jetsunma Kunten, whose full name was Kunga Tenpai Nyima (1914–52). Jetsunma Kunten was very close to the fifth and youngest sister, who was named Kalzang Chodron (1917–62), just like her older sister, but who was known as Jetsunma Chungwa (Younger One).[284] Jetsunma Chungwa didn't talk, and people thought that she was mute, but she wasn't. She died in her labrang when the Chinese took over (see below).

Dagmo Trinlei Paljor, who was an avid storyteller, once related how the three oldest sisters—Jetsunma Kunga Wangmo, Jetsunma Kala, and Jetsunma Chime Wangmo—went on pilgrimage to Lhasa and Lhoka, or south Tibet. When they arrived at the ancient and famous Samye Temple established in the eighth century, they did not tell anyone that they were Sakya jetsunmas. They did not want to receive the special attention that was normally given to members of the Khon family. Appearing as ordinary pilgrims, they only had two horses—one to carry their things, and one to ride if someone was tired. Mostly they all walked. Jamyang Khyentse Chokyi Lodro Rinpoche (1893–1959), a highly realized master and the teacher of most of the most eminent lamas during the twentieth century, was also at Samye during this time.[285] He asked them, "Where are you from?" They replied, "We are from Tod [the area of West Tibet]." He persisted, "Where in Tod?" They replied, "Lhatse [a town in West Tibet]."

Jamyang Khyentse Rinpoche's tents were near their tent. While they were doing their practice inside the tent, he overheard them doing the Hevajra sādhana with *torma* offerings. As soon as he heard this, he entered their tent and did prostrations before them. "You are not ordinary nuns. You are Sakyapas. Ordinary people do not do this kind of

284. Though the fifth sister had the same exact name as the second sister, the Dolma Palace family members referred to the second jetsunma as Kala and to the fifth jetsunma Chungwa (Younger One). See Chapter 6.
285. Jamyang Khyentse Chokyi Lodro Rinpoche went on a pilgrimage to Central Tibet in 1926. Though there isn't any mention in the diary, it may have been at this time that the Sakya jetsunmas were in Samye.

practice and rituals." He requested a teaching from them, so the oldest, Jetsunma Kunga Wangmo, who usually gave teachings, gave him an oral transmission of some teaching. (Jetsun Kushok isn't certain which teaching it was.)

Thus they tried to keep a low profile and did not want to receive the pomp and ceremony usually given to Sakya Khon family members. One of her paternal aunts related the following story to Jetsun Kushok. A young monk recognized the youngest jetsunma, Chime Wangmo, and said, "You may say that you are an ordinary nun, but I know who you are. When I was at Sakya, you distributed food to the monks." He remembered that he had received food from her. The youngest jetsunma implored him, "Please do not say anything." He obeyed and did not tell anyone.

Jetsun Kushok relates another event: "After our father died, Jetsunma Chime Wangmo gave a long-life empowerment of Hayagrīva and Amitāyus Buddha every Friday, and on every Monday performed a purification ritual (sma 'brtsegs chu) for His Holiness [the 41st] Sakya Trizin, to protect the only son of the Dolma Palace. Jetsunma Chime Wangmo was very shy and would not allow any servants to help her. She told me, 'You be the shrine-keeper.' So I did the mandala offerings, etc." Jetsun Kushok recalls, "When my aunt Jetsunma Chime Wangmo gave teachings to my brother, if I looked at her face, she reprimanded me, 'Don't do that.' Since my brother was young, she didn't care if he looked. The other aunts did not give teachings to my brother."

Also, the 41st Sakya Trizin remembers his aunt Jetsunma Chime Wangmo as a great Vajrayoginī practitioner. He recalled:

> I visited her shortly after I finished studying the Vajrakīlaya pūjā and sacred dance. She asked me to perform the dance for her, which I did, and she was very impressed.... She asked me to pray for her to be reborn in Khecari [Vajrayoginī's paradise]. Shortly after that she passed away.
>
> When her tomb was opened after her cremation, the entire inside was covered with sindhura powder, and all her bones were yellow. [These are indicators that she was an excellent Vajrayoginī practitioner.][286]

286. H.H. the 41st Sakya Trizin, Great Sakya Women (Walden, NY: Tsechen Kunchab Ling

In their late teens, most jetsunmas move to their own residences, which were owned and maintained by either the Dolma or the Phuntsok Palace. These labrangs were passed on from one generation to the next as residences for the jetsunmas. The family provided everything. For example, Jetsun Kushok's fourth paternal aunt Jetsunma Kunten—and, earlier, her paternal great-aunt Kyabgon Pema Trinlei (Chapter 5)—lived in the Tashi Gang Labrang, located in the village of Tashi Gang, about 5 miles from Sakya.[287] In the North Monastery area of Sakya were two labrangs adjacent to each other, but with separate entrances. One was Shabten Lho Labrang (south), where Jetsunma Chime Wangmo (the third paternal aunt) and Jetsunma Chungwa (the fifth aunt) lived. The other was Shabten Byang Labrang (north), where Jetsunma Kunga Wangmo and Jetsunma Kala (the first and second paternal aunts) lived.[288]

Each labrang had two or three floors. The protector's shrine, often dedicated to the great Mahākāla, was usually on the first floor. In some labrangs, monks came daily to do pujas to the protectors; in others, they came to do them only on special days. Most jetsunmas were dedicated spiritual practitioners and did long retreats in their homes.

As a unique example of a jetsunma's life, the youngest of the five paternal aunts, Jetsunma Chungwa, stopped speaking at the age of eight. As the great Drakpa Gyaltsen, one of Sakya founding masters, says in his *The Great Song of Experience*, "All great meditators who practice, please do not enjoy engaging in idle talk."[289] Jetsun Kushok emphasizes that Jetsunma Chungwa was not mute but was, rather, a very serious practitioner. She spoke only to her older sister, Jetsunma Kunten, and to the old nun who was her attendant. Like most jetsunmas, she lived in her own residence until she died. At first, the Chinese left her alone, thinking she was dumb and could do no harm. But later they forced her to leave her living quarters on the second floor and live downstairs, in the shrine dedicated to Mahākāla, the great protector. When she heard that

---

Publications, 2017), 23–24. In this account Jetsunma Chime Wangmo is inadvertently listed as Chime Tenpai Nyima.

287. See chapter one of *Red Star Over Tibet* (London: Collins, 1974) by Dawa Norbu, who grew up in this village.

288. Benard 2015, 1–20.

289. Tseten 2008, 13.

the Chinese were planning to remove her from her labrang, she died in the protector's shrine, in 1962.

CODA

As this chapter has shown, Dagmo Trinlei Paljor was supported by the female relatives of the Dolma Palace family. In the next chapter we see that her niece Jetsun Kushok was raised in a loving environment, surrounded by paternal and maternal aunts and other strong religious practitioners.

CHAPTER EIGHT

Born to Practice:
Jetsun Kushok (b. 1938) and Her Brother
the 41st Sakya Trizin

ON NOVEMBER 14, 1938, Dagyum Sonam Dolkar (see Chapter 7) gave birth to her first child—a daughter named Jetsun Chime Osel Bukhrid Rigzin Trinlei Wangmo (hereafter Jetsun Kushok).[290] It was a very auspicious day because it was the date (according to the Tibetan lunar calendar) when the Buddha descended from Tushita Heaven after visiting his mother to impart the important teachings of Abhidharma (a systematic account of existence). Among Tibetan Buddhists, it is known as Lhabab Duchen and is commemorated annually with pujas and celebration. Most Tibetan Buddhists would interpret this as a foreshadowing of Jetsun Kushok becoming a great teacher in the future. The family rejoiced to have their first child after eleven years.

Though Dagyum Sonam Dolkar gave birth to Jetsun Kushok, she was in frail health, so it was her older sister Dagmo Trinlei Paljor (Chapter 7) who took care of the newborn and acted as her mother in many ways. As an infant Jetsun Kushok slept most of the day and stayed up most of the night. For the first month she cried at night. Dagmo Trinlei Paljor would stay awake and try to calm her. Since Dagmo Trinlei Paljor rose so often to take care of the baby, she developed the habit of taking short naps throughout the night and did her religious practices between these naps. She became known as a great meditator who took only catnaps and "slept" in her meditation box rather than on a bed. This habit continued for the rest of her life.

290. Chime = immortal, Osel ('od gsal) = luminosity/clarity, Bukhrid = bringer of sons, Rigzin = awareness- or wisdom-holder, Trinlei = activity of the Buddha, Wangmo = powerful woman.

Her aunt's reputation as a paragon of spiritual practice made a profound impression on Jetsun Kushok as she grew up. One can see that Jetsun Kushok has incorporated her aunt's resourcefulness and perseverance. For instance, when she became a mother, she developed a suitable method for managing her childcare duties, her spiritual obligations, and the need to earn a living in exile. It is known that Jetsun Kushok does not sleep much, and that her priority is to keep her commitments (*samaya*) to do her daily practices. Furthermore, her aunt had the reputation of being a very decisive person who was sharp in evaluating situations quickly. Likewise, if one has the opportunity to be with Jetsun Kushok for a day, one notices the many diverse situations she can handle and how decisive she is. She has the wonderful talent of assessing situations quickly and accurately. One of her disciples, Jennifer Harrington, reflected, "What I have always found remarkable about Jetsunma is her capacity to give individual advice in less than ten words, usually more like three words. First, I can remember it, and second, it always seems to work in lots of situations. So it is concise and comprehensive."[291] Jetsun Kushok is well known for her no-nonsense and pragmatic approach to life. She credits her aunt Dagmo Trinlei Paljor, who nurtured these abilities in her when she was young.

THE 1940S: A DECADE OF JOY AND SORROW

Jetsun Kushok's mother Dagyum Sonam Dolkar gave birth to three more children after Jetsun Kushok was born in 1938 (see Chart 4 in Chapter 6). Her second child was a son named Dungsay Jigdal Dutral, born in 1940. There was much rejoicing that a male heir had finally been born after waiting thirteen years. The future seemed promising. Moreover, in the tenth month of 1943, her second daughter was born, and was named Jamyang Bukhrid. But this happiness was fleeting. In late 1943 or early 1944, Dungsay Jigdal Dutral died of measles. Shortly afterward, the children's paternal uncle, Ngawang Kunga Gyaltsen, died.[292] It became a very

---

291. Jennifer Harrington email, January 2, 2019.

292. Though the sisters Dagmo Trinlei Paljor and Dagyum Sonam Dolkar were married to the two Khon sons, Jetsun Kushok usually refers to the older brother, Dagchen Kunga Rinchen (1902–50), as her father, and to the younger, Ngawang Kunga Gyaltsen (1904–ca. 1943), as her uncle.

sad year. Jetsun Kushok was only six years old, but she remembers well that the family decided to go on a pilgrimage to generate merit for her recently deceased uncle and baby brother, as well as to conceive another son.

PILGRIMAGE TO HOLY SITES IN TIBET AND NEPAL

This was an extensive pilgrimage to Mount Kailash, the kingdom of Mustang, and Nepal, especially the holy sites of Namo Buddha, Bodhnath, Svayambhu, and Pharping. It lasted for more than six months. The travelers included Jetsun Kushok's father Dagchen Kunga Rinchen (the surviving Khon brother married to her mother and aunt), her mother Dagyum Sonam Dolkar, her aunt Dagmo Trinlei Paljor, Jetsun Kushok, and her younger sister Jamyang Buhkrid. Wherever the family went, they performed rituals, recited chants, and offered prayers.

This pilgrimage is the first vivid memory held by Jetsun Kushok. When she speaks of this arduous journey, it assumes the dream-like quality of reliving a past that can no longer be duplicated. The pilgrimage began in the summer of 1944, when the family and their entourage traveled on horseback to the west via the vast Northern Plain (Changtang) to holy Mount Kailash.

The great Northern Plain, dotted with mountains about 14,000 feet high and scattered with freshwater and salt lakes, evokes a sense of vastness. It comprised about one-third of all Tibet and was not subdivided into agricultural plots or distinct villages. The nomads who inhabited this plain usually returned year after year to the same winter or summer pastures, but no one owned the land.[293] As the group traversed the expansive plain, they saw large herds of chestnut-colored kiangs (wild donkeys), over 4.5 feet at the shoulder and with pure white underparts; enormously powerful wild yaks; flocks of large white cranes with black necks and a touch of red at the top of their heads; and orange-colored ducks (perhaps the ruddy shelduck). "I have only seen these orange-colored ducks in Tibet, nowhere else in the world," Jetsun Kushok says, with a faraway look, as she recalls the plains filled with wild animals. These

293. Dawa Norbu describes the Northern Plain: "The four elements of snow, frost, wind and sun, in combination with undulating desolate plain and naked rocks and cliffs, create an austere grandeur and a subtle beauty unique to the Chang Thang." Norbu 1974, 25–26.

wild animals were not harmed or killed because the Tibetans believed that they belonged to the local deities.[294]

The entourage included three female servants who served as nannies, three cooks, two or three people who took care of the luggage and horses, and five male servants, two of whom were monks. Since both Jetsun Kushok and her sister Jamyang were young, each had their own nanny with whom they rode. As they traveled over the vast plain, each group member usually recited mantras, adeptly fingering their rosaries while riding their horses. The horses were calm and steady because the plain was broad and safe. The ride was so calm that sometimes people fell asleep in their saddles. Jetsun Kushok remembers that one time she saw her mother on her horse racing over to her aunt's horse. Dagyum Sonam Dolkar had noticed that her older sister had fallen asleep and that her rosary, which she was holding in her hand, was slipping. Quickly she urged her horse right up to her sister's horse and, without stopping, adroitely put the rosary over her sister's neck.[295]

Most days the group would travel for about six or seven hours, beginning at 8:00 a.m. and stopping before sundown. Since the plain was so flat, they could see the previous night's fire for hours and hours. Every night, before retiring, the family and entourage would chant the Praises to the Twenty-One Taras. According to Jetsun Kushok, "We never missed this chanting. No matter how tired we were, we chanted this praise before going to bed." The monks would lead the chant.[296] Later, when Jetsun Kushok became a teacher, she frequently recommended that her students chant this praise.

294. Unfortunately, in the 1960s when the Chinese army came, more than a hundred thousand strong, the wild yaks and donkeys were shot to feed the army. Very few remain today.

295. Most Tibetans learned to ride when they were six or seven years old. Children were not taught but simply learned by imitating their elders. This was necessary because horses, yaks, and mules were the only means of transportation. Yaks are very steady but also slow. Since mules are very strong, some high lamas preferred riding mules in difficult terrain.

296. Tara is considered important to speedily remove obstacles. She has 21 main forms, ranging from peaceful to extremely wrathful. This chant is very popular among Tibetans, and many know it by heart. In *My Life and Lives*, Khyongla Rinpoche (1996, 129) relates that when he visited the Dalai Lama's summer palace, the Norbulingka, "Suddenly I heard the deep resonant voices of the Dalai Lama's bodyguards chanting in the night the praises of Goddess Tara . . . I thought to myself that Tibet was truly a country of religion, where even the soldiers sang the praises of our goddess."

The first major destination was the sacred Mount Kailash. Kailash is a Sanskrit name that means Crystal Mountain, and for Tibetans, it is Gang Rinpoche—Jewel in the Snow. Mount Kailash is a holy site for the people of four religions—Buddhism, Bon (the indigenous religion of Tibet), Hinduism, and Jainism. Though Jetsun Kushok did not give me details of their arrival at the majestic mountain, one can only imagine the family's awe before the immensity of the holy peak, which is more than 22,000 feet high and stands alone, like a giant crystal, gleaming in the sun amidst an azure sky. Its four sheer sides each face one of the cardinal directions, so it easy to understand how Buddhists and Hindus consider it to be at the center of the universe. As such, it is the *axis mundi* where sky and earth meet.

Two lakes are nearby at an altitude of 15,000 feet. Lake Manasarovar (Lake of the Mind) is a large circular freshwater lake. Southwest of it is the smaller, crescent-shaped Lake Rakshastal (Lake of the Demon), which is a salt lake. Some say that they symbolize the sun and the moon, respectively.

As many pilgrims do, the family took about three days to visit many holy caves along the pilgrim circuit. They said prayers at many of the sacred sites on behalf of Jetsun Kushok's recently deceased uncle and baby brother, as well as for all sentient beings. One of the highest points in the circuit is the Tara Pass (18,471 feet), where one is believed to be "reborn" after passing burial grounds and visualizing one's own death by reflecting on impermanence.

From Mount Kailash, they traveled south and entered the royal kingdom of Mustang, which, although located in Nepal, is ethnically Tibetan.[297] Of the four Tibetan Buddhist traditions practiced in Mustang, the strongest one is Sakya, which was introduced in the fifteenth century.[298] The family stayed with the royal family and visited various temples in Mustang. As they continued their journey, they visited Chumig Gyatsa (Chu-mig brgya rtsa, or Hundred-Water Springs), where there are 108 waterspouts and one can be blessed with the icy water. This place is better known as Muktinath (Place of Liberation). This area, too, is sacred to

297. Though Mustang is part of Nepal, there was a king until 2008. Jigme Dorje Palbar Bista, the former king, continues to live in Mustang.
298. Lama Ngorchen Kunga Zangpo came to Mustang in the mid-fifteenth century. The famous temple in Kagbeni has a bronze statue of Ngorchen Kunga Zangpo on its altar and three walls painted with images related to the Ngor subsect of the Sakya tradition.

both Buddhists and Hindus. Tibetan Buddhists believe that in the eighth century the famous Indian yogi Padmasambhava stopped here to meditate on his way to Tibet. There is also a special statue of Avalokiteśvara there. Jetsun Kushok does not mention these.

However, she does recall distinctly caves with special fires in them. There was the earth-fire cave where some earth gave off a light-green flame. The water-fire cave had a small pond with a burning fire in it, and the rock-fire cave enclosed burning rocks. Jetsun Kushok remarks, "I remember them well because these fires were so unusual and I was very interested in watching them."[299]

From Mustang they traveled south to central Nepal, where they visited the holy Buddhist sites of Namo Buddha, Bodhnath, Svayambhu, and Pharping. Namo Buddha (sTag mo lus byin) is where the Buddha-to-be is said to have seen a tigress and her cubs stuck in a deep ravine. Knowing that the tigress was so hungry that she wanted to eat one of her cubs, he jumped into the ravine so that she could devour him instead, thus preventing her from acquiring the bad karma of eating her own offspring.

The second sacred site, Bodhnath, is located on a flat plain where there is an enormous stupa more than 118 feet high. It is believed to contain relics of the previous Buddha Kasyapa. In Sakya, in the Namgyal Stupa, which is one of the Four Wonders of Sakya, there is a relic of Buddha Kasyapa. For Tibetans, Bodhnath is one of the holiest places in the Kathmandu Valley, and many Tibetan monasteries and temples have been erected there since Tibetans fled their country in 1959.

The family's next stop was the Svayambhu Stupa and Temple across the Kathmandu valley, on the western side. Svayambhu is considered the second most important site (after Bodhnath) for Tibetan Buddhists. Unlike Bodhnath, which is built on the plain, Svayambhu is built on a hill. Nowadays, one has to climb 365 steps, which become progressively steeper and narrower as one approaches the stupa. The stupa, with large painted eyes, appears very imposing from the steps.

The last place that Jetsun Kushok remembers is Pharping, located south of Kathmandu. Next to Pharping is Yanglesho (Yang le shod). For

---

299. Under the altar of the Jwala Mai Temple (Goddess of Flames Temple, or Temple of the Miraculous Fire), natural blue flames burn. Originally there were three flames, one appearing on water, one on stone, and one on earth. The latter expired around 50 years ago, and for locals this was an ominous sign that things were changing. From https://www.pyramidkey.com/legends-of-muktinath/.

some Tibetan Buddhists, it is considered as holy as Bodhgaya, India, where the Historical Buddha attained enlightenment, because it is here that Padmasambhava, venerated as "the second Buddha," attained enlightenment. Pilgrims who wish to receive his blessings eagerly seek out his two main meditation caves.

After descending from one of these caves, one visits the ancient Vajrayoginī temple in Pharping, a very holy pilgrimage site for Sakyapas (Sakya practitioners) because in the eleventh century the Phamthing brothers lived at this shrine. The two brothers were disciples of the great Indian mahāsiddha Nāropa, the founder of the Vajrayoginī teachings taught in the Sakya tradition. Sakyapas consider Nāropa's Vajrayoginī to be one of their most important meditational deities.

After entering the temple, one must climb to the second floor, where the Vajrayoginī image is found in the inner sanctum. The circumambulation path is dark and narrow.[300] Jetsun Kushok remembers that at all these sacred sites her family did pujas, offering many butterlamps and incense offerings. Jetsun Kushok and her little sister Jamyang spent their time in play since they were very young. The long and strenuous journey was so difficult for infant Jamyang that she almost died, but luckily she received medicine that saved her.

After visiting the major pilgrimage sites in central Nepal, Jetsun Kushok's father did a divination to determine whether they should continue on to India or return to Tibet. The divination indicated that it was best to return to Tibet through Nepal and not visit India. As the group traversed the vast Himalayas, the sun's unrelenting reflection off the snow blinded young Jetsun Kushok. Since no sunglasses were available, the servants deftly cut some hair from the tail of one of their horses and made an eye covering for her, which provided relief to her irritated eyes.

TSEDONG, A SECONDARY HOME FOR THE FAMILY

After the long pilgrimage to Mount Kailash, Mustang, and Nepal, the Dolma Palace family bypassed Sakya and went farther north to one their

300. Jay Goldberg related the following in a March 16, 2016 email: "Hidden behind the main Vajrayoginī image is supposedly a statue that was passed down from Nāropa to the two Phamthing brothers. Back in the 1970s, if you gave a little *bakshish* to the temple-keepers—who are descendants of the Phamthing brothers—they would bring out the image for you to see. However, they would bring it into view and rush it back behind the main image in a flash, so it was impossible to really see it clearly."

main residences in the village of Tsedong (rTse gdong), in Tsang Province. Tsedong is located on the northern bank of the mighty Tsangpo (Brahmaputra) River, which begins near Mount Kailash and ends in the Bay of Bengal. To reach it, the family had to cross the Tsangpo River in coracles near Shigatse, the main city of Tsang and the traditional seat of the Panchen Lamas. Tsedong was about four or five hours by horseback from Shigatse and about 70 miles from Sakya.

Tsedong is in a small valley between two mountains. The village was organized as many other villages were in Tibet. The villagers lived in the valley, and the Tsedong estate, where the Khon family stayed, was higher up the mountain. Above the estate was the monastery, and on the highest section was a small shrine. Small peach trees cover the mountainsides, and the cultivated valley included fields of barley, wheat, black peas, and red mustard (not the usual yellow mustard). Tsedong was famous for its artisans. Some of the best metalworkers, sculptors, painters, and wood carvers in Tsang lived there.[301] Moreover, the area offered much lumber, some of which was brought to Sakya when buildings needed renovation.[302]

Jetsun Kushok remembers the house fondly. It reminded her of the slightly smaller Shigatse fort (dzong). Though technically the estate belonged to the Sakya government, the Dolma Palace paid the expenses to maintain it as a family residence. Thus the Dolma Palace family considered it to be their second home. It has been in the Khon family for more than five hundred years. Ngakchang Ngawang Kunga Rinchen, the great Sakya lama who revitalized the Sakya teachings and restored many important Sakya holy buildings, was born in Tsedong in 1517.[303] He was the 23rd Sakya Trizin from 1534 to his death in 1584. In 1945 the future 41st Sakya Trizin would be born in the same room in Tsedong where the 23rd Sakya Trizin had been born more than four hundred years earlier.

Jetsun Kushok describes the residence. On the third floor was the main living area for the family. There was a large central room that was so spacious it was referred to as the Potala Room (indicating that it was enormous, since the Potala is the monumental winter residence of the

---

301. See Jackson 2020, 590 n. 135.

302. Sakya and Emery 1990, 127.

303. See https://treasuryoflives.org/biographies/view/Ngakchang-Ngawang-Kunga -Rinchen/7053.

Dalai Lama in Lhasa). This Potala Room served several purposes: it was the reception room for guests and was also where religious teachings were given. On the east side of the third floor were Jetsun Kushok's parents' bedroom, her aunt's bedroom, and additional rooms for guests. On the west side were storage rooms, a toilet, some empty rooms, and a large hallway. The second floor was reserved as the living quarters of the managers and of former workers who were now retired. They could live out their days comfortably, without worrying about food and lodging.

As was the case in many Tibetan homes, the ground floor served as a barn in which to house animals and store their food. The house was so large that the ground floor was not well maintained. Since many windows were broken, birds delighted in making their nests on the ground floor. The flat earthen roof of the residence served as a place to dry eighteen different kinds of food, including peaches, turnip greens, nettles, cabbage, white radishes, and yak and sheep meat.

Above the house was Tsedong Monastery (rTse dong chos de), founded by Namkha Tashi Gyaltsen. The exact name was Sisum Namgyal Ling Monastery. At the entrance was a central courtyard facing the main assembly hall. Surrounding the courtyard were small one- and two-story monks' residences. There were more than a hundred monks, with an abbot and other monastic officials.

Later, in the winter of 1954, a young Sakya monk by the name of Tenzin Dawa (b. 1936) from Trehor, Kham, visited Tsedong for a few days.[304] Though there were only about two hundred monks, he was impressed by how well organized they were. He felt fortunate to see a Vajrakīlaya Cham dance. Perhaps five or six hundred people attended the performance. Tenzin Dawa saw the first day's performance when the monks danced without costumes, but he was unable to stay for the second day when the monks wear beautiful brocade robes and painted masks. Still, since he himself was a Cham dancer in Kham, he appreciated the opportunity to see the monks dance. Above the monastery was the Mountain Peak Temple (Lhunpo rtse), maintained by a temple-keeper. Though no one except the keeper lived in the temple, pilgrims frequented it during the day.

304. Interview with Tenzin Dawa, April 17 and 22, 2009, at Ngor Monastery, in Rongye, Sikkim. Later, Tenzin Dawa would become abbot of the Sa-ngor Chotshog Monastery in Rongneck, Gangtok, Sikkim, India. He was originally from Dongthong Monastery in Kham.

THE BIRTH OF H.H. THE 41ST SAKYA TRIZIN

After resting at the Tsedong estate, the family continued their pilgrimage to Lhasa and then farther north to Phenpo Nalendra Monastery, a principal monastery of Tsarpa Sakya, one of the subsects in the Sakya tradition. Though the purpose of the pilgrimage was to provide merit for the family's recently deceased son and uncle, it was also undertaken to gain merit, so as to successfully bear an heir to assume the Sakya throne. Jetsun Kushok's father, Dagchen Kunga Rinchen, had almost given up hope of having another son. But when the family arrived in Phenpo Nalendra Monastery, some students of his father, the 39th Sakya Trizin Dragshul Trinlei Rinchen, insisted that the Dolma Palace needed a lineage-holder. They entreated him to have a son.

At the monastery, Dagchen Kunga Rinchen met with the young Chogye Trichen Rinpoche (1920–2007),[305] who had a strong karmic connection with the family (and who would later be one the main teachers of the 41st Sakya Trizin). Chogye Trichen Rinpoche reflected upon their dilemma and suggested that they ask his teacher, the great scholar-yogi Lama Ngawang Lodro Rinchen (Ngag dbang blo gros rin chen, 1892–1959; better known as Lama Ngaklo Rinpoche), to perform the necessary rituals "to bring forth a son." Ngaklo Rinpoche was famed for achieving such goals by ritual means. At the time, however, he was conflicted: he wanted to help the Khon family by traveling with them and performing the needed rituals, but he was already instructing the young Chogye Trichen Rinpoche and wanted to finish imparting the teachings to him. In Tibetan Buddhism, a lama has the responsibility to complete a teaching. But Chogye Trichen Rinpoche urged his teacher to help the Khon family. Ultimately it was agreed that Ngaklo Rinpoche would accompany the family and perform the necessary rituals.

Jetsun Kushok emphatically stated, "His rituals always worked." He did not disappoint the family. Dagyum Sonam Dolkar became pregnant within a few months. Later, Ngaklo Rinpoche would become an important lama to Jetsun Kushok and to her brother (Fig. 15), who turned out to be the long-awaited male heir.

During Dagyum Sonam Dolkar's pregnancy, Dagmo Trinlei Paljor remembered a story told by her father-in-law the 39th Sakya Trizin Drag-

305. See Jackson 2020, which is a two-volume biography of Chogye Rinpoche.

Fig. 15. H.E. Jetsun Kushok and H.H. the 41st Sakya Trizin in Rajpur, India, 2002.

shul Trinlei Rinchen. When she herself had been trying to become pregnant, he had performed many rituals to help her conceive a child. While
he was performing these rituals, a group of Mongolians had arrived in
Sakya.

Tibetans and Mongolians have a very strong Buddhist connection.
For example, many Mongolians come to Tibet to complete their studies in Buddhist philosophy. Among Tibetans, the Sakyas have a unique
relationship with Mongolians because the Mongolian emperor of China,
Kublai Khan (1215–94), appointed an ancestor of the Khon family, Chogyal Phagpa (1235–80), to be his imperial spiritual preceptor and gave him
leadership over Tibet. In the thirteenth century, Sakya was the capital of
Tibet.

This visiting Mongolian group had promised Dragshul Trinlei
Rinchen that they would offer him a larger-than-life-sized statue of Guru
Rinpoche (Padmasambhava). Since the metal statue was very large, dif-
ferent parts were brought separately to Sakya. One day, when Dragshul
Trinlei Rinchen had completed a ritual for a male lineage-holder, the
"life stick" of the statue arrived.[306] He told Dagmo Trinlei Paljor that this

---

306. In Tibetan Buddhism, a sacred statue frequently has a life stick (*sog shing*) in the middle
of its body that represents the central axis of the subtle body. It must be made in a precise
fashion, and traditionally it was carved from juniper or from costly sandalwood.

was a very auspicious sign: "This means that only one son will come and he will hold the Sakya lineage very strongly. He will be a pillar of the Sakya lineage."

When Dagyum Sonam Dolkar had given birth to her first son, everyone had thought that he was to be this lineage-holder. When the baby died, they not only mourned his death but despaired about the succession of the lineage. Eventually, however, Dragshul Trinlei Rinchen's interpretation of the "life stick" proved to be correct: after eighteen years of hope and anguish, on September 7, 1945 (the first day of the eighth month of the wood bird year), a boy was born at sunrise in Tsedong. He was Dagyum Sonam Dolkar's final child, and in bearing him she fulfilled the dearest wish of the Dolma Palace because he would become the 41st Sakya Trizin.[307] This was the high point of the 1940s.

Being born into this illustrious spiritual family, the newborn son immediately experienced his first ritual, just as all children in the Khon family did. The 41st Sakya Trizin explains, "The very first thing, as soon as the child is born, is that the letter *dhīḥ*, the seed syllable of Mañjuśrī, who represents speech and wisdom, is written on the child's tongue with a special nectar made of saffron and many other things."[308] Thus, within hours of the child's birth, the infant is already associated with the great Bodhisattva of Wisdom, Mañjuśrī, and this creates favorable conditions for the development of the mind.

To help ensure that this young son would have a long life, many prayers were said and special empowerments and rituals were performed. Both his father and Ngaklo Rinpoche bestowed long-life rituals. Dagchen Kunga Rinchen gave his son a Sanskrit name, Ayu Vajra (Long-Life Vajra).[309] Since Buddhism came from the holy country of India and

---

307. In fact, the 41st Sakya Trizin became the longest reigning Sakya Trizin; he was Sakya Trizin for 58 years (r. 1959–2017). He is considered to be a reincarnation of both his paternal grandfather the 39th Sakya Trizin Dagchen Trinlei Rinchen and of the Nyingma discoverer of hidden texts (*terton*) Apam Orgyen Trinlei Lingpa (O rgyan phrin las gling pa, 1895–1945). Thus he has a strong connection to the Nyingma school as well as to the Sakya school.

308. Tseten 2008, 31.

309. Tibetan Buddhism is known as Vajrayana (Way of the Vajra). The vajra (or thunderbolt) symbolizes the indestructible means to enlightenment. This reinforces the method of applying compassion in order to impartially help all sentient beings realize enlightenment. Many Khon sons have a Sanskrit name. This tradition continues with both families. The 41st Sakya Trizin's older son is Ratna Vajra (Jewel Vajra), and his younger son is Gyana Vajra (Wisdom Vajra).

Sanskrit is known as the language of the gods (*devanāgarī*), it is seen as auspicious to have a Sanskrit name. Later, when his father gave his infant son his first empowerment of the long-life nine-deity Amitāyus, he conferred on him his long Tibetan name, Ngawang Kunga Thegchen Palbar Trinlei Samphel Wangyi Gyalpo.[310]

A supreme spiritual master of the time, the great abbot of Ngor Monastery Vajradhara Dampa Rinpoche (Ngawang Lodro Shenpen Nyingpo, 1876–1953), said to Ngaklo Rinpoche, "In bringing about the birth of this child, you have performed a great deed. The future of the doctrine of the Sakya Order is well assured. I am an old monk. Now, even if I die, I shall have no regrets."[311]

Though 1945 was celebrated with joy, there was sadness, too. A few months after the future Sakya Trizin's birth, Dagmo Trinlei Paljor and Dagyum Sonam Dolkar learned that their oldest brother, Kalon Bonshod, had died at the age of 58. The sisters invited their mother, who had lived with their brother in Lhasa, to come to Sakya and live with them. Their mother was blind, lived very simply, and had become a nun in her old age. Eventually she did come, but she felt so shy in front of Dagchen Kunga Rinchen that she only stayed a year. Then she returned to Lhasa. By the time the Khon family went to Lhasa in 1951, she had already passed away. She was in her seventies.

Sakya Trizin's second birthday was an occasion of lavish celebration in Sakya. Geshe Thuchey Wangchuk (1928–2018) remembered this celebration: "The Dolma Palace's son, [Dagchen] Kunga Rinchen, his young son [the future 41st Sakya Trizin], Dagmo [Sonam Dolkar, his mother], her older sister, Dagmo Trinlei Paljor Zangpo, plus many people from Tsedong arrived in Sakya in 1947 (fire pig year). In the eighth month, there was big celebration for the young son on the top floor of the Dolma Palace. When the mother picked up her son, he didn't like it. But when Auntie [Dagmo Trinlei Paljor] picked him up, he was very happy. This indicated that the young son knew that his mother would not live long, but Auntie will serve Sakya Trizin for a long time."[312]

---

310. Ngawang = powerful speech, Kunga = joyful, Thegchen = Mahayana, Palbar = glorious, Trinlei = enlightened activity or activity of a Buddha, Samphel = increasing one's wishes, Wangyi = powerful, Gyalpo = king.

311. Ratna Vajra Sakya et al. 2003, 39.

312. From a personal manuscript of Geshe Thuchey Wangchuk, n.d., p. 19.

Throughout these years, Jetsun Kushok was being trained thoroughly. When each child became six years old, their father selected the best tutors for them from among the monk-teachers of the Great Temple. The tutors conferred with the children's father, who told them what to teach. Then, following the proper protocol, the tutor visited their mother and aunt. There was one tutor for the two jetsunmas (Jetsun Kushok and her younger sister), and later another one for the 41st Sakya Trizin.

The two young jetsunmas were given one of the most eminent philosophers, Lu rigs Gyatso, who was the head of the school of philosophy, or *shedra*. Jetsun Kushok recalls, "He was very kind, quiet, knowledgeable, and a retreat teacher." At the beginning of each lesson, the tutor prostrated three times to the jetsunmas. For five or six years, he taught them how to read, and how to memorize religious texts and prayers. Each child began by memorizing short prayers to Mañjuśrī and the goddess of learning, Saraswatī. In India, where Buddhism began, it is believed that one should start with something auspicious to create beneficial effects in the future. For the Sakya Khon family members, who are expected to become religious lamas to many learned scholars, beginning one's studies with prayers to the deities of wisdom and learning lays an excellent foundation for propitious results.

Mastering the alphabet and learning to read quickly followed. The Tibetan language has many silent consonants that affect how a word is pronounced or the meaning of the word. Each syllable is separated by a dot, but one needs to know the rules of grammar and spelling to recognize specific words. The 41st Sakya Trizin states, "We Tibetans say that the more you practice spelling, the faster you will be able to read."[313] For example, if English were written as the Tibetan language is written, it would look like this—ti.be.tan.lang.u.age. Unless one knew the two words "Tibetan" and "language," one would not know where one word ended and the next word began. Thus religious teachers, who must become fast readers in order to give long textual transmissions, must be very familiar with spelling and grammatical rules.

Except for a lunch break, which they had with their teacher, each child had to study and memorize texts from 9 a.m. to 3 p.m. There was no other break or any kind of recess. The 41st Sakya Trizin stated, "I was taught

313. Ratna Vajra Sakya et al. 2003, 32.

spelling seven hours a day, six days a week, for nearly two years."[314] All the children were expected to become excellent practitioners and well versed in spiritual matters. In addition, Dagmo Trinlei Paljor taught the jetsunmas how to write. In Tibet, most children were taught to read but not to write. Learning to write was not considered important except for the daughters and sons of noble families and for the sons of officials, who would later need to write official documents and other correspondence.

Jetsun Kushok remembers that at the age of six, she was instructed in how to do her first meditations on Mañjuśrī and Saraswatī. The teacher who guided her in the meditations made certain that she did these correctly. Once he was satisfied, she was allowed to continue these meditations on her own. This laid the foundation for meditation on a daily basis that she has continued throughout her life. In spring of 1945, the abbot of the South Monastery, Khen Jampal Zangpo (1901–61; see Chapter 6), gave her the novice ordination in the Tara Temple.

Jetsun Kushok's father and aunt told the tutors that it was permissible to discipline the children with corporal punishment from the waist down only, no slapping of the face or the upper part of the body. Before doing so the tutor had to prostrate three times before the jetsunmas and dungsays. Jetsun Kushok remembers her tutor fondly. "Lu rigs Gyatso was very good—very kind. He never beat my sister and me, but he did scare us by holding up some nettles in the summer. This was effective; we made sure that we were good. Even if you are touched a bit by nettles, it hurts. If we did very well, the next day he would bring presents, such as candies, and in the winter when stores sold fruit from India, he would buy some for us. Unfortunately, he got tuberculosis and died in his late forties. There were very good signs at his death. It was a beautiful sky with many rainbows." (These are considered to be signs that he was an excellent practitioner.)

The end of 1947 was a difficult time for the Dolma Palace. In the tenth lunar month, Dagyum Sonam Dolkar, who had suffered for a long time with a disease known as a blood-wind imbalance (*khrag rlung*), became critically ill.[315]

---

314. Ibid.

315. See Jackson 2003, 625 n. 599. Symptoms of a "blood-wind" (*khrag rlung*) disease include feeling that your head is aching or bursting, pulsation in the head, episodic pain in the neck, insomnia, etc. According to Western medicine, it corresponds to hypertension.

At that time a very holy lama, the 3rd Dezhung Rinpoche (see Chapter 5), was visiting from Kham. He had good relations with the families of both the Phuntsok Palace and the Dolma Palace. Dezhung Rinpoche felt especially close to Dagchen Kunga Rinchen, whom he considered to be one of his root lamas. Dagchen Kunga Rinchen requested Dezhung Rinpoche to confer the blessings of the three long-life deities on his wife and family.[316] After receiving this request Dezhung Rinpoche had a portentous dream in which a beautiful image of the goddess Dolma broke.[317] He was deeply concerned because the ailing mother's name was also Dolma (Tara),[318] and White Tara is one of the three long-life deities; he felt that the signs were highly inauspicious. Dezhung Rinpoche revealed this dream to Dagchen Kunga Rinchen, who asked him to try to decipher its meaning. Shortly afterward, Dagyum Sonam Dolkar died; she was only 29 years old. Jetsun Kushok was nine, her little sister Jetsunma Jamyang was four, and the young future 41st Sakya Trizin was just two years old (and has stated many times that he does not remember his mother).

Though Dezhung Rinpoche was planning to visit the famous Ngor Monastery to receive the important teachings of the Path with the Result, which were taught only once a year, at the behest of Dagchen Kunga Rinchen he remained in Sakya to help him perform the required funerary rituals for forty-nine days.[319] After the final rites and cremation, he was asked to oversee the offering of a hundred thousand memorial butterlamps in the name of the departed, Dagyum Sonam Dolkar. Dezhung Rinpoche's younger sister, Ani Chime Dolma, accompanied and helped him with this task. She remembers that some of the main offerings were made at the Gorum and Rinchen Gang temples and in front of the important Namgyal Stupa built by Bari Lotsawa to the goddess Uṣṇīṣavijayā (Tib. Namgyal), who destroys obstacles (see Chapter 2). Since the condition of the stupa has a strong connection with the Khon family, it is

316. There are different sets of three long-life deities (*tshe lha rnam gsum*), but the most common set is Amitāyus, White Tara, and Uṣṇīṣavijayā.

317. Jackson 2003, 156.

318. Dolkar is an abbreviated form of Tara (*dolma*) and white (*karmo*), thus it means "White Tara." One of the three long-life deities is White Tara, so Dezhung Rinpoche is referring to this form of Tara.

319. Jackson 2003, 157. The annual teaching of the Path with the Result at Ngor Monastery began on the twenty-fifth day of the tenth lunar month and usually finished on the eighteenth day of the first lunar month.

considered crucial to include rituals at this stupa for all members of the Khon family.

In the end, Dezhung Rinpoche and his sister Ani Chime visited and performed offerings and prayers at 108 of the 130 shrines mentioned in the Sakya pilgrim's guidebook. Ani Chime remarks, "We did so many recitations and prayers that by the end, I had learned many recitations and prayers by heart."[320] The family of the Dolma Palace appreciated their efforts. Later, in India and in the United States, Dezhung Rinpoche would teach both the 41st Sakya Trizin and Jetsun Kushok. In fact, he would give them some teachings and transmissions that he himself had received from their father.

Soon after their mother's death, Jetsun Kushok began to cultivate a lifelong practice of making retreats dedicated to particular deities. From the beginning of the eleventh lunar month to the end of the twelfth lunar month, when she was ten years old,[321] she made her first retreat on Bhūtaḍāmara Vajrapāṇi, a form of Vajrapāṇi that holds a vajra and subdues demons. Her teacher stayed with her to make sure that she did everything correctly and remained focused during all sessions. All the children in the Khon families begin with this retreat because it is considered very effective to avert obstacles or difficulties in spiritual practice.

Like all Sakya retreats, it involved four sessions a day. She rose at 3 a.m. to begin the first session and went to bed at 11 p.m. after concluding the fourth session. These retreats help calm the wandering mind, focus it in beneficial ways, train the mind in a concerted and constant manner, and also create merit. Most retreats require that one repeat the main mantra (and sometimes a secondary mantra) of the particular deity a specific number of times. During her month-long retreat, the young Jetsun Kushok recited the short mantra one million times and the long mantra a hundred thousand times. According to Buddhist teachings, all phenomena are uncertain. One must make an effort to pursue spiritual practices in order to help others, as well as to be able to cope with difficult periods in one's own life.

At times, the family had visits from foreign dignitaries. The Sakya Khon family had a special status among noble families in Tibet because

320. Ibid., 625 n. 605.

321. According to Tibetan calculation, a child is one year old at birth. Previously in Tibet, everyone became one year older at the New Year. Individual birthdays were not celebrated. But nowadays Tibetans celebrate their birthday on the day they were born.

they had been the rulers of Tibet during the Yuan or Mongol dynasty (1272–1368) in China, prior to the rule of the Dalai Lamas that began in 1642. With this special status, most foreign dignitaries would visit the Khon family during their tours of south Central Tibet. The West Side Bedroom was reserved for them. Jetsun Kushok remembers that the room always contained a portrait of the Dalai Lama. From 1910 to 1948 the primary foreign guests were British political officers from India. In the early 1950s it was Chinese officials, who insisted that a portrait of Chairman Mao also be hung in the room.

The final British visitors were Arthur J. Hopkinson (1894–1953), who was the last Indian Political Officer before India became independent, and his wife Eleanor (1905–2007). In 1948 the Hopkinsons made a month-long tour of the Tibetan administrative centers of Shigatse, Gyantse, and Sakya to inform the Tibetans that the British were leaving India and that they would now have to deal directly with an independent India.[322]

Since the 40th Sakya Trizin was from the Phuntsok Palace, the Hopkinsons stayed there, but they did visit the Dolma Palace. Jetsun Kushok recalls their aunt Dagmo Trinlei Paljor remarking, "The skinny Tibetan couple who are the Hopkinsons' guides are cousins of the Dolma Palace family." Jetsun Kushok never learned their names.

She does remember that the Hopkinsons gave the Dolma Palace three phonographic records. Everyone was curious about the black discs that emitted sounds as they turned around and around. "We didn't understand them, but one record had many laughs so we thought it was funny." Also the Hopkinsons showed some movies, but since there was no electricity, they had to bring along a generator. Jetsun Kushok developed a bad headache from the fumes, so she couldn't watch much. "One was about Bhutan, showing the Bhutanese with bows and arrows, shooting arrows and riding horses." Seeing movies must have intrigued Jetsun Kushok because when she lived in India, she enjoyed seeing both Hindi and American movies with her cousin Lama Kunga Rinpoche. Even today, she has fond memories of movies such as *Rio Bravo*, and enjoys listening to the songs crooned by Dean Martin and Ricky Nelson.

The family was impressed that Eleanor Hopkinson was very tall. She

322. Indians had been demanding their independence from the British Empire. There had been constant strikes, disruptions, and peaceful protests by leaders such as Mohandas Gandhi and Jawaharlal Nehru. Succeeding in their freedom struggles, the Indians celebrated their independence on August 15, 1947.

told the family that she missed her own four children and that she would like to see their young son. But the family refused, worried that visitors might bring infectious diseases from abroad. Reflecting upon the irony, Jetsun Kushok laughs, "In Sakya, my family would not let the English even see my brother, and now my brother is teaching foreigners in English!"

The Hopkinsons showed great foresight in bringing toys for the children all the way from India. Jetsun Kushok remembers that the 41st Sakya Trizin, her younger sister Jamyang, and she liked their gifts. Even though the Hopkinsons didn't see the 41st Sakya Trizin, they gave him a present of two big metal trucks that Jetsun Kushok thinks may have been blue. She herself distinctly remembers receiving a red car and a green pickup truck, and Jamyang got a pink truck and a black car. All were made of metal, in contrast to their other toys, which were usually made of clay. Speaking with satisfaction she remarks, "They lasted a long time." Such visits were rare, and a welcome diversion from their constant studies.

In 1948 Dagchen Kunga Rinchen went on pilgrimage to visit the holy Buddhist sites in India for four months.[323] He did not take any family members, but an entourage of about ten people accompanied him. Jetsun Kushok remembers that he brought back some clay toys that were figurines of Indian women working in the fields with animals.

Before leaving, Dagchen Kunga Rinchen (Fig. 16) asked Dezhung Rinpoche to remain in the study room adjacent to the future 41st Sakya Trizin's main practice room so as to perform rites to ensure the health and longevity of his children during his absence. Already one son had died, and Dezhung Rinpoche was acutely aware of his responsibility. He constantly worried about the health of the young future 41st Sakya Trizin. Every night he performed the rite of the protector (*bskang gso*). Every Monday, he performed cleansing and purification rituals (*khrus*). Every Friday, he gave the long-life empowerment (*tshe wang*) to the family. Each night before the children retired, they would receive his blessing. Usually they all climbed up onto his lap and played with one another there. Dezhung Rinpoche remained a total of eight months at the Dolma Palace.[324]

323. Jackson 2003, 167. There is no mention why Dagchen Kunga Rinchen went on pilgrimage to India. One reason may have been to generate more merit for his recently deceased wife.

324. See ibid., 168.

Fig. 16. Dagchen Kunga Rinchen in the courtyard of the
Dolma Palace, Sakya, in the late 1940s.

To add to Dezhung Rinpoche's concern for the children, Jetsun
Kushok suffered from a recurring nosebleed. The bleeding would stop
for a while and then start up again. Dezhung Rinpoche, Khen Jampal
Zangpo (the abbot of the South Monastery), and Dhihphu Choje Rinpoche together performed a very extensive Tara ritual to repel negative
forces (*sgrol ma gyul mdos*).³²⁵ Usually this ritual is regarded as highly
effective to remove any obstacles or illness. However, the nosebleed only
stopped completely when Jetsun Kushok's father returned from India

---

325. This elaborate ritual involves making a replica of the deity's palace using interwoven
threads stretched over wooden frames. This is known as a thread-cross (*mdo*), or sometimes,
in the U.S., a "God's eye." They chanted all day and most of the night. At the end of the ritual,
Dezhung Rinpoche, accompanied by other monks, carried off the *mdos* symbolic sacrifice.

and said to her, "Now you're okay. Go to bed." Jetsun Kushok remarks, "My father's return was the best medicine, and my nosebleed stopped." Dagchen Kunga Rinchen was extremely pleased with Dezhung Rinpoche and all the rituals he had performed on behalf of the family.[326]

1949 AND THE VAJRAKĪLAYA EMPOWERMENT

In mid-1949,[327] when Dezhung Rinpoche returned to Sakya, he formally requested that Dagchen Kunga Rinchen confer upon him the Vajrakīlaya empowerment in the Khon family lineage tradition, which began in the eighth century. The Sakya Khon family is considered so skilled in this practice that, once every generation, the Sakya Trizin would bestow it upon the reigning Dalai Lama.[328] Thus to receive it from the Khon family was a rare and precious opportunity not to be missed.[329]

Every male member of the Khon family must display his understanding and connection to Vajrakīlaya by performing many ceremonies and rituals. But one distinctive display is to perform specific dances in elaborate costumes during the annual ceremony to Vajrakīlaya. The other lamas judge how well the Khon family sons perform the dance, and infer the strength of the connection to Vajrakīlaya of each individual dancer. Thus each son's public performance is an indication of his spiritual acumen.[330]

Dagchen Kunga Rinchen not only agreed to give the empowerment, but also decided that since this would be the first time he gave it to his young son, he would give the most extensive version. Dezhung Rinpoche

326. See Jackson 2003, 168.

327. This was in the third lunar month; see ibid., 163.

328. Deshung Rinpoche 1995, 499 n. 16. See also ibid., xlvi: in the late 1940s, the 40th Sakya Trizin Thutop Wangchuk went to Lhasa to perform the ancient Vajrakīlaya rite to avert obstacles to the Dalai Lama's government.

329. This practice is not exclusive to the Sakya sect, but it is a major practice for the Khon family, which has maintained it since the eighth century. In addition, this lineage has been unbroken since the time of Padmasambhava and one of his main disciples, Khon Nagendra Raksita, right up until the present. Through the centuries, the unbroken series of Vajrakīlaya lineage-holders have all had very high realization. See more at http://hhsakya trizin.net/teaching-vajrakilaya/.

330. This tradition continues with the 41st Sakya Trizin's sons, the 42nd Sakya Trizin Ratna Vajra Rinpoche and the 43rd Sakya Trizin Gyana Vajra Rinpoche, as well as Jigdal Dagchen Sakya's grandsons, Dungsay Avikrita Vajra Rinpoche, Dungsay Asanga Vajra Rinpoche, and Dungsay Abhaya Vajra Rinpoche.

was delighted to receive this empowerment from one of his root teachers. The small group, which included Jetsun Kushok and a few visiting tulkus from Kham, received the first part of the empowerment for "upper activity" (the gaining of enlightenment) in the Big Glass-Window Room on the third floor of the Dolma Palace.

The second part of the empowerment is for "lower activity"(the violent "liberating" of enemies and obstacles).[331] Both Jetsun Kushok and the 41st Sakya Trizin remember it well. Though not yet four years old, the young future Sakya Trizin, sitting on the lap of a personal attendant, remembers very clearly when his father wore the wrathful costume, including the black hat of Vajrakīlaya, as he performed the ritual dance. "I even remember who played the musical instruments then," he said sixty-seven years later.[332] After receiving the consecration, the young 41st Sakya Trizin needed to study Cham, practice the precise steps, and learn the ritual well. Jetsun Kushok helped him; they did the Cham dances together.[333]

Shortly after the Vajrakīlaya empowerment, their aunt, Dagmo Trinlei Paljor, became gravely ill, and Dezhung Rinpoche was asked to perform the long-life empowerment in the tradition of Tangtong Gyalpo's *Glorious Giver of Immortality* ('*Chi med dpal ster*) a hundred times. Tangtong Gyalpo

---

331. Jackson 2003, 163. The dancer appears in a wrathful form to tame the "rough" minds of the audience who have the negative emotions of hatred, greed, and ignorance, which may be transformed into beneficial emotions of love, generosity, and wisdom.

332. See Tseten 2008, 32, and personal interview with H.H. the 41st Sakya Trizin at Walden, New York, on May 10, 2012.

333. Later, this practice proved fortuitous: in the very difficult year of 1959, when so many Tibetans were struggling as recent refugees in India, a Khampa lama by the name of Khardo Tulku told them that although his monastery had not performed the Cham dance in Tibet, he would offer his own wealth to sponsor it in India. This conversation occurred in the seventh month, when the rituals usually took place each year in Sakya. When Khardo Tulku heard this, he asked, "Why can't we perform it now?" The 41st Sakya Trizin reports that he himself, Jetsun Kushok, Khardo Tulku, and one older monk performed the ritual. Though there was no sand mandala, all the empowerments and visualized meditations were completely performed. See http://www.hhthesakyatrizin.org/teach_vajrakilaya.html.

(1385–1509) was a Renaissance man whose range of knowledge and abilities included being a great Buddhist adept, the creator of Tibetan opera, and a builder of iron bridges.[334] His long-life empowerment is very popular because it is believed that he lived more than 124 years.[335] While Dezhung Rinpoche was performing the empowerments, Dagmo Trinlei Paljor had a vision of Tangtong Gyalpo. She thought this was a good sign and she immediately offered new clothes for a statue of Tangtong Gyalpo in their home. She recovered quickly. Her husband was very pleased with Dezhung Rinpoche, saying, "Your prayers are very powerful. Now please perform the long-life empowerment a hundred times (*tshe dbang brgya rsta*) for me and my children." Dezhung Rinpoche gladly did so.[336]

After performing all these rituals for the aunt, Dezhung Rinpoche's leg troubles flared up. Jetsun Kushok remarked, "It was as if he had taken her sickness upon himself." In Buddhism, a person who is highly developed in compassion and concern for others can take on someone else's sickness. This practice of giving happiness to others and taking on someone else's suffering is known as *tonglen* (*gtong len*).

Having been of benefit to the Khon family, Dezhung Rinpoche requested the special empowerment of Marpo Korsum, the cycle of initiations into the extraordinary forms of red Ganapati, Takkiraja, and Kurukulle. Jetsun Kushok explains that the complete set of Marpo Korsum comprises a special, secret teaching. These are deities that increase one's power. This teaching was from the lineage of the Indian adept Indrabhuti to the Tibetan translator Bari Lotsawa. The transmission has a strong lineage within the Dolma Palace family.

The 39th Sakya Trizin, Dragshul Trinlei Rinchen, had given it to his son Dagchen Kunga Rinchen, who was now giving it to his own family. This is an extremely rare teaching, and few people receive it. Dagchen Kunga Rinchen said to Dezhung Rinpoche, "We have a close relationship, so I will give them to you." Only eleven people received this empowerment, including Dezhung Rinpoche, Dagmo Trinlei Paljor, Jetsun Kushok's younger sister Jamyang Bukhrid, and Khen Jampal Zangpo, the

---

334. For an excellent biography of Tangtong Gyalpo, see Stearns 2007; see also ibid., 28–30, for the history of the *Glorious Giver of Immortality* teachings.

335. Tangtong Gyalpo has many different dates for his life, such as 1361–1480, 1385–1509, and many more.

336. See Jackson 2003, 164.

abbot of the South Monastery.[337] Later, one of the deities in the Marpo Korsum, the goddess Kurukulle, became Dagmo Trinlei Paljor's main meditational deity, or *yidam*. Over her lifetime, she recited 20 million mantras of Kurukulle.[338]

Jetsun Kushok explains that they needed eleven people, and so she was invited to join.[339] But she refused because her brother was not receiving it and she wanted to receive the teachings together with her brother. The family asked her again, and she suggested that they ask her younger sister, Jamyang Bukhrid, who then did attend. In retrospect, Jetsun Kushok believes this was important for her sister, who died in 1950. Jetsun Kushok remarks, "Perhaps this was a premonition of her imminent death." She died when she was seven years old. Jetsun Kushok continues, "Both my name, which has six words [Chime Osel Bukhrid Rigzin Trinlei Wangmo], and H.H. Sakya Trizin's name, which has eight words [Ngawang Kunga Thegchen Palbar Trinlei Samphel Wangyi Gyalpo], are long names, whereas our sister and other brother had short names. Both died young."

THE BEGINNING OF JETSUN KUSHOK'S TEACHING CAREER

By the time Jetsun Kushok was eleven years old in 1949, she was considered proficient enough to be accepted as a spiritual teacher. She relates the following situation: In 1945, lightning damaged the southwest pillar of the Great Temple in Sakya.[340] Two floors were affected, with extensive damage to books and images, many of which had to be replaced or repaired. Also it was decided to repaint everything. The burden of collecting funds for these repairs and replacements was placed on the two Sakya Khon families—but especially on the Phuntsok Palace, since the

337. Ibid.

338. Though the proper Sanskrit noun is Kurukulla, Tibetans call her Kurukulle. This is the vocative form of her name, and since in her mantra she is called Kurukulle, Tibetans use this form, rather than the nominative Kurukulla. See http://www.rigpawiki.org/index .php?title=Kurukulla.

339. Jetsun Kushok said, "For initiations it is better to have an odd number, and eleven was an auspicious number." Also it is believed that having an odd number allows for an openness or a possibility of a continuation, whereas an even number is seen as a closed system that is already complete.

340. See Cassinelli and Ekvall 1969, 200 and 392.

ruling 40th Sakya Trizin Ngawang Thutop Wangchuk[341] belonged to the Phuntsok branch of the family.

First, the Khon family requested a 10,000 *dotse*[342] loan from the Tibetan government in Lhasa. This loan was given interest-free, and the families only had to pay back 700 *dotse* a year. The Tibetan government also appointed Lobsang Yarphel Pandatsang, a fourth-rank (*rim bzhi*) official, to help with the restoration.[343] He did not personally come to Sakya but sent his secretary, Dorje Gyalpo. However, more funds were still needed, so the 40th Sakya Trizin asked the Dolma Palace to help him raise the necessary funds.

Since the Dolma Palace did not have enough on hand, Jetsun Kushok's father sent her to the nomad areas north of Lhasa, near the Namtso Lake and the Ngachuka area, to seek donations. She received permission from the Sakya government to bestow long-life empowerments of Amitāyus with Hayagrīva. She explains that this empowerment is from the lineage of Padmasambhava (the great Indian master who introduced Buddhism to Tibet in the eighth century) to Tangtong Gyalpo (a great adept of longevity who lived more than a hundred years).[344] This is a very popular Sakya empowerment.

From the fourth to the tenth month of 1949, Jetsun Kushok traveled with her teacher Ponlop Kunga Gyaltsen, a manager, her personal attendants (a girl and a boy), an older monk, her oldest maternal aunt Jampal Yangkyi, a cook, three horsemen, and three men who took care of the yaks. In addition, there were five monks who performed the rituals and provided music: two double-reed horn (*gyaling*) players, two ceremonial

---

341. Ngag dbang mthu thub dbang phyug (40th Sakya Trizin from 1936–50).

342. One *dotse* (*rdo tshad*) is approximately 4 pounds of silver in bar form, and was the highest denomination of currency. Thus this was a significant amount of money.

343. Lobsang Yarphel Pangda Tsang [sic] (Yar 'phel spom mda' tshang, b. ca. 1898) is described as follows: "The richest of all Tibetan traders, and works as agent of the Tibetan Government in India. Has a branch at Kalimpong. His firm has agents throughout Tibet, China and India. . . . The family is from Kham. Promoted to the 4th rank and appointed Tibetan Trade Agent, Yatung, in November 1940. Speaks Hindustani and Chinese fluently. Appointed in September 1947, as the Commercial Adviser to the Tibetan Trade Mission to India, China, United Kingdom and the United States of America. Appointed Lay Leader of the Tibetan Trade Mission at Kalimpong in June, 1952." From http://tibet.prm.ox.ac.uk/biography_201 .html.

344. Both Padmasambhava and Tangtong Gyalpo (see notes 334 and 335 above) came to the area that was later known as Sakya.

horn players, and one drummer. The group also had a yak and a mule to carry the ritual instruments, tents, bedding, pots and pans, and a tea churn.[345] Jetsun Kushok conferred the long-life empowerments and also the Amitābha *phowa* practice transmission for transferring one's consciousness to the Pure Land at the time of death.[346] She explains that the nomads requested this teaching and that she gave them a brief teaching that took less than an hour.

Also she performed *torma* and incense offerings. In return, she received donations (*'bulwa sdud*, "donation gathering") of more than 1,000 *dotse* and many gifts, including yaks, sheep, horses, wool, and dairy products. Her father had told her, "Don't bring animals back to Sakya. Animals die when they are brought to a new area. So please sell the animals in the same area and bring back the money." Jetsun Kushok remarks, "Everything I collected, except for the share of a few servants, I gave for the repair of the Lhakhang Chenmo [the Great Temple]. I was proud of doing this—no money was wasted."

Another skill that Jetsun Kushok developed was photography (Figs. 17 and 18). One of her cousins in Gangtok, Sikkim, gave her a camera and developing chemicals.[347] He showed her how to take pictures and how to develop them. Many monks asked her to take their photos, so she did, and gave them the prints for free. She brought some of her negatives with her when she escaped to India, and eventually brought them to Canada, where she resides today.

JETSUN KUSHOK'S EARLY PRACTICE OF DIVINATION

Jetsun Kushok acquired many skills. Her aunt Dagmo Trinlei Paljor had encouraged her to learn how to do divinations using dice. In the Tibetan tradition there are numerous forms of divination; frequently a rosary or dice are used (see Chapter 4). In 1949, during her travels in the North-

345. Interview with H.E Jetsun Kushok at her home in Richmond, BC, Canada, in 2010.

346. *Phowa* is a special practice that is done when someone is definitely dying. At this point, just prior to death, a skilled practitioner can transfer the dying person's consciousness to a favorable rebirth, such as rebirth in the Pure Land of Amitābha Buddha.

347. See Jamyang Norbu, "Newspeak and New Tibet, Part 2, The Myth of China's Modernization of Tibet and Tibetan Language," Phayul.com, Friday, June 17, 2005, 23: 42. This article discusses the fascination of the upper class with photography, and how some became expert photographers.

Fig. 17. The young 41st Sakya Trizin in Yatung, Tibet, 1957. Photo by Jetsun Kushok.

Fig. 18. The Cham dances at the Dolma Palace, May 1957. Photo by Jetsun Kushok.

ern Plain (Changtang) to collect donations, one night she stopped at a small monastery by a mountain. Later that night, some monks arrived from one of the main monasteries of the Gelug sect—Sera Monastery, on the outskirts of Lhasa—and requested an audience immediately, despite how late it was. Jetsun Kushok remarks, "I was only spending the night here, so they probably worried that I might leave early the next morning and miss their chance to request a divination." They asked for a divination concerning the imprisonment of their abbot, Khardo Tulku Kelsang Thupten. In 1947, the former regent (r. 1933–41) of Tibet, Radreng (Reting) Rinpoche,[348] had been arrested and imprisoned under suspicion of plotting to poison the current Regent Taktra. Reting Rinpoche had died under mysterious circumstances. Since the monks' abbot Khardo Rinpoche had supported Reting Rinpoche, he, too, had been imprisoned, and his monks feared the worst. Her divination with dice recommended performing the ritual of the four-mandala puja of Green Tara and reciting the Praises to the Twenty-One Taras a hundred thousand times.

348. Gyaltsap Rinpoche, Regent (1911–47). Some selected portions from the introduction of *Who's Who in Tibet* 1915/38: "The Regent, Thupten Jampel Tishey Gyantsen, was born about 1911 and was discovered to be the fifth Incarnation of the head Lama of Reting Monastery. He studied in Sera monastery for his degree of Geshe. In 1934 after the death of the [13th] Dalai Lama he was appointed Regent. In 1933 he visited the Cho-Kor-Gye Lake in search of signs of the reincarnation of the Dalai Lama. During the stay of the British Mission at Lhasa in 1936–37 he expressed the wish to resign but appeared ready to postpone this action until the reincarnation of the Dalai Lama should be discovered. He subsequently resigned the Regency after the new reincarnation had been found. He is usually addressed as the Gyaltsap (Gyetsap) Rinpoche." From https://tibet.prm.ox.ac.uk/biography_291.html.

Two years later, in 1951, when she was in Lhasa, Jetsun Kushok recalls, "A group of monks requested an audience with me. They thanked me sincerely and profusely, and when I inquired the reason for this thanks, having forgotten about the incident and the divination, they told me that they had followed my instructions, and that their abbot had been released the day after they had completed the one-hundred-thousandth recitation of the Praises to the Twenty-One Taras." When the 14th Dalai Lama (b. 1935) assumed political power on November 17, 1950, he gave amnesty to all prisoners. Khardo Rinpoche had been released on that day.

Jetsun Kushok's skill as a prognosticator developed further over the years. One of her disciples, Thrinley DiMarco (1936–2020), who was the manager of Jetsun Kushok's retreat center Sakya Kachod Choling, in Friday Harbor, Washington, for 21 years, observed, "Jetsun Kushok did *mos* or divinations for people and they always turned out to be correct."[349] This is attested to by many of her students. Jetsun Kushok tells one very clearly whether one should proceed wholeheartedly, proceed with caution, or abandon a project one is thinking of undertaking.

THE DEATH OF DAGCHEN KUNGA RINCHEN

In 1950 there was an epidemic of influenza in the Sakya area. In a single day Dagchen Kunga Rinchen had to officiate at eleven funerals.[350] On the next day, he moved into his practice room and passed away. Jetsun Kushok remembers, "I was walking in the hallway near my father's room and heard someone crying in the distance. I sat by the steps and listened. I didn't know what happened. My tutor came very quietly and took me to my auntie's room and took me onto his lap. Then my auntie came in, she was crying and suddenly fainted. Her two servants didn't know what to do. I remembered that my auntie sometimes took medicine for wind imbalance (*rlung*), so I went to her medicine box and took out the right medicine—*agar 35*. I mixed the powdered medicine with butter, rubbed this mixture on her palms and soles. Then I put some more on the fire

---

349. Thrinley DiMarco email, December 28, 2018.

350. Jetsun Kushok remarked that after her father's death, the epidemic ceased; it was sad; he had foreseen the Chinese Communist invasion and did not want to live during this future period. Jackson 2003, 631 n. 684.

pot to create smoke. Then she woke up. This how I found out about our father's death. Father died at 49 years old in the second month, eighth day of iron tiger year. I remember clearly that it was in my thirteenth, bad year—[and] a tiger year."[351]

Less than a month before, on the twelfth day of the first month, Jetsun Kushok's young sister Jamyang had died of pneumonia. For a good rebirth it was advised to create a statue of four-armed Avalokiteśvara, which was put in Jetsun Kushok's practice room. Later that same year, on the twentieth day of the sixth month (June 28), the 40th Sakya Trizin, Ngawang Thuthob Wangchuk from the Phuntsok Phodrang, died.

As soon as Dagmo Trinlei Paljor's older sister Jampal Yangkyi heard that Dagchen Kunga Rinchen had died, she came from Lhasa to console and help her younger sister. Since she was not a member of the Khon family, she was not consulted in making decisions. However, she provided good company; the two sisters would chat and relax together. She stayed for a long time. Also Jetsunma Chime Wangmo (Jetsun Kushok's paternal aunt) helped Dagmo Trinlei Paljor in making important decisions. Though she was very quiet, she was very knowledgeable in both spiritual and poitical matters.

While suffering extreme grief, the family had to handle all the funeral arrangements. Dagmo Trinlei Paljor, with the advice of Khen Jampal Zangpo (abbot of the South Monastery), was in charge of all the rituals, the offerings, the cremation, and the preservation of her husband's relics.[352]

Furthermore, she had the arduous responsibility of making certain that the best available lamas were properly training the five-year-old

351. According to popular belief, certain years are dangerous for a person, especially the year of one's birth sign. Jetsun Kushok and her father were both born in tiger years: her father in 1902 (wood tiger) and she in 1938 (earth tiger). One's 48th year, when her father died, is a dangerous year, as is one's 72nd year (Jetsun Kushok had a stroke during that year).

352. In the Khon families, the death of any son is treated with extensive rituals and a specific kind of cremation. As for most Tibetans, there is a concentration of prayers and offerings for forty-nine days. In Sakya, most people were cremated, unlike other areas of Tibet where cremation was too costly due to lack of available wood. Later a 10-foot-high, very ornate gilded stupa was made to enclose the relics of Dagchen Kunga Rinchen, which was located in the Great Temple, specifically in the Dolma Palace family shrine where stupas of other family members are located. For a classic article on this topic, see Turrell Wylie, "Mortuary Customs at Sa-skya, Tibet," *Harvard Journal of Asiatic Studies*, vol. 25 (1964–65): 229–42. See also Cassinelli and Ekvall 1969, 194.

future 41st Sakya Trizin and twelve-year-old Jetsun Kushok. In the Khon families, the father or uncle was often the children's main lama, but with the death of both the uncle and the father in this case, another lama had to be found. With the help of Khen Jampal Zangpo, the spiritual advisor to the Khon family, Dagmo Trinlei Paljor made certain that Jetsun Kushok and her brother would receive all the important teachings and necessary transmissions to maintain and preserve the Sakya tradition.

The 41st Sakya Trizin stresses that the timing was crucial because some of these great lamas died within a few years of his father's death, and later there was so much turmoil it would have been impossible to receive the teachings and transmissions. Thus it was with great foresight and excellent timing that Dagmo Trinlei Paljor fulfilled this responsibility. He emphasizes that his aunt did this despite all the difficulties she encountered in her own life.

The most important teaching in the Sakya tradition is the Path with the Result (see Chapter 1). It is imperative that all Khon family members receive this teaching early in their youth, and preferably from a lama who is considered to be an important lineage-holder of these teachings. At the time, one of the most renowned lamas in Tibet was Jamyang Khyentse Chokyi Lodro Rinpoche (1893–1959), who was residing in Kham.[353] Though he was the best-qualified teacher, Dagmo Trinlei Paljor and her advisors deemed Kham too far away and dangerous since the Communist Chinese were encroaching slowly from the east in China into Kham. It would be safer if the children stayed in the Tsang area where Sakya and Ngor monasteries are located. Some felt that the future 41st Sakya Trizin should remain in Sakya, but Dagmo Trinlei Paljor felt that one of the best teachers was at Ngor Monastery, which was less than a day away by horseback. Thus, despite protests in the Sakya community, in the autumn of 1950 she brought Jetsun Kushok and her brother to Ngor to study under the great Khangsar abbot known as Dampa Rinpoche (1876–1953; Fig. 19).

Dampa Rinpoche (whose full name was Ngawang Lodro Shenpen Nyingpo) is remembered as one of the greatest Sakya and *rime* lamas of his era. He was a very diligent and dedicated student in his youth. As a teen-

353. Although Jetsun Kushok and the 41st Sakya Trizin did not receive the Path with the Result from Jamyang Khyentse Chokyi Lodro, in the mid-1950s they were fortunate to receive other major teachings from him belonging to both the Sakya and Nyingma traditions.

Fig. 19. Ven. Dampa Rinpoche in tantric regalia.

ager, he went to Kham and met a lama who had profound understanding of the Dharma. This teacher was Khenpo Shenga (Shenpen Chokyi Nyima Nangwa, 1871–1927). His explications of texts were renowned, and he used the profound verses of a text as a way to introduce students to the nature of mind.[354] One of Khenpo Shenga's poems of insight is: "When the notions of real and unreal are absent from the mind, there is no other possibility but to rest in total peace, beyond concepts."[355]

As soon as Dampa Rinpoche encountered Khenpo Shenga, he knew that he must become his disciple and learn as much as possible. Khenpo

354. Jackson 2020, 39.

355. https://www.rigpawiki.org/index.php?title=Khenpo_Shenga.

Shenga observed Dampa Rinpoche's great diligence in staying up most of the night studying, in addition to his other good qualities, and once remarked, "He is not an ordinary person. He's a superior being (*skyes bu dam pa*)." Coming from Khenpo Shenga, who also persevered under difficult circumstances and was regarded by his own teacher as an indefatigable student, this was much more than a mere compliment. Thus Dampa (Superior) Rinpoche received this title as a teenager and was called by this title throughout his life.[356] As an example of his dedication, every day Dampa Rinpoche offered a hundred butterlamps and 25 recitations of the Praises to the Twenty-One Taras without interruption. He gave away all his goods and wealth to religious institutions.[357]

When Dampa Rinpoche conferred the esoteric Path with the Result teachings on them, the 41st Sakya Trizin remembered, "Khangsar Abbot [i.e., Dampa Rinpoche] was a very holy, very spiritually advanced lama, always very calm, very slow in movement and he did everything perfectly."[358] The young Jetsun Kushok and future Sakya Trizin did not receive the regular annual public teachings of the Path with the Result in Ngor Monastery but were given special teachings in the abbot's room. Only thirty people received these. They stayed for four months at Ngor.

Jetsun Kushok elaborates that the rules of Ngor Monastery are very strict concerning women visitors. Ngor has four residences (*labrangs*) for the abbots, and each is associated with either a reincarnation or a family lineage: Khangsar, Luding, Phende, and Thartse. The Phende and Thartse Labrangs have reincarnation lineages, and women can visit only during the day, but not overnight. The lamas in Luding Labrang are born

356. Jackson 2020, 39.

357. Ibid., 38–44. Some of Dampa Rinpoche's achievements included receiving the *Compendium of Tantras* from Jamyang Loter Wangpo in Kham in 1909. He also received the Path with the Result and Kalachakra. Returning from Kham, he became the 65th Ngor abbot and stayed primarily in Tsang for the remainder of his life. He gave many teachings innumerable times, including the Path with the Result, the *Compendium of Sādhanas*, and, perhaps more importantly, the *Compendium of Tantras*. Later, the incomparable Chogye Trichen (one of the root gurus of the 41st Sakya Trizin) would credit Dampa Rinpoche with saving the *Compendium of Tantras* from extinction. It was due to Dampa Rinpoche's diligence that significant lamas received it. He had many students, including many from the Dolma Palace: Jetsun Kushok's grandfather Dragshul Trinlei Rinchen, father, uncle, and also Jetsun Kushok and the 41st Sakya Trizin themselves, both of whom consider Dampa Rinpoche to be one of their root gurus.

358. Tseten 2008, 33.

into a family lineage, so they are more accepting of women relatives visiting. Eventually Jetsun Kushok married into the Luding family, and one of her sons has become part of the Luding lineage at Ngor Monastery in India. But as a young girl, she stayed at Khangsar Labrang because she was receiving the Path with the Result from the abbot of Khangsar.

Jetsun Kushok remembers that Khangsar Labrang included a separate two-story house near the labrang. The Sakya family stayed on the second floor of this house. Typical of many Tibetan houses, domestic animals, such as cows, goats, and sheep, were kept at night on the ground level. In this house only dairy cows were kept on the ground floor. Khangsar Labrang was farther from the center of Ngor Monastery than the other three labrangs. The place in Ngor with the strictest rules was the Ngor Lhakhang, or the main temple of the monastery, which women were forbidden to enter. Jetsun Kushok emphasizes, "It did not matter if you were a Sakya jetsunma or not, no women were allowed."

CONFIRMATION OF THE 41ST SAKYA TRIZIN

The year 1950 was a time of tremendous turmoil for both the Dolma Palace and Phuntsok Palace because the father of each palace had passed away. Jetsun Kushok remembers that, after the death of her father Dagchen Kunga Rinchen, "Some people were trying to take some of the Dolma Phodrang's land away from us. My aunt felt that we needed help from the [Central] Tibetan Government to intervene and protect this land. Also she knew that she needed to ask the [powerful] Pandatsang family and Jamyangkyi family as supporters ('tsho 'dzin) to plead our case to the government."[359] Thus it was decided that the family would go to Lhasa.

In Sakya, after the death of the 40th Sakya Trizin of the Phuntsok Palace, it was unclear who should be the successor because of the recent death of Jetsun Kushok's father of the Dolma Palace. Jetsun Kushok explained, "[The succession] alternates between the two palaces. After the Sakya Trizin from one palace passes on, the throne will go to the other palace. Then among the sons of the palace ascending the throne, it is the oldest son who will become the Sakya Trizin."[360] According to this

359. Jetsun Kushok email, August 12, 2020.
360. Ibid.

rule, Jetsun Kushok's younger brother would become the Sakya Trizin. However, the leaders of the Phuntsok Palace assumed that their oldest son, Jigdal Dagchen Sakya (1929–2016), would become the 41st Sakya Trizin since he was already old enough to rule, whereas the son of the Dolma Palace was only five years old. While the Dolma Palace family was in Lhasa awaiting a reply to their request to settle the land dispute, Jetsun Kushok recalls,

> The Sakya Government had sent a letter to Lhasa to inform the [Central] Tibetan Government that the Sakya Trizin has been chosen and that it was Dagchen Jigdal Rinpoche. However, Trinly Rinpoche, Dagchen Jigdal Sakya Rinpoche's younger brother, disputed the decision. Somehow, Dolma Phodrang's name was mentioned in this case and it was sent to H.H. the Dalai Lama. He inquired about it, asking "Why are there only two dungsays presented?" when he heard that there were three dungsays in Sakya. His Holiness' name [Jetsun Kushok's younger brother] was then given to the Dalai Lama. Upon doing a divination on the three dungsays, the Dalai Lama said his divination indicated that His Holiness would be the best choice for Sakyapas. That was how His Holiness was selected to be the 41st Sakya Trizin.[361]

Though Jigdal Dagchen Sakya did not become the Sakya Trizin, his marriage to Dagmo Jamyang Sakya thrived for more than sixty years, until his death in 2016.[362] Both he and Dagmo Jamyang Sakya became outstanding teachers worldwide.

Still, there was opposition. Some were perplexed as to why such a young boy would be given the throne when Jigdal Dagchen Sakya, who was 21 years old, was not being considered. Others who supported the five-year-old candidate wondered if such a young boy could manage the position. Jetsun Kushok recalls that the 14th Dalai Lama—himself still a teenager—said, "When I was young, my helpers helped me, so Gongma

361. Ibid.
362. See Sakya and Emery 1990. Jigdal Dagchen Sakya Rinpoche died April 29, 2016 in Seattle, Washington.

Rinpoche[363] [her little brother, the future 41st Sakya Trizin] must have people who will help him until he can manage on his own. It will be fine."

The family and its entourage had taken the northern route to Lhasa. They stayed at the residence in Lhasa belonging to Dagmo Trinlei Paljor's late brother Kalon Bonshod. It was empty because his wife and mother had also passed away. Only some servants and a few renters occupied the large mansion. The Khon family stayed there for two or three months. High-ranking Chinese officials were making their presence known in Lhasa for the first time. To ingratiate themselves to the Tibetan noble families, these officials rented noble families' residences in Lhasa at a good rate. Since the Bonshod residence no longer had family members residing there permanently, it was rented to the Chinese within a few months of the family's arrival in Lhasa, so they moved to the famous temple and tantric college of Ramoche, where they had a maternal uncle from the Changra family (Dagmo Trinlei Paljor's mother was from the Changra family). They stayed in his home. It was more convenient, too, since it was more centrally located than the Bonshod residence.

The year 1951 was a difficult one for Tibetans because China, which prior to October 1, 1949 had been in the midst of a civil war, was now governed by the People's Republic of China and sought to incorporate Tibet. In Chinese, Tibet is known as Xizang; some translate this as the Western Treasure House. The Chinese coveted the abundant natural resources of Tibet, including forests, minerals, and, most importantly, the five major rivers that provide invaluable resources to most of Asia: the Indus River in Pakistan, the Brahmaputra River in India, the Salween River in Myanmar, the Yangtze River in China, and the mighty Mekong River, which flows through Thailand, Laos, Cambodia and Vietnam. Any country that can control all these rivers controls the continent of Asia.

By late 1950, the Chinese had taken over parts of eastern Tibet and had their sights set on Lhasa, the capital. The situation was so critical that the Tibetan government decided to immediately invest the fifteen-year-old Dalai Lama as their political as well as religious leader. Thus on November 17, 1950, the 14th Dalai Lama became the political leader of Tibet. However, under the threat of a Chinese invasion, on December 16, 1950, the 14th Dalai Lama and major cabinet members secretly left Lhasa and

363. Tibetans use the title Gongma (Superior One) or Kyabgon (One Who Protects) for the Sakya Trizin. See Appendix C.

set up a temporary government in Dromo (Fig. 20), close to the border of Sikkim. This was a safety measure in case the young Dalai Lama had to flee to India for protection.

The Tibetan government further decided to send a group of delegates to Beijing in hopes of ameliorating the situation. But this move resulted in the first of many defeats for the Tibetans. Under duress, the Tibetan delegates were forced to sign the infamous Seventeen-Point Agreement on May 23, 1951, which basically surrendered all control of Tibet to the Chinese. The first point is: "The Tibetan people shall be united and drive out the imperialist aggressive forces from Tibet; that the Tibetan people shall return to the big family of the motherland—the People's Republic of China."[364]

When the young Dalai Lama heard this distressing news being broadcast by Radio Beijing, he nearly fainted. He could not believe that his delegates had signed such an agreement without consulting him. Some of his advisors suggested that he flee Tibet and seek help from the newly formed United Nations. Though Tibetans did seek international help, few countries cared about their plight.[365] In the end, the 14th Dalai Lama decided to return to Lhasa, arriving there on August 17, 1951.

The 41st Sakya Trizin remembers this day well. His family and entourage had arrived in Lhasa few days earlier, and they were told that the Dalai Lama's return was imminent. "Though I was only six years old, the Dalai Lama's arrival was impressive. For miles and miles, beautifully decorated horsemen waited on both sides to greet the Dalai Lama, who was carried in a golden palanquin with bright yellow curtains in the middle of the road. Of course, I did not see him, but I will always remember the Tibetan people welcoming him home." Later, the 41st Sakya Trizin did have an audience with the Dalai Lama. He remarks that his aunt, as well as the rest of his family, had great faith in the young Dalai Lama.

The 41st Sakya Trizin and Jetsun Kushok also attended an empowerment and teachngs on four-armed Avalokiteśvara given by the Dalai

---

364. http://www.tibetjustice.org/materials/china/china3.html.

365. The first resolution on October 21, 1959: Ireland and Malaya requested consideration of "The Question of Tibet" in the UN General Assembly. Resolution 1353 (XIV) was adopted by a vote of 45 to 9, with 26 abstentions. Again on December 20, 1961 Malaya, Thailand, Ireland, and El Salvador requested a second consideration of "The Question of Tibet" in the UN General Assembly. Resolution 1723 (XVI) was adopted by the General Assembly by a vote of 56 to 11, with 29 abstentions.

Fig. 20. H.H. the 14th Dalai Lama in Dromo, Tibet, 1951.

Lama at the Norbulingka, his summer garden estate. Thirty-six tulkus[366] were given the special honor of being seated on the stage near the Dalai Lama. Each tulku had a table with his name on it. Jetsun Kushok smiles mischievously as she admits,

> I enjoyed acting like a male and wearing robes of a Sakya monk. Although I had strict rules to follow as a jetsunma, I wanted to wear men's clothing. My aunt was not pleased but she did not say much. Only my close family knew that I had disguised myself as a monk. Even people in Sakya thought I was a monk since I acted like a boy. In Lhasa, the Tibetan government thought that I was the Sakya son who was a monk and my brother was the son who was a householder.

She reiterates, "People thought that I was a tulku; that I was a monk-dungsay. Everyone called me 'Rinpoche' and I was put in the tulku section. My name card on the table read 'Sakya Dungsay.'"[367]

366. *Tulku*, "recognized reincarnation," literally means "emanation body," but it refers to people who have the ability and deep-rooted concern to return to the world to help others.

367. Though Jetsun Kushok did not explicitly say so, one can surmise that being considered a Khon son was more prestigious than being a Khon daughter.

The 41st Sakya Trizin remembers that he, too, was in the front. He was one of the few who threw the flower stick[368] (one of the rituals during the empowerment) and received a blessing directly from the Dalai Lama. As he was receiving the blessing, he turned his head away from the Dalai Lama to get a better view of the large microphone. It was the first time that he had ever seen one. The 41st Sakya Trizin chuckles, "Since I was a young child, I was very interested in the large microphone."

Though the Chinese were not invited, they insisted on attending the ceremonies and were filming everything with big movie cameras. The Tibetans were not pleased. At the end of the first day of the empowerment, everyone was given two pieces of kusha grass to be put under their bedding in order to promote prophetic dreams, which would be interpreted on the second day of the empowerment. The 41st Sakya Trizin recalls, "So many people attended and each was holding stalks of kusha grass.[369] It felt like I was in a field."

During their four months in Lhasa, the family took the opportunity to visit many temples and monasteries in the city and its environs, including the more distant Sakya Phenpo Nalendra Monastery and the ancient Samye Monastery, the first monastery established in Tibet in the eighth century. On their way home, they stopped to see relatives. One such relative was Lama Kunga (Ngor) Thartse Rinpoche (b. 1935), a great lama who is the reincarnation of Sevan Repa, a heart disciple of the renowned yogi Milarepa. He presently lives in Kensington, California, and remembers: "When H.H. Sakya Trizin was six years old, the Khon family was returning home from Lhasa. My father invited them to visit us at our estate—Gushi Peling Estate in Nar Village, near Shigaste. My father was born on this estate in 1904.[370] I remember that I met the entire family and

368. In two-day empowerments, one of the rituals is throwing the flower stick on a mandala of the five Buddhas and recording the Buddha on which it lands. This indicates some propensity with this Buddha. For example, if the flower lands on Akshobhaya Buddha (the Immutable One), this indicates that one will develop mirror-like wisdom.

369. Kusha grass is a common Indian grass used to make meditation mats by yogis; so in Tibetan Buddhism it is associated with spiritual endeavor and practice. For the empowerment, one puts it under one's bedding to evoke propitious dreams, which may indicate one's affinity with the deity and the practice of the empowerment.

370. Nar Village is one day by horse from Ngor Monastery. For the life story of Lama Kunga's father, see Summer Carnahan with Lama Kunga Rinpoche, *In the Presence of My Enemies* (Santa Fe, NM: Clear Light Publications, 1995).

Ngawang Lodro Rinpoche [Ngaklo Rinpoche] during their visit." Lama
Kunga continues:

> H.H. Sakya Trizin was very playful and enjoyed playing as if he
> were performing a ritual dance. I think that their aunt Dagmo
> Trinlei Paljor Zangmo was about 45 years old. I was 16 years
> old. I was nervous in her presence because she had the reputa-
> tion of being authoritarian and strict. I wanted to do the right
> thing in front of her. I wanted to do prostrations to H.H. Sakya
> Trizin and to the aunt. When I began to do prostrations to her,
> she scolded me and said, "Don't be silly, don't do prostrations
> to me." Though I was apprehensive, the aunt treated me very
> well. She said that she loved me, cared about me, and wanted
> me to behave well and study hard. I felt that she did care about
> me.[371]

Dagmo Trinlei Paljor was also an aunt on Lama Kunga's mother's side of
the family.[372]

The family stayed for a few days. The Khon family gave some blessings, but it was mostly a social visit. Lama Kunga was happy that the
family had come to visit. Today Jetsun Kushok and Lama Kunga have a
very amiable relationship and enjoy visiting each other in California and
Canada. Their conversations range from memories of Tibet and India
to esoteric explanations of particular spiritual practices. In 1953, one of
his older brothers, the Ngor Khangsar abbot Ngawang Lodro Tenzin
Nyingpo (1929–ca. 1956),[373] would teach the esoteric Path with the Result
to both Jetsun Kushok and the 41st Sakya Trizin at Ngor Monastery.

Throughout their travels and after returning to Sakya, though the
future 41st Sakya Trizin was only six years old, he felt much pressure
because he had to memorize one of the principal texts for the Sakyas,
the long Hevajra Root Tantra, which is about 60 folios long. Whether
or not they were traveling, he had to keep memorizing the text. Later, in
Sakya, in early 1952, he was enthroned as the Sakya Trizin designate. (He

371. Interview with Lama Kunga Rinpoche in Walden, New York, June 21, 2011.

372. Jetsun Kushok explained that she is related on both sides to Lama Kunga. His paternal
grandfather and Jetsun's paternal grandmother were brother and sister. Also Lama Kunga's
maternal grandmother and Jetsun's maternal grandmother were sisters.

373. See Fig. 21 and note 385 below.

was still too young to be enthroned as the actual Sakya Trizin.) In this first ceremony, he had to prove that he had the ability to memorize the Hevajra Root Tantra; this was required of all Sakya monks. He remarks, "I am glad to say that I passed by reciting it correctly."[374] Of course, this remark is a modest one because for many people, Sakya Trizin is considered to be an emanation of the Bodhisattva of Wisdom, Mañjuśrī. From a very young age, he has impressed people with his capacity to understand quickly and thoroughly. As he matured, his reputation has grown as an extraordinary teacher who can explain esoteric and philosophical subjects with acuity and clarity.

The 41st Sakya Trizin elaborates that only the Dalai Lama, as head of the Central Tibetan Government in Lhasa, has the authority to recognize the Sakya Trizin. The Sakya government cannot do this. It is the Dalai Lama who confers the title and position. First, the Central Tibetan Government provides a formal letter conferring this position on the person who has been selected. When he visited Lhasa in 1951 as a six-year-old, he received such a letter, and after returning to Sakya, there was a public ceremony to confirm this recognition. On the day of the public ceremony, he touched the letter to his head to show respect to the Dalai Lama and his authority. He then gave the letter to Sakya Shape, the head of the Sakya government, who read it in front of a public assembly, thereby confirming the Dalai Lama's approval of the next Sakya Trizin. The actual enthronement was held in early 1959.

Since the Dolma Palace's son had been selected as the next Sakya Trizin, the family had the privilege of moving from their summer home, the Dolma Palace, to the winter home of Sakya Trizins in the Zhitog building.[375] Zhitog had five floors. Jetsun Kushok explains, "For most of my childhood, we did not live in Zhitog since my father was not Sakya Trizin. Only when my brother was selected as Sakya Trizin did the family move to Zhitog for the winter." She continues, "On the top floor was H.H. Sakya Trizin's main room, which was known as the Golden Window Room because the window was decorated with gold." This room served as a reception room where guests and dignitaries were received. Jetsun Kushok states, "We all slept together—His Holiness, my aunt, and I—in the room next to the Golden Window room, which was much smaller.

374. Tseten 2008, 33.

375. In the word Zhitog, *gzhi* = "base," not "four."

Some other rooms were very big, but mostly empty. On the third floor was a Vajrayana room where empowerments were bestowed. The Sakya government owned other rooms on various floors, and their offices were on one side of the second or third floor. On the third floor were shrine rooms, including one large shrine room dedicated to Vajrayoginī. The second floor was the kitchen and a monks' residence. On the ground floor was a small prison."

Throughout these years and events, both Jetsun Kushok and the newly designated 41st Sakya Trizin continued their studies and their practices, which trumped all other activities. One is reminded that the Khon family is foremost a spiritual family.

1952

At the age of seven—when other children are playing with toys and amusing themselves with games—the newly designated Sakya Trizin was being trained in both spiritual and political matters. In the summer of 1952 (the fifth month), he went to Tashilhunpo Monastery, the seat of the Panchen Lama, in the city of Shigatse, Tsang Province, to attend the enthronement of the 10th Panchen Lama.[376] This was the first time he traveled with all the pomp and accoutrements of a recognized Sakya Trizin. Jetsun Kushok, Dagmo Trinlei Paljor, and his entourage accompanied him.

The Panchen Lama and the Dalai Lama have a special relationship. The title Panchen combines the Sanskrit *pan* (an abbreviation of *pandita*, meaning "scholar") and the Tibetan *chen* ("great"). Thus Panchen Lamas are known to be great scholars, and for many centuries they were teachers to the Dalai Lamas. The Panchen Lama is considered to be an emanation of Amitābha Buddha, the Buddha of Boundless Life, and the Dalai Lama is regarded as an emanation of Avalokiteśvara, the Bodhisattva of Compassion. In Mahayana Buddhist iconography, Amitābha Buddha sits atop Avalokiteśvara's head, thereby protecting him. Hence the Panchen Lama has a unique position with respect to the Dalai Lama.

Though it seems that the Panchen Lamas and the Dalai Lamas had amicable relationships, strife existed occasionally between the adminis-

---

376. Isabel Hilton, *The Search for the Panchen Lama* (New York: W.W. Norton and Company, 1999), 84.

tration of Shigatse, the seat of the Panchen Lama, and the government in Lhasa, the seat of the Dalai Lama. The 9th Panchen Lama (1883–1937) fled to China in 1923 due to disagreements with the Central Tibetan Government over taxation and other matters. He only returned as his new reincarnation, the 10th Panchen Lama (1938–89), when he was fifteen years old. With the Panchen Lama living outside Tibet for 29 years, it was a long-awaited homecoming for his devoted followers and for the monks of his main monastery. The 10th Panchen Lama arrived at Tashilhunpo Monastery on June 23, 1952, with much ceremonial pageantry.

However, his return was not without controversy, because numerous Chinese officials and a contingent of Chinese troops accompanied him. This did not seem to have an effect on the enthronement of the Panchen Lama, nor on his guests of honor, but it did make an impression on the seven-year-old Sakya Trizin, who likewise had to juggle the responsibilities of both the political and religious aspects of being the Sakya Trizin.

From 1952 until the present, some Tibetans have doubted the loyalty of the 10th Panchen Lama. When many Tibetans sought exile in 1959 and the early 1960s, he remained in Tibet. Within a few years, he became a prisoner of the Chinese government and lived in Beijing under house arrest. He was forced to disrobe, marry, and serve as the "puppet spokesperson" for Tibet in China. He did try to help the Tibetan people, but he was extremely constrained by his house arrest and under constant surveillance by the Chinese government. Allowed to return to Tashilhunpo Monastery on January 28, 1989, he died under mysterious circumstances. Many think that a Chinese official poisoned him.

The 11th Panchen Lama, Gendun Chokyi Nyima, was born on April 25, 1989, and on May 14, 1995, the 14th Dalai Lama recognized the new reincarnation. But on May 17, 1995, the Chinese government kidnapped the young boy of six from his home in Tibet. He disappeared, and no one knows whether he is still alive. The Chinese government has selected their own 11th Panchen Lama who serves as their spokesperson; but Tibetans do not accept him as the true reincarnation of the 10th Panchen Lama. The fate of the institution of the Panchen Lama is in jeopardy.

Late Summer/Autumn 1952 and Winter 1953

Their teachers told both the 41st Sakya Trizin and Jetsun Kushok that it was imperative to continue their Path with the Result teachings with the

abbot of Ngor Khangsar, Dampa Rinpoche, so they returned to Ngor
Monastery to continue their studies of the exoteric and the esoteric Path
with the Result. They began their studies and practices of the esoteric
teachings on the twenty-fifth day of the sixth month of 1952. They had
many breaks before completing them on the auspicious Dharmacakra
Day of the fourth day in the sixth month of 1953.[377] They also received
other important teachings, including commentary and explanations
about Vajrayoginī and the teaching on *Parting from the Four Attachments*
(see Chapter 1) by Sachen Kunga Nyingpo. In addition, from the abbot of
Ngor Phende Labrang, Ngawang Khedrup Gyatso (1917–69),[378] considered
to be one of the greatest disciples of Dampa Rinpoche, they received the
biography of Ngorchen Kunchok Lhundrup (1494–1557),[379] the 10th abbot
of Ngor Monastery. Known as a great Path with Result practitioner, he
gave the Path with the Result more than 35 times in his life. In addition,
he wrote a commentary on it that emphasizes the key tenet of the non-
differentiated view of liberation and cyclic existence (see Chapter 1).[380]
His biography would have inspired both the 41st Sakya Trizin and Jetsun
Kushok in their practice of these teachings.

They studied at Ngor for a year, until the Chinese asked the young
Sakya Trizin to attend talks at Sakya.[381] Though there were such occa-
sional interruptions by the Chinese government insisting that Sakya
Trizin or a member of the Khon family attend political meetings, Sakya

377. H.H. the 41st Sakya Trizin email, December 8, 2018. His Holiness explained that they
were unable to complete the esoteric Path with the Result with Dampa Rinpoche because
he passed away. Khangsar Shabdrung (see Fig. 21 below), who was Dampa Rinpoche's main
disciple, completed it. He was Lama Kunga Rinpoche's older brother. Dharmacakra Day is
celebrated annually to commemorate the first sermon of the Historical Buddha after his
enlightenment.

378. Ngawang Khedrup Gyatso died in Rajpur, India, in 1969 or 1970. He was abbot from 1948
to 1951. See Jackson 2020, 121.

379. See the short biography of Ngorchen Kunchok Lhundrup at http://rywiki.tsadra.org
/index.php/Ngorchen_Konchog_Lhundrup.

380. See Deshung Rinpoche 1995.

381. The Chinese government was slowly asserting its authority in Tibet. It employed differ-
ent techniques to influence the Tibetan people in accepting its legitimacy to control Tibet.
One technique was to insist that Tibetan leaders become spokesmen for the Chinese. In the
Sakya area, where the Khon family enjoyed enormous respect and Tibetans trusted them,
the Chinese compelled both the Phuntsok Palace Dagchen Rinpoche and the Dolma Palace
Sakya Trizin to attend meetings where they were told what to say to the Tibetan people. The
Tibetans considered this to be complete coercion by the Chinese officials.

Trizin and Jetsun Kushok concentrated on their studies. The Tibetan author Dawa Norbu (1949–2006), who grew up in Sakya during this time, writes in his book *Red Star Over Tibet*, "Ten strange-looking khaki-clad horsemen rode past in a line. They certainly were not Tibetans: they were Chinese."[382] He continues to relate an amusing incident: Some Tibetans were carrying manure when they met the Chinese near the Dolma Palace. Immediately they started clapping their hands. Very pleased because they felt that the Tibetans were welcoming them, the Chinese joined the Tibetans in clapping. Unbeknownst to the Chinese, however, Tibetans clap to expel enemies.[383]

Despite these interruptions, Dagmo Trinlei Paljor never forgot her main task of securing a proper religious education for her nephew and niece. Jetsun Kushok has frequently echoed the words that the 41st Sakya Trizin spoke at their beloved aunt's funeral ceremonies in India in 1975: "Starting from learning the alphabet to receiving the ocean of profound and extensive Dharma teachings from the masters who are Buddhas in human form and acquiring the ability to be a part of the group of those noble people, was all the result of the great kindness of my late Aunt."[384]

Sadly, Dampa Rinpoche passed away in his room on the twelfth day of the holy fourth lunar month of 1953.[385] His successor as abbot of Ngor Khangsar (Shabdrung) was Ngawang Lodro Tenzin Nyingpo (1929–ca. 1956; Fig. 21).[386] The 41st Sakya Trizin emphasized that Ven. Khangsar Shabdrung was the heart son of Dampa Rinpoche. He was deeply attached to his lama, who had recently passed away. At the beginning of the Path with the Result empowerment, one recited the guru transmission lineage. "When the time came to recite Dampa Rinpoche's name, he couldn't say his name without choking and breaking into tears, and he cried for a long time," said the 41st Sakya Trizin.[387]

382. Norbu 1974, 107.

383. Ibid.

384. Ratna Vajra Sakya et al. 2003, 31.

385. The fourth lunar month is known as Sakadawa, the Buddha (*Saka*) month (*dawa*). See note 194 above.

386. Ngawang Lodro Tenzin Nyingpo (also known as Yeshe Tenzin) was one of the older brothers of Lama Kunga Thartse Rinpoche. See Carnahan with Lama Kunga Rinpoche 1995, 80. On this page is a list of Shuguba's sons and daughters.

387. H.H. the 41st Sakya Trizin email, December 13, 2018.

Fig. 21. Ven. Khangsar Shabdrung.

LATE 1953

Having received the main transmissions of the Path with the Result and the entire requisite accompanying teachings, the 41st Sakya Trizin and Jetsun Kushok were ready to undertake the required long retreat of Hevajra and his female counterpart, Nairatmya. Jetsun Kushok was 15 years old when the retreat began in the end of the seventh lunar month of 1953. They performed the retreat in their own practice rooms in the

Dolma Palace, having decided that they would begin and end the retreat on the same days. The retreat involved the chanting and visualizations of the Hevajra sādhana during four sessions each day, as well as completing the required recitations of the mantras of Hevajra and Nairatmya.

The 41st Sakya Trizin relates that during the retreat their teacher Kunga Tsewang, who guided them both and was the chanting master (*dbu mdzad*) of the Northern Monastery, was very strict and only allowed them to see their aunt and two servants. Though he and Jetsun Kushok did not see each other, they were able to pass notes via the servants. They did encounter some difficulties because their teacher was very ill for the first half of the retreat. Both the 41st Sakya Trizin and Jetsun Kushok were in good health, but their teacher could not guide them as well as he had hoped. Fortunately, the retreat ended successfully, and eventually their teacher recovered his health completely.[388] To perform all the obligations, they stayed in retreat for seven months, completing the retreat in the second month of 1954.

SUMMER 1954

In the summer of 1954, beginning in the fifth month, the abbot Ngawang Lodro Tenzin Nyingpo came from Ngor Monastery to Sakya. He conferred on Sakya Trizin and Jetsun Kushok the transmission of the *Compendium of Sādhanas* (see Chapter 5). These transmissions were given at the Relaxation House in the park of the Dolma Palace. Sakya Trizin remembers, "This lasted for three or four months and was a very pleasant occasion . . . taught in a very leisurely fashion."[389] Jetsun Kushok remembers that some lamas, including the abbot of the South Monastery, Khen Jampal Zangpo, were present. Many monks and three laypeople also attended the transmission. The biography of Khenpo Sangye Tenzin (1904–90), abbot of the Sakya Monastery in Ghoom, India, states that he, too, received these teachings at the Dolma Palace.[390]

388. Tseten 2008, 34.

389. Ibid., 35.

390. Though there is not a specific date, it must have been at the same time.

AUTUMN 1954

The 41st Sakya Trizin participated in the month-long Vajrakīlaya ceremonies in the seventh lunar month of 1954. He attended nearly every day of the ceremonies and participated in the meditative dance, but he was not master of ceremonies that year.[391]

After the conclusion of the Vajrakīlaya ceremonies, Jetsun Kushok and Sakya Trizin received secret Mahākāla teachings from Ngaklo Rinpoche (Lama Ngawang Lodro Rinchen, 1892–1959). It was he who years before had left his monastery of Phenpo Nalendra, traveled with the family, and performed the rituals to "bring forth a son" that were followed by Dagyum Sonam Dolkar giving birth to the future Sakya Trizin. Sakya Trizin recalls of Ngaklo Rinpoche: "He was a wonderful lama, very strict in his observance of the Vinaya, rules of monastic discipline; and [according to the rules he] would never eat after lunch or wear animal skins or shirts with sleeves. His arms were always bare, no matter how cold it was. . . . [Though] Sakya is a really cold place—his room was always warm. . . . We could keep water. Elsewhere, we could never keep water in the winter: if we put water in a bottle, it would freeze within a few minutes and crack the bottle."[392] This implies that Ngaklo Rinpoche was a master of *tummo* who could control his external bodily temperature.

Immediately upon the conclusion of the teaching, they did a month-long retreat to meditate on the great Dharma protector Mahākāla, thereby solidifying their practice and understanding of the teachings. Then Sakya Trizin received some more teachings, and after a brief interval began a three-month retreat on Vajrakīlaya.[393]

THE FOURTH AND YOUNGEST JETSUNMA TO TEACH THE PATH WITH THE RESULT

In the winter of 1955, a large group of monks came from Kham (southeast Tibet) to visit Sakya. Their hope was to receive the Path with the Result transmission from the young Sakya Trizin, who was then ten years old. However, he was in retreat as part of the preparation to be able to give the

391. Tseten 2008, 35.

392. Ratna Vajra Sakya et al. 2003, 32.

393. Tseten 2008, 35.

major empowerment of Vajrakīlaya. Dagmo Trinlei Paljor, well versed in Sakya history, knew that previous jetsunmas had taught the Path with the Result. Thinking that Jetsun Kushok, who had recently completed the extensive retreat, should follow in the footsteps of her paternal great-aunt Kyabgon Pema Trinlei (Chapter 5),[394] she urged her niece to bestow the transmission on the monks from Kham. It was decided that she would bestow the short version of the Ngor Path with Result lineage by Ngawang Chodrak (Nga dbang chos grags),[395] together with the accompanying empowerments and other rituals.

The teaching lasted for three months. Jetsun Kushok was the fourth woman—and, at the age of eighteen, the youngest Khon family jetsunma to date—to confer the Path with the Result. By presenting these prestigious teachings, her status was elevated and she was treated with more pomp and ceremony on special occasions. Significantly, she donned the red and gold hat worn by high Sakya lineage-holders.

As Jetsun Kushok was conferring the Path with the Result, the ten-year-old Sakya Trizin was completing all the mandatory preparations for giving his first major empowerment, the Vajrakīlaya initiation. When the Path with the Result teachings were completed, he was ready to confer the Vajrakīlaya empowerment in the spring of 1955. More than a thousand people wanted to receive it. In the Sakya tradition, some empowerments can only be given to 25 people at one time. He gave the consecration numerous times for many days. Jetsun Kushok and Dagmo Trinlei Paljor were in the first group to receive it.

Also in spring/summer 1955, Jetsun Kushok relates that she and her brother received secret teachings from Ngaklo Rinpoche, who was staying in the Relaxation House of the Dolma Palace. She emphasizes that "only the two of us received these teachings. Rinpoche had received them from the Phenpo Nalendra lama, who in turn had received them from our paternal grandfather. Some of these teachings included the Three Red Deities, three Vajrayoginīs, and two main Sakya protectors.

394. Though jetsunmas were well trained in the Path with the Result teachings and practices, it seems only four jetsunmas conferred the transmission: Jetsunma Chime Tenpai Nyima (Chapter 3); the Phuntsok Palace Jetsunma Tamdrin Wangmo (Chapter 4); the Dolma Palace Kyabgon Pema Trinlei (Chapter 5), and her niece, Jetsun Kushok Chime Luding (Chapters 8 and 9).

395. For his biography, see https://treasuryoflives.org/biographies/view/Ngawang-Chodrak /10548 (1572–1641).

Fig. 22. The young 41st Sakya Trizin and Khen Jampal Zangpo in the Pandatsang's shrine room in Lhasa, 1956.

Others were Hevajra from different traditions, Yamāntaka, Guhyasamāja, Mañjuśrī, Chod teachings, the medical texts known as Yuthok Nyingtig." These empowerments, commentaries, and teachings were presented in the Dolma Palace and lasted for five months.[396]

AUTUMN 1955 MEETINGS AND TEACHINGS

In autumn of 1955, Sakya Trizin, Jetsun Kushok, Dagmo Trinlei Paljor, and numerous Sakya officials and monks (a total of about thirty people) traveled to Lhasa to meet with the Dalai Lama. Every Sakya Trizin visits the Dalai Lama after being recognized as the Sakya throne-holder. The journey began in the same way as their visit in 1951. The group rode horses from Sakya to Shigatse. When they arrived in Shigatse, however, the Panchen Lama offered them the use of some Chinese trucks and a jeep. This was the first time Jetsun Kushok and the 41st Sakya Trizin rode in a car. They remember that everyone was excited and a bit apprehensive because they didn't know what to expect. The ride was smooth and they arrived in Lhasa quickly. This time they stayed at the Pandatsang Residence (Fig. 22), owned by one of the Sakya family's main sponsors and located in the southeast corner of the Barkhor, the innermost sacred circuit near the Jokhang Temple in Lhasa.

396. Tseten 2008, 36, and also H.H. the 41st Sakya Trizin, email dated December 15, 2018.

Pilgrims who finally arrive in the holy city of Lhasa become spellbound when they see the Potala, the winter palace of H.H. the Dalai Lama. In *My Life and Lives,* the young Khyongla Rinpoche, who approached Lhasa after a long journey on horseback that had begun several months earlier, in Dagyab, Kham, describes the scene:

> On a beautiful autumn afternoon, we finally arrived in the great valley of Tsangpo, where Lhasa is located. The sky was like a vast turquoise canopy overhead, and as we rode through the broad valley I could see off in a distance a light blazing from a high hill in the center of the plain. When Dongye [his guardian] pointed out the contours of a huge building on top of that central hill I could see that the blaze was from the sun striking the golden roofs. The building was the Potala, the palace of H. H. the Dalai Lama; and the largest building in Tibet.[397]

As the earthly representation of the heavenly residence of the Bodhisattva of Compassion embodied by H.H. the Dalai Lama, the Potala is one of the great wonders of the world. A building of immense magnitude and magnificence, it inspires awe. The Great Fifth Dalai Lama (1617–82) gave orders to his regent to construct the Potala. The construction began in 1645 and lasted until 1694. The Great Fifth never saw its completion.

The central section is painted in red and has 13 stories. Each side wing is painted in white and has nine stories. The building rises more than 1,000 feet above the surrounding valley; it seems to touch the celestial realm of the gods. In fact, the name Lhasa means "Place of the Gods." This massive building has sloping stone walls averaging a thickness of 10 feet on the upper levels and 16 feet at its base. No concrete or cranes were employed during its construction.

The Potala was divided into two main sections. The top floors, with the outside walls painted red, symbolized the spiritual domain and were the winter palace of the Dalai Lamas. The bottom floors, with white walls, represented the affairs of the secular domain and held the offices of the Tibetan government. The Potala exemplifies the combination of the spiritual and the political roles of the Dalai Lama. Before the modern period, the first thing travelers saw as they approached Lhasa by horse or

397. Khyongla Rinpoche 1996, 43, 52–53.

on foot was this huge, mountain-like palace. With more than a thousand rooms, the building housed countless shrines and holy statues.

Since the 41st Sakya Trizin had already been officially recognized, the family was granted a private audience with the Dalai Lama in the Potala. To reach the top floors of the Potala is both arduous and breathtaking. By horse one can ride up to some of the lower levels from the rear of the Potala. Then, as one ascends on foot by climbing many high stone steps, one can see parts of Lhasa and the golden roof of the Jokhang, the holiest temple, in the distance. Snow-capped mountains encircle the Lhasa valley. The higher one climbs, the smaller the pilgrims appear as they circumambulate the Lingkor, the holy circuit that encircles the Potala.

Finally, one reaches a broad courtyard, but this is only a stop to catch one's breath. One then begins to enter the actual building by ascending a narrow, dimly lit wooden staircase. Once inside the sacred area, there seems to be a maze of rooms in all directions, many of which are shrines. The highest floors are reserved as the Dalai Lama's personal residence. One can only imagine the feelings of the Sakya family members as they approached the Potala and slowly ascended to the top floors to meet with Kundun (The Presence);[398] they must have been filled with joy, excitement, and veneration.

The 41st Sakya Trizin requested an extensive Lamrim teaching,[399] but since the Dalai Lama did not have much time, he offered to give the family the shortest Lamrim teaching. They changed their request, asking for the middle-length Lamrim teaching instead. The Dalai Lama agreed and presented this teaching to them in the Potala.

When a group requests a teaching, they are the sponsors of the teaching and are also the principal group to offer the mandala.[400] Usually the

---

398. Tibetans use the title Kundun for the Dalai Lama.

399. *Lamrim* means "the graduated path to enlightenment." It consists of different texts, but the founder of the Gelugpa sect, Je Tsongkapa (1357–1419), wrote some of the most important ones. For a wonderful translation, see Tsong-kha-pa, *The Great Treatise on the Stages of the Path to Enlightenment*, trans. Lamrim Chenmo Translation Committee, ed. Joshua Cutler and Guy Newland (Boston: Snow Lion, 2014).

400. In Tibetan Buddhism, there are different kinds of mandalas. This mandala symbolizes the entire universe according to Indian cosmology. When one requests a teaching, practitioners must show their sincere appreciation in receiving something precious. As one is offering this mandala, one describes the universe and all the symbolic gifts accompanying it. The patron and all the other participants should visualize with deliberation and good intentions that they are really offering everything to the lama to receive the precious

group offers the mandala without explanation, but in this case the young Sakya Trizin gave an extensive explanation of the meaning of the mandala in front of the Dalai Lama, his monks from Namgyal Monastery, and the lay assembly, which included high-ranking officials and even some cabinet members. Everyone was impressed by his knowledge. He was only eleven years old.

The teaching lasted seven days. Present were Sakya Trizin, Jetsun Kushok, Dagmo Trinlei Paljor, their cousin Lama Kunga Thartse Rinpoche from Ngor Monastery, Khenpo Gyatso, the Dalai Lama's younger brother Lobsang Samten (1933–85), Bakula Rinpoche from Lhadak, India,[401] the Dalai Lama's monks from the Namgyal Dratsang (the oldest monk was an elderly geshe to whom the Dalai Lama showed much respect), some Sakya monks who served the family, and some Sakya noble families. In total there were about 50 participants.[402] The teachings were concluded with an empowerment of the protector Mahākālī (Palden Lhamo) or Magzorma,[403] with the accompanying special offerings, or tsok (the thanksgiving offering to the protector). Jetsun Kushok remembers that the tsok offering, made of roasted barley flour, brown sugar, and butter, had a "beautiful taste."[404]

In early 1956, after the great Monlam (Great Prayers) festival in Lhasa, held for the first fifteen days of the first lunar month, the 41st Sakya Trizin and his entourage had gone south on pilgrimage. They visited many Sakya monasteries and established a good connection with the monks and abbots of the monasteries. But the trip was curtailed when Chinese officials requested that he attend a ceremony on April 22, 1956 for the Preparation Committee of the Tibetan Autonomous Region established by the Chinese government in Lhasa. The Chinese were becoming more and more confident that they could dictate their demands to the Tibet-

---

teaching. Further, at the conclusion, another mandala is offered in thanksgiving for having receiving the teaching.

401. Bakula Rinpoche (1917–2003) later became Lhadak's minister to the Indian parliament in Delhi, India, and Indian ambassador in Mongolia.

402. Interview with Lama Kunga in Walden, New York, June 2011.

403. The 41st Sakya Trizin explained that in Sanskrit the names are the same but in Tibetan, they are two different deities. (Palden Lhamo has four arms and Magzorma has two arms.)

404. By this statement of a "beautiful taste," Jetsun Kushok is implying that the Dalai Lama has a special connection with the goddess Magzorma and that the goddess blessed the offerings, thereby transforming them and giving them an exquisite taste.

Fig. 23. Ven. Jamyang Khyentse Chokyi Lodro.

ans. The Tibetans believed that they were an independent nation and that the Chinese were invading their country. The Chinese saw it differently and insisted that they were helping the Tibetans liberate themselves from oppression and imperialism.

To establish this so-called Tibetan Autonomous Region, or TAR, the Chinese government created the Preparation Committee and then held this inauguration ceremony with much fanfare. The ceremony infuriated the Tibetans because the Chinese government, while insisting that it was liberating Tibet, was slowly asserting its claim that Tibet had always been a part of China. Many high-ranking lamas and Tibetan officials were compelled to attend. The 41st Sakya Trizin remembers that since he was young and was forbidden to bring any attendants, he felt uncomfortable. Fortunately, the 16th Gyalwang Karmapa carried him through the crowd.

The one silver lining was that, because they were in Lhasa, Jetsun Kushok and Sakya Trizin had an extraordinary opportunity. Staying near them in Samdrup Podrang was the highly realized master Jamyang Khyentse Chokyi Lodro (1893–1959; Fig. 23), the heart of the ecumenical movement known as *rime*. Decades earlier (as mentioned in Chapter 7), Jamyang Khyentse had met Jetsun Kushok and Sakya Trizin's paternal aunts at Samye.[405] The 41st Sakya Trizin remembers, "Of course, I had already heard many stories about him, as he was so famous. But when I actually got to meet him, it was an extraordinary experience. By merely being in his presence, I felt such great devotion. He was a very great master; there are very few lamas who receive respect from every tradition."[406] For the first time, Jetsun Kushok met his young consort, Khandro Tsering Chodron (1929–2011), who was considered to be a highly realized being and a ḍākinī.[407]

Jamyang Khyentse Chokyi Lodro was secretly making his way into exile in Sikkim. Jetsun Kushok and Sakya Trizin requested the full Nyingma transmissions of Long Chen Nying Tik,[408] which he agreed to give them. He was considered a major holder of this transmission and bestowed the entire teaching over eleven days at the Pandatsang home.[409] About 200 people received it. By receiving this teaching, a strong spiritual connection was established between Jamyang Khyentse Chokyi Lodro and Jetsun Kushok and Sakya Trizin.[410]

---

405. Tseten 2008, 59. The 41st Sakya Trizin relates, "When I was very young, my aunt asked some monks to do a prediction involving a mirror. They saw a strange lama in the mirror and myself in front of him. The lama had long ears, and the space between his upper lip and nose was very wide. He had a scar. We didn't know who it could be but later discovered it was Khyentse Rinpoche."

406. H.H. the 41st Sakya Trizin email, December 5, 2018.

407. For the Sanskrit term ḍākinī (Tib. *khandro*, "sky-goer"), see note 263 above.

408. Long Chen Nying Tik is considered the innermost secret teaching of the Dzogchen path and is imparted only to students with the highest capacity to understand—and, more importantly, to experience—the nature of mind. The great Nyingmapa master Dilgo Khyentse Rinpoche described Dzogchen as follows: "The practice of Dzogchen or Atiyoga, is to realise the buddha nature, which has been present in our nature since the very beginning. Here it is not sufficient to concentrate on contrived practices that involve intellectual efforts and concepts; to recognise this Nature, the practice should be utterly beyond fabrication. The practice is simply to realise the radiance, the natural expression of wisdom, which is beyond all intellectual concepts. It is the true realisation of the Absolute Nature just as it is, the ultimate fruition." http://www.rigpawiki.org/index.php?title=.

409. H.H. 41st Sakya Trizin email, December 5, 2018.

410. As noted earlier, H.H. the 41st Sakya Trizin is considered a reincarnation of the Nyingma Apam Tulku.

Their connection was further strengthened when Jamyang Khyentse Chokyi Lodro came to Sakya later that year, in the autumn of 1956, to teach the 41st Sakya Trizin and Jetsun Kushok the Four Unbreakable Practices in the Big Glass-Window Room of the Dolma Palace. About a hundred people received this teaching, including Dagmo Trinlei Paljor.[411]

It seems that Jamyang Khyentse Chokyi Lodro wanted to make an even stronger connection with Jetsun Kushok because he requested a reading transmission (Tib. *lung*) from her. As Jetsun Kushok recalls:

> At that time when Khyentse Rinpoche was in Sakya, he stayed in my father's room. My aunt instructed me to serve tea to Khyentse Rinpoche, and to serve him well. So I obediently went into the room to serve tea to him on several occasions. On one occasion, when I was holding the teapot to serve Rinpoche, he held up some pages of a text he was reading and asked me to give him the *lung* for that. It was a short long-life sādhana. I replied that I couldn't do so, telling him that I thought I might not have received the appropriate empowerment for it. Khyentse Rinpoche told me that he was sure I must have had the transmission because I had already received the complete *Collection of Sādhanas*. With no choice, I obliged him and read it. Then Khyentse Rinpoche suddenly made the mandala *mudra* and offered me a mandala during the reading transmission.[412]

Furthermore, Jetsun Kushok's friendship with Khandro Tsering Chodron was strengthened since they would see each other frequently. They enjoyed singing songs together and being playful with each other as young women. They remained friends until Khandro Tsering Chodron passed away in 2011.

LATE 1956 PILGRIMAGE TO INDIA

In November 1956, at the invitation of the Indian government, the Dalai Lama and the Panchen Lama (Fig. 24) arrived in India to participate in

411. H.H. the 41st Sakya Trizin email, December 14, 2018. The Four Unbreakable Practices (Chak mey nam zhi) are the Lam dus Hevajra sādhana; the Vajrayoginī sādhana; the Bir sung, or Virūpa protection meditation; and the Lam zap, or profound path of Guru Yoga meditation.

412. Jetsun Kushok email, August 12, 2020.

Fig. 24. H.H. the 14th Dalai Lama and the 10th Panchen Lama in Sikkim, 1956.

the commemoration of the 2500th anniversary of the Buddha's pari-nirvana. They visited the major Buddhist sites, such as Bodhgaya, where the Buddha became enlightened, as well as many other places, including Prime Minister Nehru's home in Delhi.

The Chinese government was putting much pressure on the Indian leaders. In fact, Zhou Enlai, premier of the People's Republic of China, made a sudden visit to India to insist that Indian officials not provide refuge for the Dalai Lama and the Panchen Lama. Despite the constraints, the Dalai Lama and the Panchen Lama were able to participate in some of the commemorative activities and also see many areas of India, from north to south.

The 41st Sakya Trizin, Jetsun Kushok, Dagmo Trinlei Paljor, and their entourage, including their tutor, Khen Jampal Zangpo, went on pilgrimage to India soon after the Dalai Lama's departure. It was a short trip, lasting only about two months. Jetsun Kushok has never forgotten their very first train ride, which she loved, with so many new landscapes, people, and animals to see out the window of their railway carriage.

Like most Buddhist pilgrims, they visited the four major sites associated with the life of the Historical Buddha. The 41st Sakya Trizin remembers that it was difficult because no one in the group spoke Hindi or English. Luckily, in Sarnath, they met two fellow pilgrims named Lama

Lobsang and Thutop, who were from Lhadak and spoke Tibetan. They were studying at Benares Hindu University. Sakya Trizin did some divinations for them. The Khon family also met a Gelugpa monk named Thupten Jungney, who wanted to build a monastery in Sarnath. At the time he only had a small hut on his land, and he asked Sakya Trizin to bless the monks and him, which he did. Twelve years later, in 1968, the monastery was host to very first Path with Result teachings that the 41st Sakya Trizin gave.[413]

The next place is Bodhgaya, where the Buddha became awakened and realized reality. The Tibetans call this sacred site Dorjeden (Vajra Seat). This signifies that the Buddha's mind was no longer wavering. No one and no thing were able to disturb the Buddha's meditation until he became enlightened. The Buddha sat under the famous Bodhi tree until he understood the truth. The family made thousands of offerings at the Bodhi tree where the Buddha became enlightened, and they also meditated there. For all Buddhists, this place is filled with holiness and spiritual presence.

Decades later, in 2002 and 2004, Jetsun Kushok brought some of her disciples to Bodhgaya on pilgrimage (Fig. 25). Linda Lawrence remembers that when they arrived, after a long and exhausting drive, it was very dark. Linda thought they would visit the holy sites on the following day, but after everyone checked into their rooms, Jetsun Kushok announced that they would visit the Mahabodhi temple immediately. Linda reminiscences, "It was a still, dark night and the sky was very clear. After we removed our shoes at the entrance of the temple, we entered. It was phenomenal and otherworldly. I heard Carolyn [Swan] say, 'This must be what heaven looks like!'"[414]

The Sakya group continued on to Rajgir at Vulture Peak, where the Buddha taught the Perfection of Wisdom sutras, and visited nearby Nālandā University. The famous university produced many Buddhist scholars, including the great highly realized Virūpa, the abbot known as Dharmapala who later taught the precious Path with Result teachings that were brought to Sakya, Tibet. The fourth and last site was Kushinagar, where the Buddha died. Everywhere, the family performed rituals, chanted prayers, and made extensive offerings.

413. H.H. the 41st Sakya Trizin email, December 13, 2018.
414. Linda Lawrence email, December 28, 2018.

Fig. 25. H.E. Jetsun Kushok praying to Tara at the Mahabodhi Temple, Bodhgaya, India, 2002.

The 41st Sakya Trizin remembers that at every sacred place, they would chant the Sixteen Arhats puja because it is believed that doing so generates much merit and that one's understanding of the Dharma is increased. Jetsun Kushok remembers the pilgrimage well, and I asked her if she had endured any hardships. In her detached manner, she replied, "My mind is even-minded; not many things affect me. But I remember that I had trouble finding places to wash in the jungle and I was worried about snakes."

Also while they were in India, Jetsun Kushok first conceived of the idea of learning English in a Western-style school. Her tutor was scandalized and dismissed the idea: she must concentrate her efforts on her spiritual practices, not on frivolous pursuits such as learning a foreign language.

Before returning to Tibet, like many Tibetans, they stopped to visit Calcutta, the former capital of the British Raj, which teemed with Indians, Chinese, and pale-skinned foreigners with light eyes. Many Tibetans had never seen a European before coming to Calcutta. There were tall buildings, iron bridges, motor vehicles, ships, and shops packed with goods. Indeed, it was the place to shop for all kinds of Indian goods, from gold watches, radios, silk, and brocades to flashlights, black tea, sugar, dried fruit, nuts, and cotton cloth. Most likely, many goods were bought for the coming enthronement of the young 41st Sakya Trizin. Dagmo

Trinlei Paljor must have been extremely busy with such purchases and orders.

The family stayed at the Broadway Hotel, which was established in 1937 and continues to operate today. Jetsun Kushok remembers that while she was in her brother's room, she was told that the Gyalwa Karmapa (1924–81) was coming to see him. In her haste to leave before the Karmapa arrived, she bumped right into him as she was leaving the room. Embarrassed, she retreated with her head bowed to show her respect to such a high lama.

The Queen Mother of Sikkim met the family in Calcutta and took Jetsun Kushok, the 41st Sakya Trizin, and their tutor Khen Jampal Zangpo to a movie. Sakya Trizin chuckles, "It was a movie from the West, and it had a fair amount of dancing and kissing. Guru Khenchen Jampal Zangpo was scandalized and vowed never to go to the movies again. On another day, we went to the circus and our tutor really enjoyed it. Most of the time we went shopping. Also we visited Kali Ghat, the Hindu shrine. It was very crowded and difficult to enter."[415]

From Calcutta, the family went to Gangtok, Sikkim, to visit family and friends and to celebrate Losar. Sakya Trizin recalls that the family and their tutor went to give their New Year's greeting and present a *khata* to Jamyang Khyentse Chokyi Lodro, who was then living in Gangtok. After celebrating Losar, they returned to Sakya to begin the extensive preparations for the enthronement of Sakya Trizin.

1957 AND BRIEF STAYS IN JETSUN KUSHOK'S OWN LABRANG

As already mentioned, each jetsunma received her own residence, or *labrang*. In the distribution of residences, Jetsun Kushok had received the Tashi Labrang in the Northern Monastery complex in Sakya. In addition, her father had given her the Ngatse (Nags rtse) Labrang, which had larger landholdings and was close to the Dolma Palace. Geshe Thuchey Wangchuk, a lama who lived in Sakya from 1938 to 1961, described half of Ngatse Labrang as being three stories tall and the other half being two stories. On the lower level was a private protector's shrine room, plus

---

415. H.H. the 41st Sakya Trizin email, December 13, 2018.

rooms where the attendants lived. The two upper levels were reserved for the Khon family. It also had a pleasant garden with tall trees.[416]

Dagmo Trinlei Paljor advised Jetsun Kushok to take Tashi Labrang, but Jetsun Kushok did not want to stay there. Tashi Labrang was not so pleasant since it stood in the town and was situated below and west of the political/spiritual Zhitog building. On the ground floor was a protector deity shrine room that was popular with visiting pilgrims. Jetsun Kushok felt that the area was too busy and too many people lived near it. Furthermore, it looked like an ordinary house. She reiterated her desire to live in the Ngatse Labrang, but her aunt needed more convincing. Jetsun Kushok explained that the Ngatse Labrang looked like the other religious buildings in Sakya: it was painted in grey and had the distinctive Sakya vertical stripes in red, white, and blue.

Finally her aunt relented, but added, "Since you are one nun, you don't need all of Ngatse's land for your income. Stay in Ngatse Labrang, but switch its land with that of Tashi Labrang." Jetsun Kushok accepted. She wanted to stay in Ngatse Labrang because it was separate, quiet, and next to the Dolma Palace, where her brother lived. As she remembers wistfully, "Unfortunately, within two years, we lost Tibet; so I never had a chance to live there and only stayed briefly in 1957 and 1958."[417]

1958–59: THE ENTHRONEMENT OF THE 41ST SAKYA TRIZIN

To enthrone the Sakya Trizin is a very long and costly affair. Being the key person in the family after the death of her husband, Dagmo Trinlei Paljor was in charge of everything. Since Sakya had its own local government and administrative offices, many Sakya officials helped her make all the arrangements and invite the important guests. The managers in charge had to collect the money and goods needed for all the ceremo-

---

416. Interview with Geshe Thuchey Wangchuk in Seattle, with the kind help of Jeff Schoening, November 2, 2016.

417. Jamyang Thubten Zangpo, a younger brother of Jetsun Kushok's paternal grandfather, built Ngatse Labrang. He originally built it as his residence, but later it became a jetsunma's *labrang*. According to popular belief, his reincarnation was the Phuntsok Palace's second son, Trinly Rinpoche (1934–97). This labrang is also known as Nalatse in the long form, or sGrol steng bla brang. (Nalatse is an important temple in Gungtang where Sachen met Mal Lotsawa.)

nies, many of which took place far from Sakya. To accomplish all these tasks would have required two years of traveling to various sites in Tibet.

Some disagreements arose among the advisors as to when the actual enthronement ceremony should be held. In early 1958, some managers insisted that everything must be done within two years, but the 41st Sakya Trizin felt it was imperative to hold the ceremony sooner. Everything in Tibet was in flux. Chinese troops and officials were exerting pressure in many areas of Tibet.

To settle the matter, a divination was performed in the Gorum shrine, in front of the famous mask of Mahākāla, one of the Four Wonders of Sakya (see Chapter 2). Jetsun Kushok explains, "Whenever there was an important decision to be made by the Khon family or Sakya government, they would go to the Gorum shrine and ask their question in front of the mask. The mask was not normally displayed, so the public could not see it. It was reserved for these special situations."

The divination indicated to hasten the preparations. Many pujas were done in the protectors' shrines in Sakya to prevent obstacles from arising. Thousands of blessing pills, containing special herbs and other precious substances and blessed by eminent lamas, were made. Since Tibetans eagerly sought these pills, many of them would be given to the guests attending the enthronement ceremony.

One of the last rituals to be completed before the enthronement was that of the extensive Vajrakīlaya ritual, which is held annually from the twenty-third to thirtieth days of the twelfth lunar month. The soon-to-be 41st Sakya Trizin presided over the Vajrakīlaya ceremonies in early 1959. This ritual is understood to be a powerful purification ceremony that "cleans up" any harmful residue accumulated during the year. By performing this, one can begin the new year afresh.

Day by day, Sakya was swelling with people arriving from all over Tibet to participate in this joyous and propitious event. People erected tents; most households were overflowing with relatives and friends. Pilgrims thronged to the Great Temple, eager to see its grandeur, its enormous blessed statues of the Historical Buddha, the Future Buddha, the Bodhisattva of Wisdom, the Bodhisattva of Compassion, Goddess Tara, Goddess Vajrayoginī, the stupas of the former Khon family members, the massive pillars, and, of course, the famous conch given by the Mongolian Kublai Khan to his spiritual mentor, Sakya Chogyal Phagpa (see Chapter 2). For many, it was their first and only time in Sakya. At the time, it seemed inconceiveable that this was the final enthronement in Sakya, because the ceremony had been performed there for more than eight hundred years.

After the New Year celebration of three days, the enthronement rituals began with an extensive seven-day ritual honoring Pañjaranātha Mahākāla (Gurgyi Gonpo), one of the Khon family's main protectors. Every Sakya monastery has a shrine dedicated to Pañjaranātha Mahākāla, the main protector of all Sakya monasteries. In Sakya, one of these shrines is located at the top of the Great Temple, but the most important one is in the Gorum building in the North Monastery area. Thus pujas were performed in these shrines as well as in others. This specific ritual dispels potential obstacles or disturbances to the enthronement.

The North Monastery area of Sakya was buzzing with excitement and anticipation. The actual enthronement took place in the Zhitog building. Dignitaries from all over Tibet came to participate and were seated according to position and rank. These included the highest government official in the Sakya government, the Shape; more than sixty noble family officials of the high rank of *kudrak* (*sku drag*), or fourth rank;[418] monastery abbots; scholars from Ngor and Tsarpa monasteries; and members of the noble families. All were wearing silk or brocade according to their rank and position. Representatives of the Dalai Lama and of the Panchen Lama, and even some Chinese officials, attended the ceremony.

The 41st Trizin Sakya recounts, "I was accompanied by my attendants as I entered the temple. I ascended the political throne of Chogyal Phagpa, which was placed on the spiritual throne of Sakya Pandita." Sakya Pandita's teaching throne was made of unfired brick and was like a long, wide platform.[419] On top of this brick platform was an old wooden throne decorated with gold filigree called the white lotus throne. The placement of these two thrones indicated that the spiritual base informs the political aspect of the Sakya Trizin. Sakya Trizin continues, "Shortly after I was installed on the thrones, I taught the famous text *Elucidating*

---

418. In the Tibetan government, there were seven ranks. The first rank was the Dalai Lama; the second to the fourth ranks were considered high ranks.

419. Sapan's throne had three names: the great throne of Dharma (*chos khri thang mo che*), the throne of turning the three wheels of Buddhist teachings (*'khor lo gsum ldan*), and reducing the pride of scholars (*mkhas pa gdzil gnon*). Dragshul Trinlei Rinchen 1974, vol. 1, 99. In his diary entry describing the throne, Dragshul Trinlei Rinchen was describing his father Kunga Rinchen's enthronement as the 37th Sakya Trizin in 1883.

Fig. 26. Ven. Chiwang Tulku at the Sakya Centre, Rajpur, India.

the Sage's Intent (Thub pa'i dgongs gsal) by Sakya Pandita. This text is a summary of the Mahayana sutrayana path."

A young tulku by the name of Chiwang Tulku (Fig. 26)[420] arrived in Sakya for the enthronement. It was his first visit in Sakya. He remembers that Dagmo Trinlei Paljor was very well dressed in a beautiful brocade *chuba*. She wore an enormous and elaborate headdress typical

---

420. Chiwang (Tsewang) Tulku is considered to be a siddha, or adept, in Vajrayoginī practices.

Fig. 27. Dagmo Trinlei Paljor wearing a Tsang headdress, 1959.
Inset is of her brother Tashi Palrab in India.

of Tsang women, a pair of fancy earrings, and a necklace replete with pearls, coral, and turquoise (Fig. 27).[421] With an attendant on each side of her, she looked very pleased. After the celebration of the enthronement, Dagmo invited Chiwang Tulku to visit her in her private audience room. Upon entering, he immediately prostrated before her as a sign of respect. Dagmo indicated to him to take a seat, and he was offered refreshments as they chatted about the ceremony and other topics.

Later, in exile, Chiwang Tulku would get to know the Khon family very well, when he was the director of the Sakya Centre in Rajpur and

421. See note 277 above for an extensive description of the headdress and jewelry.

the Dolma Palace family lived there in the early 1970s. He remembers that "Dagmo was a very good lady. She did many pujas and did not sleep much at night. She loved to tell stories about the North and South Monasteries of Sakya. She enjoyed telling stories about His Holiness' [Sakya Trizin] root lama Dampa Rinpoche and about Lama Ngawang Lodro Rinpoche [i.e., Ngaklo Rinpoche], whose rituals brought forth the birth of His Holiness. Also she praised Khen Jampal Zangpo, who helped her tremendously after the death of her husband."

A great procession concluded the main events of the enthronement. This was followed by seven days of Tibetan opera (Lhamo) to celebrate this momentous occasion. After all the festivities, the Buddhist protectors were thanked with special offerings presented at the protectors' shrines. During the thanksgiving offered to the protector Mahākāla, sad news came—Lhasa was lost.

CHAPTER NINE

Traversing Cultures:
Jetsun Kushok in India and the West

D AGMO TRINLEI PALJOR (Chapter 7) was considered to be a very intel-
ligent and courageous woman. She said to her niece and nephew,
"We must listen to the news. If we hear that Gyalwa Rinpoche[422] [the 14th
Dalai Lama] has left for India, then we can no longer stay here—we must
leave for India. If we hear H.H. the Dalai Lama is brought to China, we
must stay here. There is no use to go [implying that other nations would
not recognize the plight of Tibetans]."

Jetsun Kushok listened to the radio for any news from India. In Delhi,
All-India Radio hired a Tibetan as a broadcaster, Lobsang Lhalungpa,
who had previously worked as the private secretary of Kalon Bonshod,
Dagmo Trinlei Paljor's older brother. Tibetans trusted him and felt he
would tell the truth, unlike the Chinese newscast, which was mostly pro-
paganda. One day Jetsun Kushok heard Lobsang Lhalungpa announcing
that the Dalai Lama had left for the south, though it wasn't clear exactly
where he was. Most people expected him to go to southern Tibet, as he
had in 1950.[423] Also, in south Tibet courageous Khampas were defending
the area; these Khampas would lay down their lives for the Dalai Lama
because no one was more precious to them than their beloved Kundun
(The Presence).

In 1959, no one was certain whether the Dalai Lama would return to
Lhasa or seek exile in India. The Tibetans waited for an indication that

422. Gyalwa Rinpoche is not a title exclusive to the Dalai Lama, but in this instance it does
refer to the Dalai Lama.

423. In 1950, the young 14th Dalai Lama and his major cabinet members had secretly left
Lhasa for Dromo in southern Tibet. The Tibetans feared a Chinese invasion and decided to
stay close to the border near Sikkim in case they needed to flee to India. They then returned
to Lhasa in the following year.

he had made a definite decision to stay or to flee. The 41st Sakya Trizin was listening to Radio Beijing, and there was no news about the Dalai Lama from them. The family felt this was a good sign. If the Chinese government had captured him, they would have boasted about his capture. Fortunately, Radio Beijing was silent.

After hearing the broadcast by Lobsang Lhalungpa, Dagmo Trinlei Paljor decided that it was best to be ready to flee to India. She began to prepare for this implausible journey—an exile that would compel the family to quit their ancestral home, abandon relatives and servants, and leave behind precious possessions blessed by the deities and by many spiritual lamas over the course of more than a thousand years. Most of their material possessions became useless, even a burden. Secretly, Dagmo Trinlei Paljor sent certain trusted servants with some of the family valuables, such as jewelry and Chinese silver coins (*dayan*), to one of their main sponsors, the Pandatsang family, who had a house in Kalimpong, India. This was all that could be sent; it was a pittance compared to the vast treasures left in Sakya. But it was saving themselves that was paramount, especially the young Sakya Trizin, the head of the Sakya school.

The second time they heard the news from Delhi, Lobsang Lhalungpa announced that H.H. the 14th Dalai Lama had arrived in Bomdila, India. Jetsun Kushok reiterates their aunt's words: "If we hear that H.H. Dalai Lama is in India—we must leave for India." Preparing their departure covertly and quietly, they announced to the people of Sakya that the 41st Sakya Trizin was going for a few days to Khau Drak Dzong to perform some pujas for the protector Mahākāla. This temple is a few hours away from Sakya.

The family members agreed that they themselves would wait a few days and then tell everyone they were going to the hot springs. Since the hot springs were close to the Mahākāla Temple, the 41st Sakya Trizin would rejoin the family nearby. The family concurred that the group had to be small to avoid attracting attention. The family selected a trader who knew the route well between Tibet and Sikkim to be their trusted guide. The group consisted of the 41st Sakya Trizin, Jetsun Kushok, Dagmo Trinlei Paljor and her great-niece Zangmo (Appendix A), and some servants—just fifteen people in all. To avoid detection Jetsun Kushok disguised herself as a man, and to be more convincing she carried a large shiny pistol on each side. One of the guns was loaded. Luckily, Jetsun Kushok did not have to use it during this perilous escape.

The family asked the Dolma Palace manager to come, but he indicated that he wanted to stay in Sakya to protect the palace. For him, it was inconceivable that a thousand years of creating and establishing Sakya would come to an end. The manager and many other servants would do their utmost to protect the Dolma Palace.

A few years later, at great personal risk, Aja Dolkar (Appendix A), an attendant and great-niece of Dagmo Trinlei Paljor, courageously broke the Chinese seals on the doors of the Dolma Palace and retrieved some of the important ritual instruments needed for performing pujas. No one asked her to do this, but she felt that she needed to bring these ritual objects to her treasured Sakya Trizin. After years of unbearable suffering, having been imprisoned and having her baby die in jail, Aja Dolkar escaped to India. When she was reunited with the family in India, she was overwhelmed with emotion; she wept tears of joy and relief. Aja Dolkar says, "It felt that I was in a dream." She served her great-aunt Dagmo Trinlei Paljor in India until the latter passed away, and continues her service today to the rest of the family through three generations.

Escape to India

Some of the family's traders who frequently did business in India knew the different routes to go to Sikkim. It was decided to go to Lachen in northern Sikkim, which had a large Sikkimese army camp. It took the family only three days on horseback to arrive there at the border of Sikkim. Though a three-day journey was considered a very short trip for Tibetans, this was a one-way journey with scant hope of returning to their cherished Sakya. They stayed a month in Lachen, relieved to be safe, and assessed their options. Then they moved to Gangtok, the capital of Sikkim. Since the wife of the king of Sikkim was from the Ragashar family, as was Dagyum Chime Kunga Dolma, the paternal grandmother of Jetsun Kushok and Sakya Trizin, the royal family received them well. Later, when Dagmo Trinlei Paljor was sharing her stories with Chiwang Tulku, the director of the Sakya Centre, she said, "I could not take valuable things from Tibet, but I brought the Jewel Gyalwa Rinpoche [the 41st Sakya Trizin]. This is most important."

Needless to say, the Khon family was concerned for all the Tibetans who could not escape. Many family members, abbots, and government leaders were "paraded" by the Communist Chinese, who forced the people of Sakya to denounce them as traitors and reactionaries. As Sakya Khon family members were being dragged by their hair through the streets, the Tibetans were told to humiliate them by jeering at them, spitting on them, and kicking them. Of course, most Tibetans were horrified at the thought of such action toward their spiritual leaders and advisors.

Tsultrim Gyatso, a young monk from the Northern Monastery who performed rituals for the Sakya family and people, was put in prison. He remembers that sixteen monks from his monastery were arrested and jailed. After a month, they were released because they were considered unimportant. Four monks plus Tsultrim Gyatso decided in jail that if they were released, they would try to get over the border. Also they heard that the Chinese were planning to do struggle sessions (wherein one must denounce and beat the accused person) with the abbot of the South Monastery, Khen Jampal Zangpo. "We monks thought, 'He is such an illustrious monk, we could never participate in a struggle session against him.' So we were determined to escape."[424] Fortunately they were able to reach India. Within a year or two, many Tibetans, including Khen Jampal Zangpo, had died from imprisonment and torture. This was the source of the agony and even guilt felt by many exiled Tibetans, who were powerless to help their fellow Tibetans in Tibet.

The family's stay in Sikkim was bittersweet. Not only were they refugees, but one of their most revered teachers, Jamyang Khyentse Chokyi Lodro Rinpoche, was dying. Hearing the sad news within a week of their arrival in Gangtok, Sakya Trizin and Jetsun Kushok,[425] together with other eminent lamas, recited incessant prayers and performed rituals and pujas to prolong his life. Jamyang Khyentse Rinpoche died on June 12, 1959 (the sixth day of the fifth month). One of his close disciples, Dodrupchen Rinpoche (b. 1927), wrote a poignant poem upon hearing the sad news. In many ways this evocative poem reflects the feelings of Tibetans about the loss of their homeland:

> The whole world is changing before us like a magic show.
> Appearances are unreliable like bubbles.

424. This is from Voice of America–Tibetan section "Reconstructing the 1950's," a series of interviews of Tibetans. This one is from Tsultrim Gyatso, who lived in Sakya during this time.

425. Jetsun Kushok was perhaps the only woman present, except for his consort Khandro Tsering Chodron, to perform the prayers and participate in the other funeral rituals for Jamyang Khyentse Rinpoche.

The monasteries, the loved ones in the Dharma, and our kin—
All have become mere memories.[426]

The 3rd Dezhung Rinpoche, the Phuntsok Palace's Jigdal Dagchen Rinpoche, and the Ngor Thartse abbot Sonam Gyatso (1930–88, later known
as Hiroshi Sonami, an older brother of Lama Kunga Rinpoche) rushed
from Kalimpong, India, to participate in the funeral and show their devotion to their beloved teacher. According to his biography, Dezhung Rinpoche had received precious teachings from Jamyang Khyentse Chokyi
Lodro Rinpoche a few years before in Tibet, and as a thank-you gift, he
had wanted to present more offerings to his teacher. Thus, Jamyang Khyentse Rinpoche had requested some gold for gilding Buddhist statues.

During the following years, Dezhung Rinpoche accumulated 30
ounces of gold, a considerable sum for him in his situation as a refugee.
Others might have used it for their own food and shelter, but Dezhung
Rinpoche immediately offered it for the reliquary stupa of Jamyang
Khyentse Rinpoche. Dezhung Rinpoche remarked to his sister Ani
Chime Dolma, who had accompanied him into exile, "This gold would
not support us for more than a few months. Anyway, we probably will
not go hungry. . . . Better to offer it to the Lama."[427]

As previously mentioned, Jamyang Khyentse Rinpoche had a young
consort, Khandro Tsering Chodron (1929–2011), who was considered to
be a ḍākinī. She remained by his side until he died and was involved in
the funeral rituals. On this sad occasion, she and Jetsun Kushok saw each
other again; they remained lifelong friends. Later, when the stupa that
held his bodily remains was constructed near the royal palace of Sikkim,
Khandro Tsering Chodron came daily to say prayers, circumambulate
the stupa, and perform other acts of devotion.

Now, as refugees, Dagmo Trinlei Paljor was trying to determine the
best place for the family to live. Some relatives suggested that the family settle in Gangtok. Dagmo Trinlei Paljor thought that the 41st Sakya
Trizin should be educated, and considered a private school. However,
when informed that he would have to cut his hair and remove his earrings, she changed her mind, saying, "No, it is against the Sakya tradi-

---

426. https://www.shentongkalacakra.com/2020/01/05/part-ii-on-the-sikkimese-trail-of
-jamyang-khyentse-chokyi-lodro-the-golden-stupa-of-tashi-ding-and-the-doorway-to
-shambhala/.
427. Jackson 2003, 240.

tion." For her this would have been sacrilege, since Sakya Trizins wore the unique turquoise earrings and kept their hair long.[428]

Within a few months, the family decided to leave Sikkim and went to Kalimpong, India. Many Tibetan traders had a residence in Kalimpong because it was the first Indian town where Tibetan goods were sorted before being sent to various places in India, such as Calcutta, and even as far as Europe. As the composer Philip Glass, who visited Kalimpong in the mid-1960s, remarked, "Really, everybody who was interested in Tibet passed through Kalimpong."[429] The family stayed at a residence of the Pandatsang family.[430]

In Kalimpong, the United Nations was providing food to Tibetan refugees and different Tibetan groups were helping each other. Since the situation was better there, many Tibetans decided to stay. Chushi Kangdruk, the main group of Khampa resistance fighters, welcomed the fleeing Tibetans. They asked the 41st Sakya Trizin to pray for those who had died. Hearing all the names of the deceased, Sakya Trizin, being still young, cried. Dagmo Trinlei Paljor reprimanded him and told him that he shouldn't cry.[431]

The family decided that they needed to help their fellow Tibetans both inside Tibet and in exile. Being a great spiritual family, they could be most effective by going on a Buddhist pilgrimage (Fig. 28). The 41st Sakya Trizin stated:

> Going to the holy places of the Buddha is very important. The Buddha himself said that "after my entering parinirvana, the sons and daughters of my followers should visit the four places." By these four places, the Buddha was referring to Lumbini, the place where He was born, Bodh Gaya where He became enlightened, Sarnath where He first turned the Wheel of Dharma and Kushinagar, where He entered into Parinirvana.[432]

428. This information was provided by Tenzin Dawa, the former abbot of Ngor Monastery, in Rongye, Sikkim. The interviews were on April 17 and 22, 2009 at Ngor Monastery.

429. Philip Glass, *Words Without Music* (New York: Liveright Publishing Company, 2015), 174.

430. The family was extremely wealthy since they had a monopoly on the wool trade between Tibet and India. They were significant sponsors of the Sakyas.

431. Interview with Tenzin Dawa in Sikkim, April 17 and 22, 2009.

432. *Melody of Dharma* 2013, no. II: 7.

Fig. 28. The Dolma Palace family and entourage at Sarnath, India, 1960. H.E. Jetsun Kushok is standing next to H.H. the 41st Sakya Trizin, who is seated.

Thus during the winter, the family went on a Buddhist pilgrimage to generate merit for all the Tibetans and to pray for the Tibetans who had died by performing many pujas and reciting many prayers. The family and their entourage began their pilgrimage from Darjeeling. They went to Bodhgaya, Sarnath, Kushinagar, Lumbini, and Kathmandu. The 41st Sakya Trizin distinctly remembers that

> On their way to Kathmandu, there is a high pass. The [hired] bus broke down on top of the mountain. The driver had to get to Kathmandu to buy some parts. They waited a long time for him to come back, and again a long time for him to fix the bus. By the time they reached Kathmandu, it was the middle of the night and everything was closed. So the driver invited them to sleep at his house, which was an old style house with elaborately carved wooden windows and doors. The next day they visited Swayambu and Boudha. The Nepal part was easy because so many people spoke Tibetan. Their interpreter (Hindi) was a married Sikkimese monk who had little need for food or drink, but who would carry his box of pan (betel nut) everywhere.[433]

433. H.H. the 41st Sakya Trizin email, December 9, 2018.

After the pilgrimage, the 41st Sakya Trizin stayed at Dakpa Monastery in Kalimpong, where Khenpo Rinchen, an expert in Buddhist logic, taught him philosophy and other subjects. One of the texts he studied was Shantideva's *Guide to the Bodhisattva's Way of Life* (*Bodhicaryavatara*). This seventh-century text is a favorite of H.H. the 14th Dalai Lama, whose favorite verse from it is:

> For as long as space endures
> And for as long as living beings remain,
> Until then may I, too, abide
> To dispel the misery of the world.

This is the ultimate wish of a bodhisattva, who intentionally returns again and again to the world to help all sentient beings be released from suffering.

While the 41st Sakya Trizin was studying and being trained to become a great religious leader, Jetsun Kushok's position and future were less clear. Times were difficult for all Tibetans. Now, as refugees in India, many had to acquire new skills—or find new ways to apply skills they already possessed. For Jetsun Kushok, who was a nun, it was especially difficult. In Indian culture, the only women who shaved their heads were widows, who were associated with inauspiciousness because their husbands had died before they did. Also, a woman wearing monastic dress was not accepted easily in India, where the dominant religions, Hinduism and Islam, considered women primarily as mothers and wives.

Jetsun Kushok recalls that she became the object of ridicule and scorn due to her shaved head and monastic robes. She sought the advice of H.H. the Dalai Lama and her brother, who advised her to give up wearing the robes. But she always says with conviction, "Though I gave up the external appearance of a nun, I have always maintained my inner demeanor of a nun."

From Kalimpong they moved to Darjeeling and stayed at another Pandatsang residence there. They stayed on the second floor; they did not have to pay rent, but they did have to pay for water and electricity. Lobsang Yarphel, head of the Pandatsang family, had an older wife who quickly became a friend to Dagmo Trinlei Paljor. His new younger wife became a friend of Jetsun Kushok, who remarks, "I tried to learn English there. I was very shy, so I did not speak a lot of English."

Fig. 29. H.E. Jetsun Kushok, Dagmo Trinlei Paljor, and Ani Freda Bedi in India in the mid-1960s.

In Darjeeling, Jetsun Kushok kept her hair short with bangs and wore traditional Tibetan women's clothes (Fig. 29). When monks would still recognize her and make prostrations to her, she would get mad. She was conflicted because although she was a jetsunma and was accustomed to receive honors such as prostrations, she felt she wasn't dressed properly for such signs of respect. Unlike her brother's status, which remained unchanged outside Tibet, it was no longer clear to her who she was and what society expected of her.

She describes herself as being quite a tomboy while living in India. Some Tibetans remember that Jetsun Kushok was developing a reputation of being wild because she wanted to dress in a more modern fashion and go to the movies. She loved movies, and, in fact, has said that she learned Hindi from watching films. But this was not proper comportment for a Khon family jetsunma.

Her aunt Dagmo Trinlei Paljor scolded her, saying, "In Tibet you were so good and gave teachings, but here you are not doing this." She cried because Jetsun Kushok was doing the wrong things. But Jetsun Kushok did continue her spiritual studies of *The Three Visions* (sNang gsum) by Ngorchen Konchog Lhundrub,[434] a text that explains the three states

---

434. See Ngorchen Konchog Lhundrub, *The Three Visions: Fundamental Teachings of the Sakya Lineage of Tibetan Buddhism*, trans. Lobsang Dagpa and Jay Goldberg (Ithaca, NY: Snow Lion, 1991), and Deshung Rinpoche 1995, which is a commentary on this text.

that sentient beings experience: First is suffering and delusion, because beings lack the knowledge of true reality. Second is having the proper methods to eliminate this suffering, for others as well as for oneself. The third and final state is the actual experience and knowledge of true reality. She also studied *A Clear Differentiation of the Three Codes* (*sDom gsum rab dbye*) by Sakya Pandita.[435] As refugees, the family had to endure many of the difficulties of being "homeless" and adjusting to new conditions in India. It was trying time for Tibetans. The Dolma Palace family was no exception.

Many Tibetans were encouraged to study English. In 1960, some members of the Khon family from the Phuntsok Palace—Jigdal Dagchen Sakya, Dagmo Jamyang Sakya, the 3rd Dezhung Rinpoche, and other family members—were invited to Seattle as scholars in Tibetan Studies at the University of Washington. The family as a whole agreed that English would be useful, whether they stayed in India or moved to the West.

Jetsun Kushok explains that, while in Darjeeling, "I was homeschooled in English by a servant of the Protestant missionary—Mr. John. He was half Nepalese and half Bhutanese. Both H.H. Sakya Trizin and I went to church every Sunday for a year or so because it made the missionary happy. The church was actually in someone's house. We sang songs and read the Bible. Most of the congregation was local Phari people." Jetsun Kushok explains this in a matter-of-fact way and does not seemed to have been impressed or influenced by the missionary. She continues, "Some people think that I met my future husband, Sey Kushok, in this church, but it is not correct. Sey Kushok was a student of His Holiness [the 41st Sakya Trizin]."[436]

Dagmo Trinlei Paljor heard about a nurse-training program, so she thought that Jetsun Kushok should learn to be a nurse in order to serve the Tibetan government. In 1962 Jetsun Kushok went to Shimla, the capital of the Himalayan foothill province of Himachal Pradesh, and worked there with children in the Tibetan nursery. She was not actually trained as a nurse and was taught only for 15 minutes how to take a child's temperature. Basically, she changed diapers, made beds, and served food.

435. See Sakya Pandita Kunga Gyaltshen, *A Clear Differentiation of the Three Codes: Essential Distinctions among the Individual Liberation, Great Vehicle, and Tantric Systems*, trans. Jared D. Rhoton (Albany: State University of New York Press, 2001).

436. Interview with Jetsun Kushok in 2013.

Together with only one other woman, she took care of 36 children. Recalling these times, Jetsun Kushok shakes her head in dismay and says, "The conditions were unsanitary and my health worsened." After nine months she got *"tipa,"* a kind of pollution that one can pick up from sick people and unhygienic places. Being exposed to this uncleanliness can make one sick. It was decided that she quit this job and return to the family. Fortunately, the *tipa* ceased after she left the job.

In autumn 1962, war broke out at the border between India and China. China attacked India in the northwest in the area of Ladakh, and in the northeast in Arunchal Pradesh. The Chinese intentionally chose the time of the Cuban Missile Crisis so that India would not receive any immediate help from the prevailing world superpowers. Fortunately, the Chinese withdrew in less than a month. However, this showed the Indian government how vulnerable India was. It made people nervous, especially the Tibetans, who wondered how safe they were in India.

The family decided to move from Darjeeling and settle in Mussoorie—another former British hill station, closer to New Delhi, the capital of India. They rented a house on the quiet and picturesque Camel's Back Road in Mussoorie,[437] where one could see the Himalayan mountains to the north, including Mount Kamet. The family loved looking at the mountains and thinking about the Land of Snows, Tibet. Here the 41st Sakya Trizin continued his studies and spiritual training. Dagmo Trinlei Paljor ensured that he had the best teachers, such as Appey Rinpoche (1926–2010; Fig. 30), a great master in both sutra and tantra and a disciple of the famous Jamyang Khyentse Chokyi Lodro. Appey Rinpoche taught Sakya Trizin different tantras that Jamyang Khyentse had received from his own teacher, the first Deshung Ajam Rinpoche, a great Tibetan mystic. Appey Rinpoche also taught him Madhyamaka philosophy, as well as poetry, grammar, and arithmetic.[438] The family lived in Mussoorie until 1971.

Since the family was living in a small and isolated place, they had few social responsibilities compared to when they had lived in Sakya,

---

437. See Germaine Krull and Marilyn Ekdahl Ravicz, *A Promise Kept: Memoir of Tibetans in India* (Xlibris, 2018) for a detailed account of the extensive time Krull spent with Chimey-la (as she calls Jetsun Kushok), the 41st Sakya Trizin, and other members of the Dolma Palace family during these years. (Unfortunately, I only learned of this book after I wrote about Jetsun Kushok. I highly recommend it.)

438. Tseten 2008, 39.

Fig. 30. H.H. the 41st Sakya Trizin and his teacher Appey Rinpoche in the 1960s.

so Dagmo Trinlei Paljor's energies were redirected. Being an industrious woman, she had more time to devote to spiritual practices, and she enjoyed doing beadwork. In Sakya, Jetsun Kushok's paternal aunts had been skilled at beadwork and had enjoyed it as a hobby. Both Dagmo Trinlei Paljor and Jetsun Kushok had learned to do beadwork in Sakya from Jetsun Kushok's paternal aunt, Jetsunma Chime Wangmo (see Chapter 6).

The beadwork done by the Sakya jetsunmas was not a usual pastime of aristocratic Tibetan women. It was done primarily to make coverings for ritual vases or for mandalas depicting the eight auspicious symbols or the eight offerings of the royal symbols. When Dagmo Trinlei Paljor first arrived in India, she busied herself by making a stunning beaded mandala that she offered to the 14th Dalai Lama. Later, she made another beautiful beaded mandala of freshwater pearls and tiny corals. The Sakya Centre in Rajpur continues to use it in some ceremonies. Both Dagmo Trinlei Paljor and Jetsun Kushok enjoyed this work but did not consider it a way to earn money. Rather, it was a way to show their devotion to the Buddhist teachings.

Though the Khon family had little wealth or political influence in India, Tibetan refugees still expected help from the family. As conditions deteriorated in Tibet, more and more Tibetans sought exile in India.

Tibetans expected important lamas, such as the 41st Sakya Trizin, to help them in their plight, but he did not own any land or have abundant wealth to distribute to the new arrivals.

Lobsang Lhalungpa, the Tibetan radio broadcaster for All-India Radio, was in demand. Since he was both a representative of the newly formed Tibetan Government in Exile and the broadcaster based in Delhi, he had access to important Indian officials. He remembers that Jetsun Kushok came south to Delhi as a representative of her brother Sakya Trizin when they lived in Mussoorie. In 1964, she informed the Government in Exile that more than five hundred Sakya monks had followed the Khon family from Darjeeling to Mussoorie in 1963 and needed a place to live. Mr. Lhalungpa introduced her to some influential Indian officials and also told her to seek the Dalai Lama's approval.

Within several months, the 41st Sakya Trizin and Dagmo Trinlei Paljor were asked to choose some land for a settlement. This settlement, which continues to exist today, is Puruwala, in Himachal Pradesh State, located a few hours' drive from Dehradun in present-day Uttarakhand State.[439] It consists of 112 acres, of which 92 acres were converted to farmland, with the remaining 20 acres for housing and a monastery. It was inaugurated in 1968, originally provided land for 900 refugees, and remains a thriving community today.[440] The Dolma Palace family built a home in Puruwala that is used primarily for special occasions, such as marriages and celebrating the Tibetan New Year.

H.E. Jetsun Kushok's Marriage

As the family was settling in India, the Khon family reassessed their situation. Dagmo Trinlei Paljor was satisfied that the 41st Sakya Trizin was being raised properly and receiving many teachings from eminent lamas. However, Jetsun Kushok's future was less clear, and Dagmo Trinlei Paljor thought that she should marry. When Jetsun Kushok heard this, she was against marriage regardless of who her future husband might be.

439. Interview with Mr. Lobsang P. Lhalungpa (1926–2008) at his home in Santa Fe, New Mexico, October 2007.

440. See the interview with the 41st Sakya Trizin in Tseten 2008, 39, in which he credits Ven. Thutop Tulku (d. 1970) for organizing the Puruwala settlement "practically single-handed." See also Krull and Ravicz 2018, 169 and passim, on "Lama Thuthop." Thutop Tulku was the brother of Chiwang Tulku.

Chart 5. The Dolma Palace, Mid-20th to 21st Century

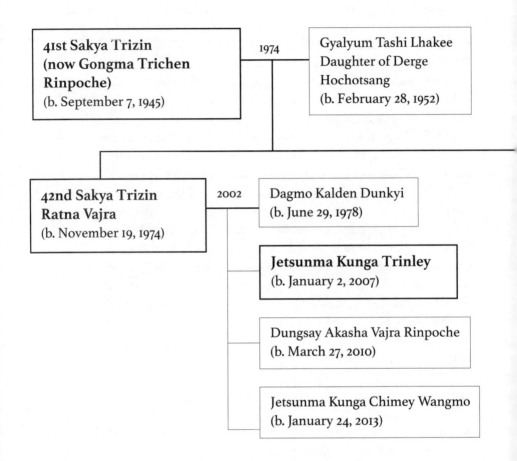

41st Sakya Trizin (now Gongma Trichen Rinpoche) (b. September 7, 1945)

1974

Gyalyum Tashi Lhakee Daughter of Derge Hochotsang (b. February 28, 1952)

42nd Sakya Trizin Ratna Vajra (b. November 19, 1974)

2002

Dagmo Kalden Dunkyi (b. June 29, 1978)

Jetsunma Kunga Trinley (b. January 2, 2007)

Dungsay Akasha Vajra Rinpoche (b. March 27, 2010)

Jetsunma Kunga Chimey Wangmo (b. January 24, 2013)

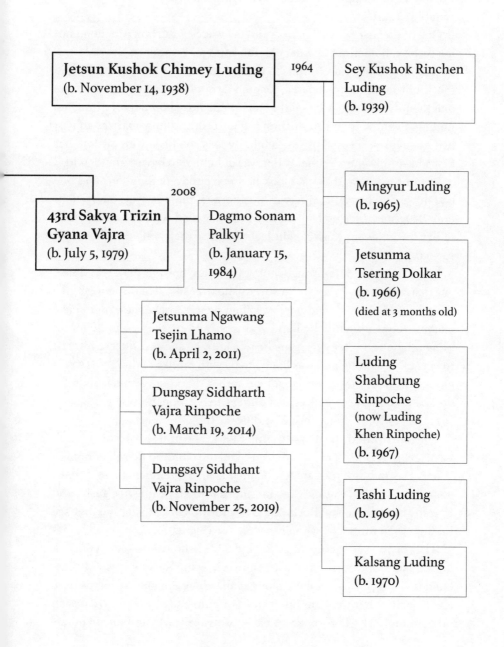

Jetsun Kushok Chimey Luding
(b. November 14, 1938)

1964

Sey Kushok Rinchen
Luding
(b. 1939)

2008

**43rd Sakya Trizin
Gyana Vajra**
(b. July 5, 1979)

Dagmo Sonam
Palkyi
(b. January 15,
1984)

Mingyur Luding
(b. 1965)

Jetsunma
Tsering Dolkar
(b. 1966)
(died at 3 months old)

Jetsunma Ngawang
Tsejin Lhamo
(b. April 2, 2011)

Dungsay Siddharth
Vajra Rinpoche
(b. March 19, 2014)

Dungsay Siddhant
Vajra Rinpoche
(b. November 25, 2019)

Luding
Shabdrung
Rinpoche
(now Luding
Khen Rinpoche)
(b. 1967)

Tashi Luding
(b. 1969)

Kalsang Luding
(b. 1970)

She protested and told her aunt that she wanted to remain a nun. But Dagmo Trinlei Paljor did not heed her protest and proceeded to find a suitable spouse for her.

One of the 41st Sakya Trizin's students was Sey Kushok Rinchen Luding (b. 1939, hereafter Sey Kushok), the younger brother of Ngor Monastery Luding Khenchen Rinpoche (b. 1931). Since the Luding family and the Khon family were related, Dagmo Trinlei Paljor and some of the older family advisors decided that Jetsun Kushok should marry Rinchen Luding. Eventually Jetsun Kushok acquiesced, and they married in 1964 (Chart 5). It was a small private affair. By 1965 she had given birth to her first son, and Dagmo Trinlei Paljor was delighted to have a grandchild.

Jetsun Kushok and Sey Kushok had five children: four sons and one daughter. The first son, Mingyur, was born in India in 1965. Sadly, their only daughter, Tsering Dolkar, born in 1966, died within a few months of her birth. Jetsun Kushok still feels sad that their only daughter died so young.

Their third child, Jamyang Chokyi Gyaltsen, born in 1967, was different than the others (Fig. 31). Jetsun Kushok recalls, "He did not act like the other children. He did not cry. When he was awake, he would make *mudras* (religious symbolic hand gestures), and he seemed to be mumbling religious texts. By the time he was four, he showed sincere interest in becoming a monk and was happy to be with monks. If there was a religious ceremony, he wanted to attend rather than play as most children do." Later, he was recognized as Luding Khen Rinpoche, and today he is the abbot of Ngor Monastery, Manduwala, India.[441]

The fourth child, Tashi, was born in 1969. The fifth is Kalzang, born in 1970. Jetsun Kushok stated, "I delivered all the children myself at home." When the family emigrated to Canada on September 21, 1971, their youngest, Kalzang, was only ten months old. Today Mingyur, Tashi, and Kalzang live near Jetsun Kushok and Sey Kushok in Canada, and they see Luding Khen Rinpoche whenever they can (Fig. 32).

It has been a very good marriage, and Sey Kushok helps Jetsun Kushok both at home and when she teaches abroad. Jetsun Kushok says, "My husband is very good—he is not jealous at all, whereas some husbands have a very jealous nature. I am not jealous of him, either, and we trust each other completely. This makes it easy for me to travel and teach; other-

---

441. For more on Luding Khen Rinpoche, see note 447 below.

Fig. 31. H.E. Jetsun Kushok and her son Luding Khen Rinpoche in the mid-1990s.

Fig. 32. H.E. Sey Kushok and H.E. Jetsun Kushok in India, 2002.

wise, if my husband were a jealous person, it would be quite difficult. He has many good qualities and supports me completely."[442]

While still in India, Jetsun Kushok received a sweater-knitting machine from the United Nations, which was donating these machines to refugees. She was sent to Dehradun to learn how to use it. Jetsun Kushok admitted, "I was terrible." Her husband learned how to make designs much better than she. Since his English was better, he showed her how to improve her designs by reading the instructions clearly. After a year, the UN wanted a report of how much money she had earned from making sweaters. Jetsun Kushok remarked, "I didn't sell any. I made one for H.H. Sakya Trizin and other family members. I didn't make any money."

In 1971 the entire family moved from the hill station of Mussoorie down to the small town of Rajpur and stayed at the Sakya Centre, established in 1964 as a monastic institute where refugee monks could receive a Buddhist education with emphasis on the Sakya tradition. The institute also provides instruction in Buddhist rituals, ritual music, religious dance, and art. It continues to be an important monastic institution for training Sakya monks.

Jay Goldberg, a longtime student of the 41st Sakya Trizin recalls, "The entire family stayed there, including H.E. Jetsun Kushok, her husband

442. Interview with Jetsun Kushok in 2013.

and four sons. In September 1971, H.E. Jetsun Kushok and her family moved to Canada. Peter Della Santina and I had just started studying the *Suhṛllekha* (*Letter to King Gautamīputra*) with His Holiness in May 1971 at the Sakya Centre in Rajpur. Also, Chogye Trichen Rinpoche arrived that summer to begin giving His Holiness the *Compendium of Tantras*."[443]

The 41st Sakya Trizin has praised his teacher Chogye Trichen Rinpoche as follows: "There are many who have attained the wisdom arising from the study of the Scriptures. There are some who have attained the wisdom arising from contemplation of the Dharma. There are few who have gained wisdom arising from meditation. His Eminence Chogye Trichen Rinpoche is one who has attained all three wisdoms. One should consider oneself fortunate just to meet him, which is in itself a great blessing."[444]

Jay Goldberg continues, "His Holiness lived in an old house at the Sakya Centre, but by autumn, a temple was built on that site and two rooms on the second floor above the temple became His Holiness' living and audience quarters. Dagmo Trinlei Paljor Zangmo stayed in a small room on the side of the temple."

H.H. THE 41ST SAKYA TRIZIN'S MARRIAGE

Though Dagmo Trinlei Paljor continued to do extensive religious practices, she still was thinking about maintaining the lineage of the Dolma Palace. Since the 41st Sakya Trizin was the only surviving son, he needed to marry to have a future heir. In consultation with some lamas, she looked for an appropriate wife for him. She succeeded (see Chart 5). In early 1974, Tashi Lhakee (b. 1952), daughter of Derge Hochotsang, a noble family from the kingdom of Derge in Kham, Tibet, married the 41st Sakya Trizin (Fig. 33). According to tradition, it was a quiet and simple affair.

Jay Goldberg (Fig. 34) recalls: "A few of us foreigners [who were] living in Rajpur and assisting His Holiness would always go to Puruwala for Losar (Tibetan New Year) celebrations. In 1974 Jared Rhoton, John Tate, and I were in Rajpur when it was time for His Holiness, Mo-mo-la or Dagmo Kusho—His Holiness' aunt, we called her both names—and

443. Jay Goldberg email, April 16, 2017.

444. https://www.tsechen.org/index.php/english/about-sakya/sakya-masters/45-his -eminence-chogye-trichen-rinpoche. See also Jackson 2020.

Fig. 33. After the wedding of Gyalyum Tashi Lhakee and H.H. the 41st Sakya Trizin in Puruwalla, India, February 1974.

entourage to go to Puruwala. We were explicitly told that we were not allowed to accompany His Holiness this year to Puruwala and that we must remain behind in Rajpur. We all thought this quite strange. About a week or 10 days later, we received word that we were finally allowed to journey to Puruwala to join the celebrations. Upon arrival, we learned that a wedding ceremony had concluded and we were introduced to the new young Dagmo, Tashi Lhakee."

In November 1974, Gyalyum[445] Tashi Lhakee gave birth to her first son, Dungsay Ratna Vajra (the future 42nd Sakya Trizin). Dagmo Trinlei Paljor was overjoyed. Gyalyum Tashi Lhakee remembers, "Auntie was so happy to see her grandson. He would give her a big smile. She said, 'My only regret is that he cannot call me Mo-mo-la [Grandmother].'" They lived together in Puruwala for only a few months; then the family moved back to the Sakya Centre in Rajpur. Having the opportunity to buy a house very close to the Sakya Centre, the Dolma Palace Society

---

445. Gyalyum is a title given to the wife when her husband becomes the Sakya Trizin.

Fig. 34. Jay Goldberg (far left) with the Dolma Palace family in
Kuching, Sarawak, Malaysia, ca. 1977.

purchased it.[446] Now that Sakya Trizin was married, it was decided that
it was best to stay there since the Sakya Centre is a monastic institution.

THE DEATH OF DAGMO TRINLEI PALJOR

A few months later, the family went to Nepal to pay a visit to Tharig Monastery in Bodhnath. Upon their return, Dagmo Trinlei Paljor became
sick. She was only sick for a few months. Gyalyum Tashi Lhakee recalls,
"She wasn't in pain but she needed to sleep on a bed for the first time
in many years. Dagmo said, 'I am very happy to have you as a Dagmo
[i.e., as the wife of H.H. Sakya Trizin] and I am extremely happy to see a
grandson.' Dagmo made a prayer that he would grow up well and serve
the Sakyas well. She was very satisfied with me."

At this time, Dagmo Trinlei Paljor remarked that she had raised so
many children—Jetsun Kushok and Sakya Trizin; her attendant and
great-niece Aja Dolkar (Appendix A) and, later, Aja Dolkar's son Tsering
Dorje (Appendix B); Jetsun Kushok's oldest son Mingyur; and (for eight
months before she died) the little Dungsay Ratna Vajra. Jay Goldberg
recalls,

> Dagmo Kushok [Trinlei Paljor] also looked after Jetsunma's
> second son, Luding Shabdrung, who was left behind in India

---

446. The Dolma Palace Society was formed to carry on the spiritual and benevolent work of
the Sakya tradition and the Khon family.

when Jetsunma and the rest of her family moved to Canada. The son stayed in India in order to become the Luding Shabdrung [the successor to his uncle Luding Rinpoche, b. 1931], and he is now the Luding Khenpo [the abbot of Ngor Monastery, Manduwala, India].[447] The former abbot [his uncle] is retired and known as the great abbot, or Khenchen.

Dagmo stated that her life was fulfilled and complete. She raised H.H. Sakya Trizin, gave him love and care, made him a great master, found him a Dagmo who bore her first son.[448]

When Dagmo Trinlei Paljor was ailing, her younger brother Tashi Palrab visited her from Dharamsala, where he worked for the Tibetan Government in Exile. Usually he would visit her several times a year, and most years they celebrated Tibetan New Year's together. She was very happy to see him and told him, "Now I do not have the regret of not seeing you. You don't need to come anymore. Don't worry. H.H. Sakya Trizin and some attendants are helping me."

Aja Dolkar, her main servant (see Appendix A), who took care of her during her brief illness, reported that Dagmo Trinlei Paljor told her that the goddess Tara came to her, and that when she recited the goddess Kurukulle mantra, Kurukulle appeared. Sangye-la, a senior family servant, explained she kept talking about a red-clothed woman appearing again and again. He said that he knew she had other visions as well, but she didn't discuss them.

The 41st Sakya Trizin gave Dagmo Trinlei Paljor many initiations before she died. For instance, he gave her a special Sakya form of the Sarvavid Vairocana (Kunrig) empowerment that is for purification of nega-

---

447. The position of Head Abbot of Ngor Monastery was traditionally held for a three-year period in which extensive teachings are given almost non-stop. The three-year periods alternated among the four monastic houses (labrangs)—Luding, Khangsar, Thartse, and Phende. Due to the Chinese takeover of Tibet in 1959 and the disruption to the Ngor monastic system, His Eminence Luding Khenchen Rinpoche Jamyang Nyima (kLu sdings mkhan chen rin po che 'jam dbyangs nyi ma, b. 1931), the 75th head of the Ngor tradition, effectively led and maintained the Ngor school up to March 16, 2000. It was then that his nephew, Jetsun Kushok's second son, was enthroned at Ngor Pal Ewam Choden Monastery, Manduwala, as the 76th abbot of the line. He is now known as His Eminence Luding Khen Rinpoche, while his predecessor the 75th is now addressed as Luding Khenchen Rinpoche.

448. Jay Goldberg email, March 16, 2016.

tive karma, thus preventing rebirth in one of the three lower realms. He also gave her the Hevajra and Amitāyus initations. At death, he gave her the Vajrayoginī initiation; she died as he was invoking the wisdom deities' (*jñānasattva*) descent into one's consciousness. The 41st Sakya Trizin finished the initiation. She died in 1975, on the twenty-fifth day of the fifth month. (It was in July, so it was very hot.) She stayed in the Clear Light for four days. This is a sign that a person is a highly realized practitioner and has control over her subtle consciousness (*sems*).

Before the cremation, which occurred seven days after passing away, Dagmo Trinlei Paljor was dressed in the crown and ornaments of a deity, with her hands holding a bell and dorje. Her body, which was in the lotus posture, was placed in large earthen stupa-like structure with an opening in front. On the very bottom of the earthen structure were painted mandalas on paper of her main meditational deities. For some lamas there is only the Sarvavid Vairocana mandala, but in this case there was was a second layer above it for the Vajrayoginī mandala, then a third layer with the Hevajra mandala. On top of the mandalas was the wood, and above the wood a large metal "basin" which holds the body. (The basin collects the ashes and any *ringsels*, unique residues that are small crystal-like beads. These are considered to be holy relics and are treasured by devotees. From the ashes, *tsa tsas*, or reliquary molds, are made.) Those present at the cremation ritual offered white scarves to the body before the wood was lit. During the cremation, the 41st Sakya Trizin was doing the Hevajra practice; Luding Khen Rinpoche, abbot of Ngor Monastery, the Vajrayoginī practice; and Khenpo Appey Rinpoche, the abbot of Sakya College, the Sarvavid Vairocana practice. The smoke went straight up in a clockwise fashion. This was an excellent sign that her subtle consciousness was freed. Small reliquary clay stupas (*tsa tsas*) were made from the ashes and put in the water on a mountain or hill as a final offering of her body.

JETSUN KUSHOK IN CANADA

Jetsun Kushok has said that neither her brother nor her aunt nor she herself had considered her moving to Canada. It was one of their friends, Germaine Krull (see Fig. 33), who made the suggestion: "I thought that I was doing well, that I was very rich—but I guess she thought that I was very poor. She asked me if I wanted to go to Canada." Knowing the

Fig. 35. Sey Kushok and H.E. Jetsun Kushok at Jigdal Dagchen Rinpoche's home in Seattle, ca. 1976.

Canadian ambassador in India, their friend helped them secure immigrant visas to Canada.[449]

The transition from Tibet to India had already been demanding and difficult for Jetsun Kushok, but at least she was now with her immediate family in the sacred land of India, the birthplace of the Buddha. Also, Tibetans in India knew that she was a daughter in the Khon family and showed their respect for her. In Canada, however, Jetsun Kushok, Sey Kushok, and their children were simply new immigrants. Almost no one knew about Tibet, and certainly no one knew about the Khon family and their illustrious history.

In Canada, both Jetsun Kushok and Sey Kushok had to find jobs (Fig. 35). As Jetsun Kushok recalls, "While my husband worked on a farm, feeding the cattle, I was working in the house, cooking the whole day and feeding the kids—a terrible experience because it never finished the whole day long."[450] Later, they both worked on a mushroom farm, where they had to fill many 20-pound boxes with mushrooms. When they came home from this back-breaking work, Jetsun Kushok had to cook, take care of the house, and help her young sons with their homework.

Eventually Sey Kushok became a custodian in a school in West Vancouver, British Columbia, where he worked until retirement. Jetsun

449. Much of this information can be found in "Interview with Jetsun Kushab" (i.e., Jetsun Kushok) at https://vajrasana.org/chime1.htm.
450. See "Interview with Jetsun Kushab" https://vajrasana.org/chime1.htm.

Kushok also helped clean schools in the afternoons and during the summertime. Later, when their sons were older, she worked as a weaver for the fashion designer Zonda Nellis.

Despite all these demands and challenges, Jetsun Kushok emphasizes that she always does her practice. She said, "These days [when she was working], I try to get up around 4:00. After my practice I go to work between 7:30 and 8:30, and then I work for eight hours. Then I come home and cook for the kids. My kids are very nice and helpful."[451]

When Jetsun Kushok was asked, "How do you suggest integrating Dharma into daily life?," she responded. "You have to make time .... If you really want to practice, then you have to give up things .... You must slowly eliminate distractions .... At work, or when I do my house duties, I do a lot of prayers: sometimes I do mantras, sometimes I sing songs." Thus, for Jetsun Kushok, there are no excuses for not being able to practice. One needs to make it a priority.

As Jetsun Kushok and her family settled into their lives in Canada, her brother the 41st Sakya Trizin came to North America for the second time, in 1979, to give teachings. While he was teaching at the Buddhist center established in Seattle by the 3rd Dezhung Rinpoche and Jigdal Dagchen Sakya, a woman asked: "Why is it that in Tibetan Buddhism all the teachers are men, and there were no women?" The 41st Sakya Trizin replied, "No, we have women teachers too; one of them is my sister. She is hiding somewhere in Canada."

Jetsunma notes, "That's what he said at the time. Then he came to visit me .... He did not press me, but he just said: 'If you teach in the West, it would be good.' That's the only thing he said."

At that time Jetsun Kushok was teachings some students privately, but not publicly. The 41st Sakya Trizin asked her to look after his centers in Los Angeles, Minneapolis, Boston, and New York. Jetsun Kushok stated, "Whenever these centers ask me to come, I go, and most of the time I do not talk a lot, but give empowerments and instructions."[452] She has bestowed empowerments and teachings on Tara, Mañjuśrī, Avalokiteśvara, Vajrapāṇi, Vajrayoginī, long-life deities, prosperity deities, and many others.

Jetsun Kushok travels the world to confer empowerments and teachings. She teaches in Australia, Brazil, Great Britain, Germany, Hungary,

451. Ibid.
452. Ibid.

Malaysia, Singapore, and elsewhere. One of the first places she taught was Australia. The 41st Sakya Trizin encouraged her to go and teach. He explained that, in the West, most practitioners are laypeople, unlike in Tibet, where many are monks or nuns. He said to his sister,

> You, a lay person, have a very similar lifestyle to the people you teach. You have a household, a working position, and so when you teach ... Western women can look at you and think: "If she can do it and get enlightened, so of course we can do it and get enlightened, too." It is beneficial for you and it is beneficial for other beings.[453]

The more Jetsun Kushok taught, the more her reputation as a lama rose. Many people are thrilled to meet and study with a female lama who is knowledgeable, competent, and accessible.

Also Jetsun Kushok has taught eminent lamas such as Dzongsar Khyentse Rinpoche (b. 1961), the reincarnation of Jamyang Khyentse Chokyi Lodro. He requested her to bestow the complete Vajrayoginī blessing and seven-day teachings on him. She gave him this teaching in the 1990s when he came to Vancouver. It was done at her center in Richmond. He also received other initiations from her. There was the White Tara empowerment in 1998 in Vancouver, when she, Dzongsar Khyentse Rinpoche, and Sogyal Rinpoche offered a joint program where Jetsun Kushok gave the initiation and the other two teachers taught on the practice. Dzongsar Khyentse Rinpoche often encourages his students to see her when they have the opportunity because he regards her as an enlightened being.

Not only was she invited to teach at many established Buddhist centers, but she also established some new centers in North America. Near her home in Richmond, British Columbia, she established Sakya Tsechen Thubten Ling, where she gives many empowerments and often joins the weekly Tara puja as well as the monthly Vajrayoginī *tsok*. Also, she knew there was a need for a proper place where practitioners could perform sustained retreats. In 1987 she established a retreat center, Sakya Kachod Ling, on San Juan Island in Washington State. Located on a dead-end road in the forest, it is conducive to practice with minimal distractions. The name means "Sakya Place of Vajrayoginī," and practitioners come

453. Ibid.

Fig. 36. The Dolma Palace family celebrating Losar in Puruwala, India, 2020.

there from all over the world to do three-month Vajrayoginī retreats, as well as individual retreats. Jetsun Kushok has given the seven-day Vajrayoginī teaching numerous times at the retreat center.[454] Another of her centers is Sakya Dechen Ling (Sakya Place of Great Joy), located in Albany, California.

Furthermore, as the Sakya centers expanded in the West, accurate translations of texts were needed. Jetsun Kushok made a profound contribution in the translation of the Vajrayoginī practices—from the sādhana to the seven-day teaching, *tsok* offering, *torma* text, and fire puja. Over the years she worked with different students and translators to improve the translations. Her sadhanā text of Vajrayoginī compiled in 2007 is especially sought-after because of Elizabeth Napper's elegant translation and the beautiful designs of deities and Buddhist symbols to help the practitioner's vizualization. Also Jetsun Kushok supervised translations of the Tara puja, the Samantabhadra and 16 Arhats prayers, the Chenrezig, Hevajra, and White Saraswatī sādhanas, and many more. Occasionally when some younger Sakya rinpoches were giving teachings overseas and didn't have the translated sādhanas for students, they would call her Vancouver center to request that a text be sent to them so as to provide stu-

---

454. The website of Sakya Kachod Ling states that, "Today, she has a special mandate to teach and provide a role model to all practitioners, but especially to women on the path." http://sakyakachodcholing.org/jetsun-chimey-luding-rinpoche/.

dents with the necessary practice materials. Three of her main centers hosted Path with the Result teachings bestowed by the 41st Sakya Trizin and attended by students from all over the world: Sakya Kachod Choling on San Juan Island in 1995, Sakya Tsechen Thubten Ling in Vancouver in 2000, and Sakya Kalden Ling in Frankfurt in 2016.

Just as Ani Chime Dolma and Dagmo Jamyang Sakya felt transformed in the presence of Jetsun Kushok's great-aunt, Kyabgon Pema Trinlei (see Chapter 7), so many of Jetsun Kushok's students experience joy and calmness of mind in her presence. Laetitia Sonami, who married Hiroshi Sonami,[455] Lama Kunga Rinpoche's brother, feels extremely close to Jetsun Kushok. Laetitia recalls:

> In 1984, Jetsun Kushok was visiting southern California. My husband bought for Jetsunma the most beautiful earrings that he could afford with the little money that we had at the time. I did not know Jetsunma, and was surprised to learn how important she was for him. He was always very undemonstrative of other teachers, except for His Holiness and Chogye Trichen. However, Jetsunma was extremely important to him and he asked Jetsunma to come when he would pass away, which she did. It was always very clear to me that she would be there for us, looking after my daughter and me, which she has. Jetsunma is always available whenever we need her—a hundred percent of the time.[456]

Jetsun Kushok excels at soothing people who are anxious and have worries, by giving them clear and concise advice in a decisive, no-nonsense manner. She is like a laser beam that is precise and knows exactly the source of the confusion. If she has time, she will invite you to have tea and a chat. When leaving her home, many have a wonderful smile on their faces and feel serene; these are signs of her blessing.

Today, her older nephew, the 42nd Sakya Trizin Ratna Vajra (see Chart 5), who is married to Dagmo Kalden Dunkyi, has two daughters and a son. The oldest is Jetsunma Kunga Trinley Palter (b. 2007; see Epilogue),

---

455. Hiroshi Sonami (1930–88) was an abbot at Ngor Monastery; his full name and title was Ngor Thartse Khenpo Sonam Gyatso Rinpoche.

456. Laetitia Sonami email, January 10, 2019.

followed by Dungsay Akasha Vajra Rinpoche (b. 2010) and Jetsunma Kunga Chimey Wangmo Sakya (b. 2013). Her younger nephew, the 43rd Sakya Trizin Gyana Vajra, who is married to Dagmo Sonam Palkyi, has a daughter and two sons. The oldest is Jetsunma Ngawang Tsejin Lhamo (b. 2011), followed by Dungsay Siddharth Vajra Rinpoche (b. 2014) and Dungsay Siddhant Vajra Rinpoche (b. 2019). Jetsun Kushok sees them frequently at teachings, empowerments, and family visits at the Dolma Palaces in Rajpur and in Purkul (the Summer Palace),[457] and often celebrates the Tibetan New Year with them at the Dolma Palace in Puruwala (Fig. 36).

Jetsun Kushok does not directly teach her great-nieces since their grandfather (the 41st Sakya Trizin) and their own fathers (the 42nd and 43rd) are themselves great teachers. All the young jetsunmas are undergoing all the religious preparation that is relevant to their role as jetsunmas. As the Khon family continues its centuries-long activities as a spiritual family dedicated to helping beings become free from suffering and gain insight into true reality, the jetsunmas continue to be powerful partners in achieving this goal for all beings.

457. The 43rd Sakya Trizin Gyana Vajra established the Sakya Academy for young monks, and the family resides there. See http://sakyaacademy.org. The exact location is Purkul Road, Bhagawantpur, Dehradun.

Jetsunma Kunga Trinley (b. 2007), The First Vegan Jetsunma

TIBETAN BUDDHISM has a tradition of recognizing a person who intentionally takes rebirth in a particular place for the benefit of sentient beings. These people are known as *tulkus*, or recognized reincarnations. Female tulkus are rare in Tibetan Buddhism (Fig. 37). None of the biographical material on which the preceding chapters are based states that a jetsunma was a recognized reincarnation. However, in the case of Jetsunma Kunga Trinley Palter (b. January 2, 2007), the 14th Dalai Lama recognized her as the reincarnation of Khandro Tare Lhamo (1938–2002), a Nyingma practitioner who is remembered as a *terton* (one who discovers hidden Buddhist texts, or *terma*). Another unusual fact is that Jetsunma Kunga Trinley's grandfather, the 41st Sakya Trizin, is the current reincarnation of Khandro Tare Lhamo's father, Apam Orgyen Trinlei Lingpa (1895–1945).[458]

Jetsunma Kunga Trinley's father is the 42nd Sakya Trizin, Ratna Vajra Sakya (b. 1974), who is the older son of the 41st Sakya Trizin, and her mother is Dagmo Kalden Dunkyi, b. 1978).[459] Dagmo Kalden recalls:

> I had a very calm pregnancy. I spent many of the months with my Ngondro practice[460] and performed countless Vajrasattva

458. See Holly Gayley, *Inseparable across Lifetimes: The Lives and Love Letters of the Tibetan Visionaries Namtrul Rinpoche and Khandro Tare Lhamo* (Boulder, CO: Snow Lion, 2019). The 41st Sakya Trizin was recognized as two different reincarnations simultaneously. One was the Nyingma master O rgyan phrin las gling pa (1895–1945) from Amdo. However, contrary to tradition, the Nyingma family did not request him to return to Amdo but accepted his remaining in Sakya and being raised as a Sakya throne-holder.

459. For a brief biography of Dagmo Kalden, see http://hhsakyatrizin.net/wp-content/uploads/2017/02/Melody of Dharma 10.pdf.

460. The *ngondro* ("preliminary") practices are: purification through precise visualizations of

Fig. 37. Jetsunma Kunga Trinley (far left) with her father
H.H. the 42nd Sakya Trizin and her family.

mantra recitations, which helped me to feel light and pure
during the whole pregnancy.... I went for countless *kora* [cir-
cumambulations in a clockwise manner] around the Boudha-
nath stupa [in Nepal]. While I was pregnant I was blessed by
Luding Khenchen Rinpoche and received special protective

_____

the deity Vajrasattva; accumulation of merit by offering the mandala as the symbol of the universe; development of humility by doing prostrations; and strengthening one's faith through
guru devotion. These four precise practices need to be done at least 100,000 times each.

chakras [amulets] from Dzongsar Khyentse Rinpoche that were blessed and empowered by him for me to wear during the entire pregnancy.[461]

This is the first biography in this book that clearly states some of the religious practices that a mother underwent during her pregnancy.

Jetsunma Kunga Trinley's great-aunt, Jetsun Kushok (Chapters 8 and 9), was born on the day when the Buddha descended from Tushita Heaven after visiting his mother to impart the important teachings of the Abhidharma (the systematic account of existence).[462] Similarly, Jetsunma Kunga Trinley was born on an auspicious day—in her case, on the parinirvana day of her illustrious ancestor, Sakya Pandita (1182–1251), one of the five founders of the Sakya school and a renowned scholar-practitioner. This has been interpreted as a foreshadowing of her future greatness. Like all children born into the Khon family, Jetsunma Kunga Trinley received her first blessing very soon after she was born, in the form of Mañjuśrī's seed syllable, *dhīḥ*, being traced on her tongue with nectar water by her grandfather, the 41st Sakya Trizin. Before she was brought home from the hospital, her own father, the future 42nd Sakya Trizin, also blessed her to protect her and remove any potential obstacles. Jetsunma Kunga Trinley is the oldest of the six grandchildren to date of the 41st Sakya Trizin and his wife Gyalyum Tashi Lhakee (see Chart 5).

When the family arrived home, according to tradition everyone was served auspicious buttered rice and tea, to create an excellent beginning for the baby girl. In addition, H.E. Dzongsar Khyentse Rinpoche (b. 1961) ordered "twelve magnificent baskets of flowers" to "signal her welcome into the world." As Dagmo Kalden recalls,

> Over the next few days and weeks Jetsunma continued to receive mandala offerings from every monastery and nunnery as well as monks, nuns and lay people. One thing I did notice was how often she would receive gifts over the next few years. [We received] gifts from friends, family and many anonymous

461. Dagmo Kalden email, August 21, 2019. Much of the information that follows is from this email.

462. In Tibetan, this day is known as Lhabab Duchen.

people. Every time I wished I had something for her like a nice sleeping bag during the winter, I would suddenly get one in the mail! It was quite miraculous![463]

She continues:

We noticed as a child that she would call her father Aba, and however much we encouraged her to say Yabla (honorific for father) she would insist on saying Aba. She would insist on calling two monks not by their names, but by unfamiliar names like Amo and NuNu. We did not quite understand where all this was coming from, until she was recognized by His Holiness the 14th Dalai Lama as the reincarnation of Khandro Tare Lhamo. We then understood that Aba was the term used by Khandro Tare Lhamo for her father! And we believe that the monk names were also names of monks she knew in her past life.

Were she in Tibet, she might have had an upbringing that kept her isolated from most people, confined mostly to the rooms of her house and undergoing a daily rigorous training with a teacher or two. Today, Jetsunma has a rigorous schedule but one that is filled with books that open her eyes to the world, with people whom she can interact with, and with places she can visit and explore. Each has its plus points and minus, but I think that in this day and age, such exposure is vital.

Just like any young lady her age, she likes handicrafts, lettering and creating things with her hands. She enjoys reading, gymnastics, physical activities and strength training! She has already traveled to many countries and is fluent in many languages.[464]

Jay Goldberg, longtime student of the 41st Sakya Trizin, was asked by Jetsunma Kunga Trinley's father the 42nd Sakya Trizin to tutor her in English when she was visiting Walden, New York.[465] He wrote,

463. Dagmo Kalden email, August 21, 2019.
464. Ibid.
465. Jetsunma Kunga Trinley has stayed several times at Tsechen Kunchab Ling, the seat of the Dolma Palace in North America, located in Walden, New York.

We didn't have many sessions together, but in any case her English was very good and her general knowledge of various subjects was widespread. For example, we discussed Indian history and she was quite knowledgeable in that field. We discussed the life of the Buddha, and also she had a keen recognition of that. She mentioned that she was being taught to play the Indian flute (*bansari* flute). As you know she speaks several languages (Chinese, Hindi and English) as well as Tibetan.[466]

Jetsunma Kunga Trinley has many firsts as a jetsunma. Besides being the first jetsunma to be a recognized reincarnation (*tulku*), she is the first to be brought up in India and educated both in the traditional Sakya manner and by attending a small private school in Dehradun. Her very early life was documented online, through her photographic journal at http://www.jetsunma.blogspot.com. There are YouTube videos about various events in her young life. She is probably the first jetsunma who can speak four languages well. From birth, she has eaten only vegetarian food, and at a young age she became a vegan for the spiritual reasons of trying to minimize harm and show compassion toward sentient beings. On a video of June 3, 2019, she and her younger brother are seen asking others to become vegetarian during the holy month of Sakadawa, or even longer if possible.[467] Jay Goldberg states, "She seems very reserved, gentle and pure."[468]

From an early age, Jetsunma Kunga Trinley has been educated in the way all Khon children are trained. Dagmo Kalden states:

> She has received many empowerments from her grandfather, His Holiness the Sakya Trichen as well as her father His Holiness the Sakya Trizin including numerous Hevajra empowerments, Vajrakīlaya empowerments, Long Life empowerments, the entire Common Lamdre twice, Oral Transmissions of the Sakya Kabum and Ngorchen Kabum (Collection of Five Founding Sakya Masters and Ngorchen Dorjechang), Vajrayoginī

466. Jay Goldberg email, November 17, 2019.
467. https://www.youtube.com/watch?v=ly6R_jc3DSo.
468. Jay Goldberg email, November 17, 2019.

Blessings, and various initiations and teachings of Dharma Protectors.[469]

Jetsunma Kunga Trinley is following the same method of developing spiritual acumen we have seen in the life stories of earlier Sakya jetsunmas profiled in this volume. She often attends the major teachings when her father or grandfather publicly bestows the empowerments, commentaries, and practices of the Path with the Result. For example, in May 2012, at Tsechen Kunchab Ling, the seat of the Dolma Palace in North America (located in Walden, New York), the 41st Sakya Trizin imparted the Path with the Result (Lamdre). He was seated on the main throne facing the audience. His son, Ratna Vajra Sakya, was seated on a lower throne facing his father, and Jetsunma Kunga Trinley was on a slightly lower throne. Her seat was higher than those of other important lamas attending the teachings. During these extensive teachings, she seemed focused and immersed in listening to the instructions and commentary. She was only five years old.

Later that year, in October 2012, she went on a pilgrimage with her paternal grandparents, the 41st Sakya Trizin and Gyalyum Tashi Lhakee; her own father and mother; her maternal grandmother, Yang Dol Tsatultsang; and her baby brother.[470] Her mother Dagmo Kalden relates that they went "on an extensive pilgrimage to Lumbini, Bodhgaya, Varanasi and Kushinagar, the four main Buddhist Pilgrimage sites, and then the four lesser sites, Sankissa, Sravasti, Rajgir and Vaishali." The family performed many prayers at all these holy sites, just as the young Jetsun Kushok and the future 41st Sakya Trizin did when they went on a Buddhist pilgrimage in India in 1956 and 1961. In some photos of the pilgrimage, one sees the five-year-old jetsunma distributing alms, offerings flowers, and sitting by her father as they performed pujas and recited prayers at the sacred areas.

From a very young age, Jetsunma Kunga Trinley "asserted with pride and conviction that she was to be a nun."[471] On March 6, 2017, when she was ten years old, her aspiration was fulfilled. In an intimate ceremony held at the Dolma Palace family's second home in Puruwala, India, she

---

469. Dagmo Kalden email, August 21, 2019.
470. See *Melody of Dharma*, April 2013, no. 11: 19–41 for many photos of the pilgrimage.
471. *Melody of Dharma*, December 2017, special edition: 53.

received the refuge vows from her grandfather, the 41st Sakya Trizin. Her immediate family and her great-aunt Jetsun Kushok were present at this momentous occasion and congratulated her on reaching this milestone. In *Melody of Dharma*, it states:

> Endowed with outstanding moral qualities, sound judgment and poise, Jetsunma promises to be an exemplary Lama. She has already begun her career as a representative of the Khon family, and has thus far done so with remarkable grace and aplomb.[472]

In September 2018, the young jetsunma, her mother, and attendants visited Kham and Amdo in Tibet. They were welcomed with tremendous enthusiasm and emotion by many Tibetans. When they visited some of the important monasteries and temples near Derge and Dzongsar in Kham, the young jetsunma, as an accepted lama, bestowed transmissions of Guru Rinpoche, Tara, and Mañjuśrī. Wherever she went, hundreds of people lined up to receive her blessings. The special issue of *Melody of Dharma* that records some of her work during this historic visit states, "In spite of her young age, Jetsunma fulfilled her duties impeccably . . . she gave blessings and performed consecrations . . . visited schools and hospitals . . . duties that are normally the preserve of more mature lamas."[473]

After visiting both Kham and Amdo, the party traveled to some of the holy Buddhist sites in China. They visited and prayed at the famous five-peak mountain area of Wu Tai Shan connected with the Bodhisattva Mañjuśrī; went to the colossal eighth-century Future Buddha statue at Leishan; and ascended to the top of Emei Shan, associated with Samantabhadra Bodhisattva. Their final stop was Beijing, where they said prayers at the stupa of the Khon ancestor Chogyal Phagpa (1235–80), who was the main lama of the Mongolian emperor Kublai Khan.

On December 21, 2018, both Jetsunma Kunga Trinley's father the 42nd Sakya Trizin Ratna Vajra and his younger brother the 43rd Sakya Trizin Gyana Vajra presided over a celebration of Sakya Pandita's parinirvana and of Jetsunma Kunga Trinley's birthday at the Sakya Nunnery in

---

472. Ibid., 54.

473. *Melody of Dharma*, May 2018, no. 17: 71.

Fig. 38. Jetsunma Kunga Trinley (back left) at an initiation given by her grandfather H.H. the 41st Sakya Trizin in the shrine room of the Dolma Palace, Rajpur, India.

Dekyiling, which is close to Rajpur, where the Dolma Palace is located.[474] One of the video posts on the 42nd Sakya Trizin's Facebook page showed Jetsunma Kunga Trinley being greeted and blessed by her grandfather the 41st Sakya Trizin and receiving birthday greetings from her grandmother Gyalyum Tashi Lhakee and other family members. Later in the day, she is seen distributing food to the needy. The post concluded with:

> May you grow wise like Manjusri, compassionate like Avalokitesvara, fearless like Vajrayogini, magnetic like Kurukulle. May you continue to touch the lives of many. Happy Birthday Precious One![475]

A few days later, on December 23, her grandfather bestowed a private empowerment of the Vajrakīlaya *torma* on the Phuntsok Palace Dungsay Asanga Vajra Rinpoche (b. May 1, 1999), Jetsunma Kunga Trinley's brother Dungsay Akasha Vajra Rinpoche, her younger sister Jetsunma

---

474. Her birthday is calculated according to the Tibetan lunar calendar, so it will be different dates in every year.

475. https://www.facebook.com/SakyaTrizin42/posts/yesterday-was-jetsunma-kunga -trinley-palters-12th-birthday-may-everyone-also-be-/2226860137534461/.

Kunga Chimey Wangmo, and Jetsunma Kunga Trinley herself at the Dolma Palace in India (Fig. 38).[476]

Though Jetsunma Kunga Trinley is still young, she has already shown herself to be deeply involved in the Dharma and very caring toward people and animals. She is well on her way to becoming an esteemed lama, following in the footsteps of both her great-aunt Jetsun Kushok (Chapters 8 and 9) and of her great-aunt's great-aunt, Kyabgon Pema Trinlei (Chapter 5). For more than a millennium, the Khon family has continued to train and nurture their daughters to be excellent practitioners and lamas. Today, with global media access, perhaps the future jetsunmas' lives will no longer be hidden.

476. https://www.facebook.com/sakya.dolmaphodrang/posts/1911122955666650.

APPENDICES

Interview with Aja Dolkar, Longtime Attendant of the Sakya Family

The Dolma Palace, Rajpur, India, December 2007

M Y NAME IS Sonam Dolkar Pod Shol [Bonshod]. I was born in the earth tiger year (1938), in Gyantse, Tsang Province, Tibet. Dagmo Trinlei Paljor Zangmo's father and my grandmother were brother and sister. From my mother's side, there were many children, five brothers and five sisters. Dagmo took three sisters, including me, to serve the Dolma Palace family. I am the oldest and came to the Dolma Palace when I was about 14 years old. My other two sisters are Tseyang, who recently moved to Pennsylvania, and Zangmo, who was a nun.

In 1956, when I was 18 years old, Dagmo arranged my marriage. As was the tradition, the families arrange the marriage and the future bride is unaware that her marriage is being planned. One day, I was told to dress nicely since we were going to some festivities. Only when I arrived at my future husband's home did I find out that this was my wedding day. I wasn't prepared for this. [It seems that she didn't like the arrangement.] I had two sons, Tsering Dorje in 1958 (Fig. 39), and one in 1959.

In 1959, I stayed behind after the family left for India. My sister Tseyang had already left and was no longer in the Dolma Palace, and [my sister] Zangmo, who was a nun, accompanied the family when they escaped.

Shortly after the family escaped, the Chinese came to the Dolma Palace and affixed Chinese seals on all the doors, rooms, and chests. Many attendants were taken to jail; there were ten main ones, including me. I had to take my newborn baby with me in jail; Tsering, my older son, was with his [paternal] grandparents. During the day, the prisoners had to make roads, and at night we were locked up in jail. The Chinese interrogated me many times. They asked me repeatedly, "How did the family

Fig. 39. Aja Dolkar and her son Tsering Dorje at the Dolma Palace, Rajpur, India, 2002.

escape, who helped them, who was with them when they escaped?" They wanted all the details of the escape. Also they wanted to know about all the belongings—what was in the sealed chests, were there other chests, where are the jewels, did I know of other treasures? They asked these questions repeatedly.

After six months I was released, but then I was again detained. The Chinese demanded a new investigation that lasted another six months. They attempted to make me into a cruel landlord who beat the "serfs." Because I was blameless, I was finally released. During these two years of being in and out of jail, working so hard and receiving such scant food, my baby died in jail.

After my release in 1962, when I was 24 years old, I felt free and did not return to my husband. Though many Chinese security guards surrounded the Dolma Palace, I secretly entered it. Surreptitiously I broke the seals on some of the chests and sent the contents to some of the family's private attendants. Though I would be executed if the guards found me, I had strong conviction that I would be protected since I was helping the family. With this faith, I took those risks. When I prepared my escape, I broke the seal of a chest that contained ritual implements—some silver mandalas, bells, and dorjes that the family did not have in India. The family is still using them today, so I am very pleased.

In the Sakya area, the Chinese guards allowed the people to collect firewood during the day. With the ritual instruments hidden in my chuba, I pretended to go to collect firewood. The family had arranged for an attendant to meet me at a secret place and he would take me to India. We walked at night and rested during the day since the Chinese were looking for escaping Tibetans. After crossing the plains and a few mountains that were not too high and without snow, we arrived at the Sikkimese border. It took five days. Once in Sikkim, we encountered more difficult terrain and snow mountains, but we were already in free territory.

Finally I was reunited with the family at Pandatsang's home in Darjeeling. When I was in prison, I thought that I might die and never see the family again. When I was finally reunited with them, I hoped that it was not a dream. With tears of happiness, I recall this day as one of the most memorable days of my life.

The family was overjoyed. They inquired about my journey, my difficulties, and were so glad that this was all behind me now. We were united again. I decided to stay in Darjeeling with other families who came from the Sakya area. I worked with this community for a few years. I finally rejoined the family in Puruwala in 1969.

I liked one of the family's main attendants, Tsepon Nyandak, and we lived as husband and wife. Unfortunately, two years after H.H. Sakya Trizin established Puruwala, Tsepon Nyandak, Thutop Tulku,[477] and the driver were killed in a car accident. The mainstay for many Tibetan refugees was to make rugs. They were returning from Delhi after purchasing wool to weave carpets.

Author's Note: After Aja Dolkar had sketched her life story, I asked whether her great-aunt Dagmo Trinlei Paljor (Chapter 7) had been like a mother to her. This is what I learned:

Aja Dolkar[478] replied, in her humble manner, that she couldn't compare herself to Dagmo Trinlei Paljor's niece and nephew H.E. Jetsun Kushok and H.H. Sakya Trizin (whom Dagmo had raised). She herself was closely

477. For Ven. Thutop Tulku, see note 440 above.

478. Aja (Elder Sister) is a respectful term used for older women.

related to Dagmo, and Dagmo did take care of her as her child. As she grew up, Dagmo trusted her very much.

Dagmo had many abilities, she said. In Tibet, Aja Dolkar saw that Dagmo had much paperwork. Since Aja is not literate, she did not know what the papers contained. The Dolma Phodrang had a special doctor for H.H. Sakya Trizin from whom Dagmo learned how to make medicine. Both in Tibet and in India, Dagmo gave away medicine that she made to people who needed it.

Dagmo stitched very well. She enjoyed making golden ornamental decorations for ritual instruments, such as the ritual vase (*bumpa*). Also she did beadwork. The Sakya Centre still uses one of the beaded mandalas that Dagmo made. She liked to cook. She was famous for making beautifully designed Tibetan cookies (*kapse*) for Losar; she made all the *kapses* when they were in India, and she learned how to make mango jam in India. She chatted with all kinds of people and was a good storyteller. At Losar and other holidays, she played cards with the attendants; everyone enjoyed themselves.

Aja Dolkar said: "Even in the early days in India, when the Dolma Phodrang did not have very much, we were all happy. Much of this was due to Dagmo. She had a noble presence. Her decisions were clear, and whatever decision she undertook, she followed through completely."

I asked Aja-la what Dagmo Trinlei Paljor's main influence on her had been. This is an American kind of question, so she was surprised by it.

She replied, "Dagmo managed to get the family safe to India, managed to get H.H. Sakya Trizin and Jetsunma all the proper and essential teachings; this made them great masters. She raised everyone and handled everything single-handed. She always thought what she could contribute to the Sakya community, not thinking about her personal interests." Aja Dolkar said that she stayed with the Sakya family because of Dagmo.

I also asked Aja Dolkar about Tashi Palrab, Dagmo's younger brother, who was an army general and a bodyguard of the H. H. the Dalai Lama during his escape.

She replied that he was a practitioner—a Gelugpa, H.H. Sakya Trizin had said—but not like Dagmo. He was a very admired general in Tibet, unlike some who would bully their underlings; he was always polite and helpful. People remember him fondly and he was very dedicated to the Tibetan Government in Exile. Though they came from a big family, only Dagmo and Tashi escaped to India. Already they were very close in Tibet, and they remained close in India.

Interview with Tsering Dorje, the Son of Aja Dolkar

The Dolma Palace, Rajpur, India, December 2007

Author's Note: Tsering Dorje was born in Sakya in 1958. When his mother Aja Dolkar was put in jail in Tibet for serving a noble family, his paternal grandparents took care of him. About two years later, when his mother was released from jail for the second time, they escaped to India.

SINCE MY MOTHER was working [in India], Auntie [Dagmo Trinlei Paljor] thought that she could take care of me. She was my "godmother." Auntie accepted me as one of her children. . . . Then, after a few months of being in Darjeeling, the family decided to move to Mussoorie.

In Mussoorie, I recall that the elder attendants remarked that I was one of the luckiest children. During this time when all Tibetans were refugees and many had to endure tremendous difficulties and hardships, I was with the Khon family. Since I was the only small child, everyone took care of me, especially Auntie. She was very close and attached to me. Being her special child, I was kept happy; everyone in the household took very good care of me. I was a very naughty child; it was difficult for the elderly attendants to discipline me. To keep me content, I was given so many sweets that I became very ill. From seven to nine years old, I was sick and needed an operation to remove a stomach tumor. The family paid half and the Christian missionaries paid half. I was so naughty that I removed the stitches and almost died before they could re-stitch everything. I feel that Auntie and the Dolma Palace saved my life.

Auntie really spoiled me and would give me everything I wanted. The attendants used this to their advantage. When they wanted to go to a movie, they would talk about it in front of me and get me interested. I would ask Auntie to see the movie and, of course, the attendants had to accompany me. Once Jetsun-la had her first son, Mingyur [in 1965], I was no longer the only child. He was considered very precious, and Auntie loved him very much. I became jealous of him and showed him a scary but harmless insect. He became so afraid, and cried. I remember that Auntie reprimanded me for being mean to Mingyur.

She was a great and dedicated practitioner and did *torma* offerings daily. When she finished her pujas, she asked me to pour the water out and dispose of the *tormas* in a clean area. She wanted me to do the job in a perfect way so I could get some merit. The birds and insects ate the *tormas*. Sometimes I helped her with her water and butterlamp offerings.

Also I remember that she stressed not to waste food. I especially remember that she said that since so many insects were killed in plough-ing, growing, and harvesting rice, I should eat every grain. To this day, remembering her words, I eat every grain.

My mother stayed in Darjeeling and worked in road construction. The Khon family thought that I should get a proper education and perhaps later I could help the family. I went to the new Tibetan Homes School in Mussoorie for two years, from six to eight years old. When H.H. Sakya Trizin moved to Rajpur at the Sakya Centre, H.H. Sakya Trizin sent me to a Catholic school in Rajpur for one year. Then I was chosen among students by the Swiss Aid to Tibetans organization to go to school in Dehradun. Most of my education was in Dehradun. Since I was an aver-age student, I did not go for higher studies after completing ten grades. I showed an interest in *thangka* painting, so Auntie arranged for me to be an apprentice in the new *thangka* school in Dharamsala. I studied *thangka* painting for seven years and stayed for an additional two years.

In Dharamsala, I met a Tibetan doctor and we got along well with each other. I wanted to marry her, but in the end she decided to go abroad. My mother also encouraged this marriage, but I realize that I was lucky that it did not work out. It seems my life is to serve the family; if I were mar-ried, it would have been very difficult to do. While I was in Dharamsala, Auntie's younger brother, Tashi Palrab, who lived in Dharamsala and had the Gakyi Vegetarian Restaurant, would come and check on me. He was always happy to see me. He encouraged me to help the Sakya family. H.H. Sakya Trizin requested that I paint the Sixteen Arhats based on a collection in the Luding Labrang that he liked. Before I finished these, the Khon family requested that I join the family and help them. Since I am busy with my tasks of taking care of the mailing, the checkbook, driving the family, and accompanying H.H. Sakya Trizin wherever he goes in India, I do not paint anymore.

My mother and I are treated as good friends and as people whom the family can trust. We are considered to be very reliable and dedicated to family. I feel that I am doing guru yoga; my motivation is to help the [Dolma] Palace and do whatever they need.

The Sakya Trizins and the Dungsays

THE TRIZINS

In the Sakya Khon families, each member has a specific title and responsibility. The most prestigious and important title is that of Sakya Trizin (*khri 'dzin*, "Throne-Holder of the Sakyas"). Though nowadays the title Sakya Trizin is ubiquitous, it is a new title. As Jigdal Dagchen Rinpoche (1929–2016), the elder son of the Phuntsok Palace, explained to Jeffrey Schoening, an earlier title was simply Trichen (*khri chen*, "Holder of the Great Throne"). But because the head of the Sakya school now lives in exile rather than in Sakya, Tibet, where the throne existed, the term was changed to Sakya Trizin.[479]

Prior to the 1700s, the main title was Gongma (*gong ma*, "Superior One"), which had been popular for many centuries. Though it is no longer the official title, many Tibetans still refer to the Sakya Trizin as Sakya Gongma. But in the late 1700s, when Sachen Kunga Lodro (1729–83) became the head of the Sakyas, the official title was changed from Sakya Gongma to Trichen, and Sachen Kunga Lodro is considered the 31st Sakya Trichen/Trizin retrospectively. The title Trichen continued until the exile in 1959. The last Trichen to be enthroned in Sakya was Jetsun's Kushok's brother the 41st Sakya Trichen/Trizin (b. 1945). Today, however, the best-known title for the current throne-holder, especially in the West, is Sakya *Trizin*. (Concomitantly, as detailed below, since the 2014 change in the succession system and H.H. the 41st Sakya Trizin's retirement in 2017, he is now known as H.H. Gongma *Trichen* Rinpoche.)

The position of Sakya Trizin is held by a male member of the Sakya Khon family. All sons of the Khon families are trained to be a Sakya

---

479. I thank Jeffrey Schoening for this information via email on July 1, 2018.

Trizin. Each must have vast knowledge and training in both spiritual and political affairs, even though only a few will actually take on this role. In most cases the Sakya Trizin remains the throne-holder until his death or until he decides to relinquish the position. No Sakya Trizin was ever forced to abdicate, and many held the position for many decades. In fact, the 41st Sakya Trizin (r. 1959–2017) was the youngest to be enthroned and had the longest reign.

Though the titles of the throne-holder of the Sakyas have changed over the centuries, a more dramatic change occurred in 2014, when the 41st Sakya Trizin of the Dolma Palace and Jigdal Dagchen Rinpoche of the Phuntsok Palace consulted together and devised a new system of succession based on the Ngor Monastery system of abbotship. The following is an excerpt from the December 11, 2014 letter announcing the new system:

> Bearing in mind that while we the elder generations are still thriving and are thus able to take the opportunity to provide guidance, I [H.H. the 41st Sakya Trizin] suggest that both generations of the Phodrangs [i.e., both the Dolma and the Phuntsok Palaces] take turns in assuming the responsibility of the role of Sakya Trizin by seniority of age and with the required qualifications of the designate for a three-year term. This agreement has great significance in that all members will have the opportunity to serve as Sakya Trizin.[480]

His Holiness the 14th Dalai Lama accepted this decision and sent his "blessed confirmation." On March 9, 2017, the elder son of the 41st Sakya Trizin, Ratna Vajra Sakya, was enthroned as the 42nd Sakya Trizin at the Sakya Institute Thupten Namgyal Ling in India. The 41st Sakya Trizin now has the title of H.H. Sakya Gongma Trichen.

Though the actual Khon family has its origins in the eleventh century, over the centuries different family branches have developed. From the fifteenth to the early nineteenth century, only the Duchod (Dus mchod) family branch remained intact, and frequently the throne was given to a son or a nephew. However, after the 32nd Sakya Trizin Thuchen Wangdu Nyingpo (Khri chen mthu chen dbang sdud snying po, 1763–1809; son of

---

480. http://hhsakyatrizin.net/official-announcement-12-11-14/.

the 31st Sakya Trizin Sachen Kunga Lodro), this unity was in jeopardy. His two sons, Pema Dudul Wangchuk (1792–1853) and Ngawang Kunga Rinchen (1794–1856), agreed to co-marry a single wife to keep the lineage intact (see Chart 1 in Chapter 3). This alliance produced one son named Ngagchang Jamgon Dorje Rinchen (sNgags 'chang 'jam mgon rdo rje rin chen), but the brothers were dissatisfied with this arrangement. It seemed that the wife favored Ngawang Kunga Rinchen, the younger brother. The two brothers decided to divide the family into separate branches (see Charts 2 and 3). Each brother built his own palace: Pema Dudul Wangchuk's residence was known as the Tara Palace (Dolma Phodrang), and Ngawang Kunga Rinchen's as the Excellent Palace (Phuntsok Phodrang). Thus the family was divided, and the succession of Sakya Trizins came into dispute.

Naturally, each father hoped that his son would inherit the throne. However, the succession was contested frequently. Two methods were employed to choose a successor: (1) selecting the oldest male regardless of which palace was currently holding the position of Sakya Trizin, or (2) alternating between the two palaces regardless of the age of the oldest male in the designated family. The result was that each family usually chose the method that favored its own son.

All sons of the Khon family are considered to be divine people, having superhuman powers as a result of their spiritual practices. They may appear to be ordinary people, but for the followers of the Sakya tradition, they are considered to be emanations of various bodhisattvas. The males are emanations of three main bodhisattvas: Avalokiteśvara, the Bodhisattva of Compassion; Mañjuśrī, the Bodhisattva of Wisdom; or Vajrapāṇi, the Bodhisattva of Power. The sons could be an emanation of one, two, or even all three bodhisattvas simultaneously. A bodhisattva vows to help all sentient beings impartially and to show them the Buddhist path to liberation from cyclic existence. Thus the followers of the Sakya tradition have great reverence, faith, and expectations that the sons of the Khon family will help everyone. Above everyone else, the Sakya Trizin is viewed as the supreme religious teacher or lama who will help in both spiritual and secular affairs.

In the Khon family, spiritual development is stressed and encouraged, but when a son becomes the Sakya Trizin, there is a major component that is political as well as spiritual. In Tibet, Sakya had its own government, independent of the Central Tibetan Government in Lhasa headed by the Dalai Lama. The Sakya government had an official, known as the Shape (*zhabs pad*), who was in charge of the day-to-day business of the government.[481] The Trichen, or Sakya Trizin, appointed the Shape, who was his main political steward and had considerable power. The title Shape literally means "Lotus Foot": *zhabs* is the honorific word for "foot," and *pad* is an abbreviation for "lotus." Usually only deities have lotus feet. When letters were written to the Shape, they were addressed to the "man of great power" (*miwang chenmo*).[482] Though the Shape had considerable power and autonomy, it was only the Sakya Trizin who initiated policy, made decisions, or revoked decisions made by his government officials. In addition, the Sakya Trizin had final control over the North and South Monasteries in Sakya and over the appointments of abbots and religious collectors, who were sent to various areas of Tibet to collect donations for the monasteries. Also, the Sakya Trizin could introduce changes in the procedures of religious observances within the monasteries. Though having this autonomy, "This freedom was limited to a range of activities circumscribed by the belief, shared by the Sakya Trizin and subjects alike, that the functions of government were minimal."[483]

In *A Tibetan Principality: The Political System of the Sa Skya*, C. W. Cassinelli and Robert B. Ekvall describe the daily activity of the 40th Sakya Trizin Ngawang Thutop Wangchuk (Ngag dbang mthu thub dbang phyug, 1900–50; r. 1936–50). To summarize, he rose at 3:00 or 3:30 a.m. and prayed and meditated until 6 a.m., when he ate breakfast. From 8 a.m. to 6 p.m. he attended to governmental and religious affairs, taking two hours for lunch. But on certain days of the month (five to six days per month) he prayed and made offerings from 8–12 p.m., and on two or three days a month, he prayed and made offerings from 2–6 p.m. On these religious observance days, he handled any governmental business during the lunch period. At 7:30 p.m. he ate dinner with the family and perhaps some friends. At 10 p.m. everyone went to bed. Each Sakya throne-holder had different interests. For example, when Ngawang Thutop Wangchuk had free time during the day, he edited religious texts that would be

---

481. Cassinelli and Ekvall 1969, 202ff. See chapter seven for a good explanation of the relationship of Trichen and Shape.

482. *mi* = man; *dbang* = power; *chen mo* = great.

483. Cassinelli and Ekvall 1969, 190.

block-printed or handwritten with the help of monks from the North and South Monasteries.[484]

Though the Khon families now live in exile, many of their spiritual responsibilities continue to be performed as they were done in Tibet. The December 11, 2014 letter that announced the change about the term limits of a Sakya Trizin also included the main responsibilities as follows:

> During the term of each Sakya Trizin, his responsibilities shall include conducting any of the major teachings of *Lamdre Ts'ogshey, Lamdre Lopshey*, the Collections of Sadhanas, and the Collections of Tantras; presiding over the important traditional annual ducho, the Commemorative Offering Ceremonies of the seat of the Sakya; overseeing the training and studies of the Sakya monasteries; seeking to find ways to promote and grow the Dharma teachings through study and practices; fulfilling the wishes of the Sakya followers; and, last, it is extremely important he carry on exceptional work that includes the improvement of all the areas of Dharma, the monasteries, and the Sakya followers.[485]

THE DUNGSAYS

The Khon sons are known as Dungsay (*gdung sras*, "Son from the Lineage of the Bone").[486] Though this is not a title exclusive to sons of the Khon family, it is the main title for them. In Tibetan theories of embryology, the bones, brain, and spine are generated from the father's reproductive substance, while the flesh, blood, vital and vessel organs are generated from the mother's menstrual blood (*zla mtshan*).[487] Thus, from the father's side, the son receives his bones. Interestingly, the daughters are not called daughter from the lineage of the bone or from any other aspect of the body, but have a completely different title. Theirs is an honorific title, Jetsunma (see Chapter 1 above).

---

484. Ibid., 197–98.

485. http://hhsakyatrizin.net/official-announcement-12-11-14/.

486. *gdung* = bone (honorific form); *sras* = son.

487. See Frances Garrett, *Religion, Medicine and the Human Embryo in Tibet* (New York: Routledge, 2008), 75.

As we have read in the biographies of the jetsunmas in the present volume, all the children, both daughters and sons, are trained from an early age to be excellent religious practitioners. They are taught by their fathers, uncles, occasionally their aunts, and by tutors selected by the family. Each child is taught the alphabet and how to read and write in Tibetan. They must become rapid and proficient readers because they will most likely become teachers who need to give oral transmissions of sacred texts. The transmission is known as a *lung* and occurs when the lama reads the text quickly but clearly aloud. Sometimes a transmission can last for days; thus a lama must be a skilled reader with a clear and strong voice. The purpose of a transmission is to introduce a practitioner to the teachings, and it is considered meritorious both to give transmissions and to hear them, since they are the words of the Buddha or another illustrious teacher.

Every child of the Khon families also receives the teachings of Lamdre (Path with the Result), which Sakyapas consider the best system of practice to follow to become enlightened and thereby be able to help all others attain the same goal (see Chapter 1 above). All sons are expected to become adept practitioners of Lamdre, to perform the requisite retreat, to know the meditations, pujas, and ancillary practices, and to be able to bestow this teaching numerous times during their lifetimes.

In addition, as already noted, all sons of the Khon families are trained to be a Sakya Trizin. Further, the sons, especially the oldest one, are expected to marry and produce an heir. Even if the oldest son prefers to remain celibate and/or be an ordained monk, he is aware of his obligation to continue the Khon lineage and will marry. As we have seen, sometimes two brothers will marry one wife (see Chapter 1 and elsewhere above).

Thus all Khon children are trained to be exceptional practitioners. The main difference between the sons and daughters is that the sons have more responsibilities, especially if they become a Sakya Trizin. As of 2017, the term of a Sakya Trizin is limited to only three years, so the twenty-first century is witnessing a new chapter in the continuum of the Khon families and of their commitment to spreading the Dharma throughout the world.

Bibliography

PRIMARY WRITTEN SOURCES

Dragshul Trinlei Rinchen (Drag shul 'phrin las rin chen). 1974. *Autobiographical Reminiscences of Sakya Trizin Dragshul Trinlei Rinchen (Rdo rje 'chang Drag shul phrin las rin chen gyi rtogs brjod)*. 2 vols. Dehra Dun: Sakya Centre.

———. 2009. *Supplement to the Genealogy and Biographies of Transmission Lineage Masters of the Sakyas (gDung rabs yang skong ngo mtshar kun 'phel sring shi'i dpal 'byor lhun grub mdzad pa po, brtan bshugs tshogs pa)*. Puruwala, India: Long-Life Offering Committee of the Golden Jubilee for the 41st Sakya Trizin.

Geshe Thuchey Wangchuk (dGe bshe thugs rje dbang phyug). n.d. *Brief Biographies of the Sakya Jetsunmas (Sa skya'i rje btsun ma rnams kyi skor phran bu bshugs so)*. Unpublished manuscript.

———. n.d. Unpublished and untitled manuscript (some information about Dagmo Trinlei Paljor).

Khenchen Appey Rinpoche, ed. 2008–10. *The Great Collection of the Lamdre Tshogse Teachings (Biographies of Lamdre Masters)*. Vol. 29, *gSung Ngag Lam 'bras Tshogs bShad Chen mo bLa ma'i rNam thar sKor*. Kathmandu: Sachen International.

Sachen Kunga Lodro (Sa-chen Kun dga' bLo gros). 2009. *Extensive Genealogy and Biographies of the Great Sakya Masters (rJe btsun Sa-skya-pa'i gdung rabs rin po che'i rnam par thar pa ngo mtshar rin po che'i bang mdzod dgos 'dod kun 'byung gi kha skong rin chen 'dzad med srid zhi'i dpal 'byor lhun grub)*. Puruwala, India: Long-Life Offering Committee of the Golden Jubilee for the 41st Sakya Trizin.

Tsering Wangyal and Yama Gonpo (Tshe ring dbang rgyal and Ya ma mgon po). 2005. *Crystal Mirror: A History of Lang Nak Monastery (gLang nag dgon pa'i lo rgyus mthong gsal shel gyi me long)*. Beijing: Mi rigs dpe skrun khang, 1–97.

INTERVIEWS

Aja Dolkar. December 2007 at the Dolma Palace, Rajpur, UK, India. (Dagmo Trinlei Paljor's attendant; see Appendix A.)

Ani Chime. November 14 and 15, 2007 and June 2010, at Tharlam Monastery, Bodhnath, Nepal. (Younger sister of the 3rd Dezhung Rinpoche and aunt of Dagmo Jamyang Sakya.)

Chiwang Tulku. 2015 at the Sakya Centre in Rajpur, UK, India. (Former director of the Sakya Centre in Rajpur, India.)

Dagmo Jamyang Sakya. June 2007, 2012, and 2018 at her home in Seattle, Washington. (Wife of the Phuntsok Palace's Jigdal Dagchen Sakya.)

Dongthong Rinpoche. February 11, 2005 at his home in Shoreline, Washington. (A reincarnated lama and historian from Ngor Monastery in Tibet.)

Drawupon Richen Tsering, with the help of his daughter, Dagmo Lhanze Sakya. August 24, 2016 in Seattle, Washington. (A great freedom fighter of Tibet who knew Kyabgon Pema Trinlei.)

Geshe Thuchey Wangchuk, with the help of Jeffrey Schoening. November 2, 2016 in Seattle. (Lived in Sakya as a monk teacher from 1938 to 1961 and eventually settled in Seattle. One of his main students is Jeffrey Schoening.)

Goldberg, Jay. Email dated March 16, 2016. (Longtime student of H.H. the 41st Sakya Trizin and H.E. Jetsun Kushok.)

Gu Yudron. December 2007 at her home in Dharamsala, HP, India. (Second wife of Tashi Palrab, youngest brother of Dagmo Trinlei Paljor.)

Gyalyum Tashi Lhakee. December 2007, at the Dolma Palace, Rajpur, UK, India. (Wife of H.H. the 41st Sakya Trizin.)

H.E. Jetsun Kushok. 2008, 2010, 2013, 2017, in Richmond, BC, Canada, and Walden, New York.

H.H. 41st Sakya Trizin. Several interviews during February 2004, December 2007, June 2012, and June 2013, and via email in December 2018 at the Dolma Palace at Rajpur, UK, India, and at Walden, New York.

Jetsunma Chime Wangmo. August 28, 2007, at her sister's home (Jetsunma Tsegen Wangmo) in Seattle, Washington. (Sister of the Phuntsok Palace's Jigdal Dagchen Sakya.)

Jetsunma Tsegen Wangmo. August 28, 2007 in her home in Seattle, Washington. (Sister of the Phuntsok Palace's Jigdal Dagchen Sakya.)

Kunga Yonten Horchotsang. April 23, 2009 at the Institute of Tibetology in Gangtok, SK, India. (Former director of the Institute of Tibetology and also first cousin of the wife of the 41st Sakya Trizin.)

Lama Kunga Thartse Rinpoche. June 21, 2011 in Walden, New York. (A reincarnated lama from Ngor Monastery in Tibet and cousin of Jetsun Kushok and the 41st Sakya Trizin.)

Lobsang P. Lhalungpa. October 2007 at his home in Santa Fe, New Mexico. (Established the first Tibetan language program of All India Radio and served as translator for Tibetans when they sought exile in India.)

Ngaklo Rinpoche. 2011 at Walden, New York. (His previous incarnation was a principal teacher of Jetsun Kushok and the 41st Sakya Trizin.)

Sho Bo Lozang Dhargey. December 12, 2007 at Norbulingka Institute, Sidhpur, HP, India. (A son of Dagmo Trinlei Paljor's youngest sister in Bonshod family.)

Tenzin Dawa. April 17 and 22, 2009, at Ngor Monastery, in Rongye, SK, India. (The former abbot of Ngor Monastery in Sikkim.)

Tsering Dorje. December 2007 at the Dolma Palace, Rajpur, UK, India. (The son of Aja Dolkar; he and his mother are attendants to the Dolma Palace family.)

Voice of America, Tibetan section. "Reconstructing the 1950's," a series of interviews with different Tibetans. Interview with Tsultrim Gyatso, who lived in Sakya during this time.

SECONDARY SOURCES

Akester, Matthew. 2004. "The Last Traces of Gyere Lhakhang." *The Tibet Journal* 29, no. 3: 55–64.

Benard, Elisabeth. 2010. "A Secret Affair: The Wedding of a Sakya Dagmo." *Tibetan Studies: Anthology*. PIATS2006: Tibetan Studies: Proceedings of the eleventh seminar of the International Association for Tibetan Studies, ed. S. Arslan and P. Schweiger, 37–63. Koenigswinter: International Institute for Tibetan and Buddhist Studies GmbH.

———. 2012a. "Tamdrin Wangmo." *Treasury of Lives*. http://www.treasuryoflives.org /biographies/view/Kelzang-Chokyi-Nyima/11883.

———. 2012b. "Pema Trinle." *Treasury of Lives*. http://www.treasuryoflives.org /biographies/view/pad+ma-%27phrin-las/13186.

———. 2015. "Born to Practice: The Sakya Jetsunma Phenomenon." *Revue d'Études Tibétaines* 34 (Décembre): 1–20. https://religiondocbox.com/Buddhism/104471150-Born-to-practice-the-sakya-jetsunma-phenomenon.html.

Carnahan, Summer, with Lama Kunga Rinpoche. 1995. *In the Presence of My Enemies: Memoirs of Tibetan Nobleman Tsipon Shuguba*. Santa Fe, NM: Clear Light Publications.

Cassinelli, C. W., and Robert B. Ekvall. 1969. *A Tibetan Principality: The Political System of the Sa Skya*. Ithaca, NY: Cornell University Press.

Chogye Trichen Rinpoche. 2003. *Parting from the Four Attachments: Commentary on Jetsun Drakpa Gyaltsen's Song of Experience on Mind Training and the View*. Ithaca, NY: Snow Lion Press.

Davidson, Ronald. 2005. *Tibetan Renaissance: Tantric Buddhism in the Rebirth of Tibetan Culture*. New York: Columbia University Press.

Deshung Rinpoche. 1995. *The Three Levels of Spiritual Perception: An Oral Commentary on "The Three Visions" (Snang gsum) of Ngorchen Kunga Lhundrub*. Trans. Jared Rhoton. Boston: Wisdom Publications; 2nd rev. ed. 2003.

English, Elizabeth. 2002. *Vajrayoginī: Her Visualizations, Rituals and Forms*. Boston: Wisdom Publications.

Freeman, Alphonso, and Gabriella Freeman. 1996. "Interview with Jetsun Kushab." *Chö Yang: The Voice of Tibetan Religion and Culture* 7: 95. https://vajrasana.org /chime1.htm.

Garrett, Frances. 2008. *Religion, Medicine and the Human Embryo in Tibet*. New York: Routledge.

Gayley, Holly. 2019. *Inseparable across Lifetimes: The Lives and Love Letters of the Tibetan Visionaries Namtrul Rinpoche and Khandro Tare Lhamo*. Boulder, CO: Snow Lion.

Glass, Phillip. 2015. *Words Without Music*. New York: Liveright Publishing Company.

Goldstein, Melvyn C. 1971. "Stratification, Polyandry, and Family Structure in Central Tibet." *Southwestern Journal of Anthropology* 27, no. 1: 64–74.

————. 1991. *A History of Modern Tibet, 1913–1951: The Demise of the Lamaist State.* Berkeley: University of California Press.

Gyatso, Janet, and Hanna Havnevik, eds. 2005. *Women in Tibet.* New York: Columbia University Press.

Haas, Michaela. 2013. *Dakini Power: Twelve Extraordinary Women Shaping the Transmission of Tibetan Buddhism in the West.* Boston and London: Snow Lion.

Havnevik, Hanna. 1999. "The Life of Jetsun Lochen Rinpoche (1865–1951) as Told in Her Autobiography." Ph.D dissertation, University of Oslo.

Hilton, Isabel. 1999. *The Search for the Panchen Lama.* New York: W. W. Norton and Company.

Jackson, David P. 1989. "Sources of the Chronology and Succession of the Abbots of Ngor E-wam-chos ldan." *Berliner Indologische Studien* 4–5: 49–94.

————. 2003. *A Saint in Seattle: The Life of the Tibetan Mystic Dezhung Rinpoche.* Boston: Wisdom Publications.

————. 2020. *Lama of Lamas: The Life of Vajra Master Chogye Rinpoche.* 2 vols. Kathmandu: Vajra Publications.

Jamgön Kongtrul. 2012. *The Life of Jamyang Khyentse Wangpo.* Trans. Matthew Akester. New Delhi: Shechen Publications.

Johnson, Sandy. 1996. *Tibetan Elders.* New York: Riverhead Books.

Kawaguchi, Ekai. 1909. *Three Years in Tibet.* Benares and London: Theosophical Publishing Society.

Khyongla Rinpoche. 1996. *My Life and Lives.* New York: Rato Publications.

Kirti Rinpoche, comp. 2013. *Gendun Chophel, Portrait of a Great Thinker: Oral Recollections about Gendun Chophel.* Dharamsala: Library of Tibetan Works and Archives.

Krull, Germaine, and Marilyn Ekdahl Ravicz. 2018. *A Promise Kept: Memoir of Tibetans in India.* Xlibris.

McGranahan, Carole. 2002. "*Sa spang mda' gnam spang mda':* Murder, History and Social Politics in 1920's Lhasa." In Lawrence Epstein, ed., *Khams Pa Histories: Visions of People, Place and Authority,* 104–124. Leiden: Brill.

————. 2010. "Narrative Dispossession: Tibet and the Gendered Logics of Historical Possibility." *Comparative Studies in Society and History* 52, no. 4: 768–797.

Melody of Dharma. 2013. Ani Jamyang Wangmo, ed. (April): 19–41.

————. 2017. Ani Jamyang Wangmo, ed. Special edition (December): 53–54.

————. 2018. Ani Jamyang Wangmo, ed. No. 17 (May): 70–72.

Ngaklo Rinpoche. 2019. *Clear Light on the Path of Liberation.* Trans. Lama Choedak Rinpoche. Canberra, Australia: Gorum Publications.

Ngorchen Khonchog Lhundrub. 1991. *The Three Visions: Fundamental Teachings of the Sakya Lineage of Tibetan Buddhism.* Trans. Lobsang Dagpa and Jay Goldberg. Ithaca, NY: Snow Lion Publications; 2nd ed. 2002. Originally published in 1987 by Golden Vase Publications in Singapore as *The Beautiful Ornament of the Three Visions.*

Norbu, Dawa. 1974. *Red Star Over Tibet.* London: Collins.

Norbu, Jamyang. 2005. "Newspeak and New Tibet, Part 2, The Myth of China's Modernization of Tibet and Tibetan Language." Phayul.com, Friday, June 17, 2005, 23: 42.

Petech, Luciano. 1973. *Aristrocracy and Government in Tibet, 1728–1959*, Roma: Serie Orientale Roma XLV, Instituto Italiano Per Il Medio ED Estremo Oriente.

Sakya, Jamyang, and Julie Emery. 1990. *Princess in the Land of Snows: The Life of Jamyang Sakya in Tibet*. Boston: Shambhala.

Sakya Pandita Kunga Gyaltshen. 2001. *A Clear Differentiation of the Three Codes: Essential Distinctions among the Individual Liberation, Great Vehicle, and Tantric Systems*. Trans. Jared Douglas Rhoton. Albany: State University of New York Press.

Sakya, Ratna Vajra, Drolma Lhamo, and Lama Jampa Losel. 2003. *Biographies of the Great Sachen Kunga Nyingpo and H.H. the 41st Sakya Trizin*. Rajpur: Sakya Academy.

Sakya Trizin, H.H. the 41st. 1982. *A Collection of Instructions on Parting from the Four Attachments: The Basic Mind Training of the Sakya Tradition*. Trans. Jay Goldberg (Ngawang Samten). Singapore: Sakya Tenphel Ling, 1982; 2nd ed. Berkeley: The Sapan Fund, 2018.

———. 2011. *Freeing the Heart and Mind, Part One: Introduction to the Buddhist Path*. Boston: Wisdom Publications.

———. 2017. *Great Sakya Women*. Ed. Chodrung-ma Kunga Chodron. Walden, NY: Tsechen Kunchab Ling Publications, 1–26.

Sankrityayan, Rahul. 2014. *My Third Expedition to Tibet (1936)*. Trans. Sonam Gyatso. Dharamsala: Library of Tibetan Works Archives.

Sarat Chandra Das. 1902. *Journey to Lhasa and Central Tibet*. Ed. W. W. Rockhill. New York: E. P. Dutton and Company.

Schaeffer, Kurtis. 2005. "The Autobiography of a Medieval Tibetan Hermitess." In Janet Gyatso and Hanna Havnevik, eds., *Women in Tibet*, 83–109. New York: Columbia University Press.

Schoening, Jeffrey. 1983. "The Sakya Throne Holder Lineage." Master's thesis, University of Washington, Seattle.

———. 1990. "The Religious Structures of SA-KYA." In Lawrence Epstein and Richard F. Sherburne, eds., *Reflections on Tibetan Culture: Essays in Memory of Turrell V. Wylie*, 11–47. Lewiston, NY: E. Mellen Press.

Shaw, Miranda. 1994. *Passionate Enlightenment: Women in Tantric Buddhism*. Princeton: Princeton University Press.

Stearns, Cyrus. 2001. *Luminous Lives: The Story of the Early Masters of the Lam 'bras Tradition in Tibet*. Boston: Wisdom Publications.

———. 2007. *King of the Empty Plain: The Tibetan Iron Bridge Builder Tangtong Gyalpo*. Ithaca, NY: Snow Lion.

———, trans. and ed. 2006. *Taking the Result as the Path: Core Teachings of the Sakya Lamdré Tradition*. Boston: Wisdom Publications.

Travers, Alice. 2006. "Women in the Diplomatic Game: Preliminary Notes on the Matrimonial Link of the Sikkim Royal Family with Tibet (13th–20th Centuries)." *Bulletin of Tibetology* 42.1–2: 91–128 (in French).

———. 2008. "Exclusiveness and Openness: A Study of Matrimonial Strategies in the Dga' ldan pho brang Aristocracy (1880–1959)." *Journal of the International Association of Tibetan Studies* 4 (December): 1–27.

Tseten, Migmar. 2008. *The Treasures of the Sakya Lineage: Teachings from the Masters*. Boston and London: Shambhala.

Tsomu, Yudru. 2014. *The Rise of Gonpo Namgyel in Kham: The Blind Warrior of Nyarong.* Lanham, MD: Rowman.

Tsong-kha-pa. 2014. *The Great Treatise on the Stages of the Path to Enlightenment: Lam Rim Chen Mo.* Trans. Lamrim Chenmo Translation Committee. Ed. Joshua Cutler and Guy Newland. Boston: Snow Lion.

Venturi, Frederic. 2013. "Creating Sacred Space: The Religious Geography of Sa Skya, Tibet's Medieval Capital." PhD dissertation, University of Indiana.

Wangmo, Ani Jamyang, and Patricia Donohue, eds. 2010. "Her Eminence Jetsunma Kunga Trinley Palter Sakya. Dharma Heir of the Great Lineage of the Khön Sakyapa." *Melody of Dharma,* no. 1: 17. Rajpur, India: The Office of Sakya Dolma Phodrang.

Wylie, Turrell. 1964–65. "Mortuary Customs at Sa-skya, Tibet." *Harvard Journal of Asiatic Studies* 25: 229–42.

Yeshi, Kim, and Acharya Tashi Tsering. 1991. "The Story of a Tibetan Yogini: Shungsep Jetsun 1852–1953." In *Chö Yang: The Voice of Tibetan Religion and Culture,* Year of Tibet Edition, 130–43. Dharamsala: Council of Religious and Cultural Affairs of H.H. the Dalai Lama. https://theyoginiproject.org/wisdom-dakinis/shuksep-jetsunma-chonyi-zangmo.

WEBSITES

https://www.facebook.com/sakya.dolmaphodrang/posts/1911122955666650

https://www.facebook.com/SakyaTrizin42/posts/yesterday-was-jetsunma-kunga-trinley-palters-12th-birthday-may-everyone-also-be-/2226860137534461/

http://hhsakyatrizin.net/teaching-great-sakya-women/

http://hhsakyatrizin.net/teaching-vajrakilaya/

http://www.hhthesakyatrizin.org/pdfs/news_11_daughter.pdf

http://www.himalayanart.org/items/54316

https://www.himalayanart.org/items/3313721

https://www.himalayanart.org/search/set.cfm?setID=178

http://jetsunma.blogspot.com

http://www.lotsawahouse.org/tibetan-masters/dudjom-rinpoche/mirror

https://www.lotsawahouse.org/tibetan-masters/jamyang-khyentse-wangpo/history-of-simhamukha

https://www.pyramidkey.com/legends-of-muktinath/

http://www.rigpawiki.org/index.php?title=Dzogchen

https://www.rigpawiki.org/index.php?title=Khenpo_Shenga

http://www.rigpawiki.org/index.php?title=Kurukulla

http://rywiki.tsadra.org/index.php/Ngorchen_Konchog_Lhundrup

https://safricachamtrulrinpoche.wordpress.com/2012/06/26/my-vital-advice

http://sakyakachodcholing.org/jetsun-chimey-luding-rinpoche/

https://www.shentongkalacakra.com/2020/01/05/part-ii-on-the-sikkimese-trail-of-jamyang-khyentse-chokyi-lodro-the-golden-stupa-of-tashi-ding-and-the-doorway-to-shambhala/

http://tenzinpalmo.com/index.php?option=com_content&task=view&id=18&Itemid=1

https://theyoginiproject.org/accomplished-yoginis/nangsa-obum
https://theyoginiproject.org/wisdom-dakinis/shuksep-jetsunma-chonyi-zangmo
http://theyoginiproject.org/yoginis-her-story/wisdom-dakinis#tabid-10
http://tibet.prm.ox.ac.uk/biography_201.html
http://tibet.prm.ox.ac.uk/photo_1999.23.1.33.2.html (Tibet Album, Oxford)
http://www.tibetjustice.org/materials/china/china3.html
https://treasuryoflives.org/biographies/view/Ngakchang-Ngawang-Kunga
    -Rinchen/7053
https://treasuryoflives.org/institution/Tengyeling
https://www.tsechen.org/index.php/english/about-sakya/sakya-masters/45-his
    -eminence-chogye-trichen-rinpoche
http://vajrasana.org/chime1.htm
https://www.youtube.com/watch?v=ly6R_jc3DS0

Figure Credits

Frontispiece: H.E. Jetsun Kushok Chimey Luding transmitting (Tib. *lung*) a religious text in the mid-1990s. Courtesy of Rosemary Rawcliffe. © Rosemary Rawcliffe.

1. Jetsunma Tsegen Wangmo and Jetsunma Chime Wangmo in the Phuntsok Palace in Sakya, Tibet. Courtesy of the Phuntsok Palace.
2. The Lhakhang Chenmo, or Great Temple, in Sakya, Tibet, 2007. Photo by Moszcynski.
3. Gyalyum Tashi Lhakee's extended family in Gangtok, Sikkim, 1964/65. Top, left to right: Pema Wangchen (son of Gyalyum's aunt); Tashi Zangpo (Gyalyum's brother); Kunga Yonten Horchotsang (first cousin of Gyalyum); Gyalyum Tashi Lhakee as a young girl (12 or 13 years old); and Yangchen (Gyalyum's older sister). Bottom, left to right: Tashi Palmo, Kunga Yonten Horchotsang's mother (d. 1975 in Darjeeling); Sheanyitsang Yangchen (maternal aunt of Gyalyum); Jamyang Senge Anjam (Gyalyum's father [1917–1986], died at Rajpur); Damcho Wangmo (Gyalyum's mother [1916–1996], died at Manduwala); and Tsering Tsomo (daughter of aunt and Pema Wangchen's sister). Courtesy of Kunga Yonten Horchotsang.
4. The main altar in the Great Temple, Sakya. Giuseppe Tucci, *Tibet: Land of Snows*, 107. Courtesy of David Jackson.
5. Ngor Monastery, Tsang, Tibet, 1939. Photo by Felice Boffa Ballaran.
6. Drawupon Rinchen Tsering in Xining, Amdo, 1953/54. Courtesy of Dagmo Lhanze Sakya.
7. Ven. Dezhung Rinpoche, Seattle, 1962/63. From David Jackson, *A Saint in Seattle*, 467. Courtesy of David Jackson.
8. H.E. Jamyang Dagmo Sakya and Ven. Ani Chime Dolma in Seattle, ca. 2003. Courtesy of Dagmo Jamyang Sakya.
9. H.H. the 13th Dalai Lama.
10. H.H. Dragshul Trinlei Rinchen, the 39th Sakya Trizin, seated on his throne in Sakya, Tibet, 1934, surrounded by his entourage. On his proper right is his younger son, Ngawang Kunga Gyaltsen, in a brocade jacket. On his proper left is the Chief Minister (from the Shar family), and in front of him is the Lord Chamberlain (from the Rangjonba family). © Frederick Williamson Memorial Fund, Cambridge.
11. Most of the Northern Monastery complex in Sakya; the Zhitog is the largest building in the center. From David Jackson, *A Saint in Seattle*, 166. Courtesy of David Jackson.

12. Dagmo Trinlei Paljor being playful. Courtesy of H.E. [Jetsun Kushok] Chimey Luding.
13. Tashi Palrab as a general in the Tibetan army, Lhasa, Tibet, mid-1950s. Courtesy of Ga Yudron.
14. The Dolma Palace, Sakya, ca. 1940s.
15. H.E. Jetsun Kushok and H.H. the 41st Sakya Trizin in Rajpur, India, 2002. Courtesy of April Dolkar. © April Dolkar.
16. Dagchen Kunga Rinchen in the courtyard of the Dolma Palace, Sakya, in the late 1940s. From David Jackson, *A Saint in Seattle*, 145. Courtesy of David Jackson.
17. H.H. the 41st Sakya Trizin as a boy in Yatung, Tibet, 1957. His Holiness commented, "This was taken in Yatung [close to the Sikkim and Tibet border] on the way back from Sikkim. We were stuck there for two weeks because of the snow." Photo by H.E. Jetsun Kushok.
18. The Cham dances at the Dolma Palace, May 1957. H.H. the 41st Sakya Trizin remarked, "This is the yearly May festival at Sakya Dolma Phodrang, during which there were Cham dances and the *gyaling* [double-reed horn] players wore special costumes." Photo by H.E. Jetsun Kushok.
19. Ven. Dampa Rinpoche (Ngawang Lodro Shenpen Nyingpo) in tantric regalia. Courtesy of Moke Mokotoff. This photo also appears in David Jackson, *A Saint in Seattle*, 173.
20. H.H. the 14th Dalai Lama in Dromo, Tibet, 1951.
21. Ven. Khangsar Shabdrung (Ngawang Lodro Tenzin Nyingpo). Courtesy of the Dolma Palace.
22. The young 41st Sakya Trizin and Khen Jampal Zangpo in the Pandatsang's shrine room in Lhasa, Tibet, 1956. Courtesy of the Dolma Palace.
23. Ven. Jamyang Khyentse Chokyi Lodro.
24. H.H. the 14th Dalai Lama and the 10th Panchen Lama in Sikkim, 1956. Photo by Homai Vyarawalla.
25. H.E. Jetsun Kushok praying to Tara at the Mahabodhi Temple, Bodhgaya, India, 2002. Courtesy of April Dolkar. © April Dolkar.
26. Ven. Chiwang Tulku in his residence at the Sakya Centre, Rajpur, India. Courtesy of Chiwang Lama.
27. Dagmo Trinlei Paljor wearing a Tsang headdress at the 1959 enthronement of H.H. the 41st Sakya Trizin. The inset is a photo her brother Tashi Palrab when he lived in Dharamsala, India. Courtesy of Ga Yudron.
28. The Dolma Palace family and entourage at Sarnath, India, 1960. H.E. Jetsun Kushok is standing next to H.H. the 41st Sakya Trizin, who is seated. Courtesy of H.E. [Jetsun Kushok] Chimey Luding.
29. H.E. Jetsun Kushok, Dagmo Trinlei Paljor, and the Western nun Ani Freda Bedi in India in the mid-1960s. Also known as Sister Palmo, Freda Houlston Bedi (1911–77) established the Young Lamas Home School in Dalhousie and was one of the first Western women to take ordination in Tibetan Buddhism. Courtesy of H.E. [Jetsun Kushok] Chimey Luding.
30. H.H. the 41st Sakya Trizin and his teacher, Ven. Appey Rinpoche, in the 1960s.

31. H. E. Jetsun Kushok and her son, Ven. Luding Khen Rinpoche, in the mid-1990s. Courtesy of Rosemary Rawcliffe. © Rosemary Rawcliffe.
32. Sey Kushok and H.E. Jetsun Kushok in India, 2002. Courtesy of April Dolkar. © April Dolkar.
33. After the wedding celebration of Gyalyum Tashi Lhakee and H.H. the 41st Sakya Trizin in Puruwala, India, February 1974. Left to right: Ven. Lama Kunga Rinpoche, the documentary photographer Germaine Krull (1897–1985), Gyalyum Tashi Lhakee, Dagmo Trinlei Paljor, and H.H. the 41st Sakya Trizin. Courtesy of Moke Mokotoff. © Moke Mokotoff. Germaine Krull and Marilyn Raviczʼs *A Promise Kept: Memoir of Tibetans in India* (2018) describes the Dolma Palace familyʼs early years in India.
34. The Dolma Palace family in Kuching, Sarawak, Malaysia, ca. 1977. Left to right: Jay Goldberg (Ngawang Samten), the monk Cho Phuntsok, H.H. the 41st Sakya Trizin, Gyalyum Tashi Lhakee, the very young Dungsay Ratna Vajra Rinpoche, and attendant Sangye-la.
35. Sey Kushok and H.E. Jetsun Kushok at Jigdal Dagchen Rinpocheʼs home in Seattle, ca. 1976. Courtesy of Chris Wilkinson.
36. The Dolma Palace family celebrating Losar 2020 at the Dolma Palace, Puruwala, India. Standing, left to right: Sey Kushok Rinchen Luding, Dagmo Kalden Dunkyi, Gyalyum Chenmo Tashi Lhakee, and Dagmo Sonam Palkyi. Seated, left to right: Jetsunma Ngawang Tsejin Lhamo, Jetsun Kushok Chimey Luding, Dungsay Akasha Vajra Rinpoche, H.H. the 42nd Sakya Trizin Ratna Vajra, H.H. Gongma Sakya Trichen (the 41st Sakya Trizin), H.H. the 43rd Sakya Trizin Gyana Vajra holding Dungsay Siddhant Vajra Rinpoche, Dungsay Siddharth Vajra Rinpoche, Jetsunma Kunga Trinley Palter, and Jetsunma Kunga Chimey Wangmo. Courtesy of the Dolma Palace.
37. Jetsunma Kunga Trinley (far left), with her father H.H. the 42nd Sakya Trizin, her mother Dagmo Kalden Dunkyi, and, in front, her brother Dungsay Akasha Vajra Rinpoche and sister Jetsunma Kunga Chimey Wangmo. Courtesy of Dagmo Kalden Dunkyi.
38. H.H. the 41st Sakya Trizin performing a Vajrakīlaya *torma* initiation in the shrine room of the Dolma Palace, Rajpur, India. From far left to right: Jetsunma Kunga Chimey Wangmo, Jetsunma Kunga Trinley, and Dungsay Akasha Vajra Rinpoche of the Dolma Palace, and the Phuntsok Palaceʼs Dungsay Asanga Vajra Rinpoche. Courtesy of the Dolma Palace.
39. Aja Dolkar and her son Tsering Dorje at the Dolma Palace, Rajpur, India, 2002. Courtesy of April Dolkar. © April Dolkar.

About the Author

Elisabeth Benard (Ph.D. Columbia University in Tibetan Buddhism) was a professor of religion and the director of the Pacific Rim/Asia Study-Travel Program at the University of Puget Sound in Tacoma, Washington. She is the author of *Chinnamastā: The Aweful Buddhist and Hindu Tantric Goddess* (Motilal Banarsidass, 1994) and numerous scholarly articles, and the co-editor, with Beverly Moon, of *Goddesses Who Rule* (Oxford University Press, 2000). Since her retirement, she has continued to pursue her interest in goddesses and spiritual women, compiling biographies of hidden yoginis in Tibetan Buddhism. Her spiritual practice has been under the guidance of the 3rd Dezhung Rinpoche, H.H. the 41st Sakya Trizin (now H.H. Gongma Trichen), and H.E. Jetsun Kushok.